RIP-OFF U.

The Annual

THEFT AND EXPLOITATION

of

Major College Revenue Producing

STUDENT-ATHLETES

by
Dick DeVenzio

The Fool Court Press
Charlotte, North Carolina

Credits:
Editing: Huck DeVenzio, Marsha Lamm
Research: Richard Ford, Dave DeVenzio, Tim Ryan
Production: Dick Edwards, Christine Townsend, Nona Latane
Printed by the Delmar Printing Company
See Page 255

Library of Congress Cataloging in Publication Data

DeVenzio, Dick, 1949-
    Rip-Off U.

    Bibliography: p.
    Includes index.
    1. College sports—Economic aspects—United States.
2. College athletes—United States. 3. College sports—
United States—Organization and administration.
I. Title.
GV350.D48   1985   796'.07'1173   85-27471
ISBN 0-910305-01-3

Official Publication Date
January 15, 1986

To all of the high school basketball and football stars who have sat on college benches and wondered what went wrong, and . . .

To all of the past, present and future student-athletes who will benefit from sweeping changes in the current, morally-bankrupt system of big-time college sports.

—TABLE OF CONTENTS—

Introduction

BEHIND THE PAPER CANNON
"Bob Cousy, John Wooden, Vic Bubas, and Dean Smith, they all came . . ."

STUDENT-ATHLETES' ENCYCLOPEDIA

On the organization of this book:

The **Introduction** offers some insight into the problems of college sports along with some biographical information explaining my personal reasons for starting a campaign to bring about sweeping changes.

Part I is a general overview of the crucial issues, the problems and solutions of big-time college sports from the student-athlete's point of view.

Part II uses the encyclopedia concept so that readers can get a clear understanding of each individual issue and be able to refer easily to specific issues.

Since many of the issues are interrelated to so great an extent, any telling of the student-athlete's story necessitates some repetition. It is hoped that the encyclopedia form makes the repetition helpful rather than annoying.

The **Appendix** includes a bibliography, and an index.

— introduction —

"It is not in the philosophy of the institutions to hire a bunch of pro athletes to represent them. Institutions are providing a means for an education for those students they recruit and that's all. They are not going beyond that."
—John R. Davis
NCAA President

"You cannot elevate blatant theft and exploitation to the level of philosophy. I will no longer sit back and watch the progressive criminalization of young athletes.
"The NCAA leadership seems to have lost sight of the fact that we, the people, ARE the institutions, and we are preparing to bring about sweeping changes."
—Dick DeVenzio
Former Academic All-American
Basketball Star
Duke University, 1971

"DeVenzio writes a monthly newsletter titled '$TUDENT-ATHLETE$.' It's his paper cannon. He aims it at the sprawling bureaucracy of big-time athletics — and fires."

—Rick Starr
Sports Editor
Valley Daily News
Tarentum, PA

"Most often, when a person comes forward with a radical, far-out, revolutionary, kooky proposal to cure all the ills in sports, the personality of the guy matches his idea. He's likely to be a kooky, far-out radical.

"Also, you can be pretty sure that the man who has all the answers on how football ought to be conducted never threw a pass or made a tackle in his life. The guy who wants to revolutionize basketball probably couldn't make a free throw in ten tries.

"Then along comes Dick DeVenzio to change that image . . ."

—Virgil Parker
Sports Editor
Lincoln (NE) Journal-Star, 5-19-85

BEHIND THE PAPER CANNON

I am proud to have graduated in four years from Duke University, one of the nation's most reputable academic institutions; and I am proud to have been named an Academic All-American for my efforts there in basketball and in the classroom. These honors, I think, place me in a position to speak in a forthright way about my feelings, observations, and insider's knowledge of big-time collegiate sports, and to some extent, at least, they insulate me from off-handed criticisms like "Oh, he's just some dumb jock who is cynical and bitter because HE failed to take advantage of HIS opportunity."

An editor-friend of mine, to whom I gave this manuscript, said "Critical readers may think it's just sour grapes." That comment exasperates me. It is used all the time against athletes who have very legitimate gripes. Basketball and football players produce revenue through gate receipts, TV contracts, concessions, alumni contributions, and increased student applications. Look at what they generate and what they get. The numbers add up to an enormous rip-off. That is why I acknowledge and do not apologize for the cynicism apparent on these pages; and I want to go a step further by saying that I believe sincerely — with all of the objectivity that my Duke education has enabled me to muster — that

it is impossible for a student-athlete, or any reasonable person who will take the time to understand the student-athlete's point of view, not to be cynical.

I have felt, but not nurtured, this cynicism for nearly twenty years of personal association with big-time collegiate sports, and I submit to you that this feeling is a concomitant, unavoidable, integral part of any examination of big-time sports from an intelligent student-athlete's point of view.

Do not mistake me. As a student-athlete, as an assistant college coach, and as an all-star camp director, sports writer, and fan, I have had many wonderful experiences as well as the opportunity to meet many wonderful people through these years. Bob Cousy, John Wooden, Vic Bubas, and Dean Smith all came to my house to recruit me. So did Larry Brown, Chuck Daly, and Digger Phelps. (Now Senator, then Rhodes Scholar) Bill Bradley wrote me a two-page letter, which I still have, from Oxford, England, talking to me about Princeton University and about life. The National League batting champion, Dick Groat, a star shortstop with the Pittsburgh Pirates, called me for Lefty Driesell to talk about Davidson College.

10

Off the court I had the opportunity to get to know and to study under professors like Ann Scott and David Paletz, two of the very best in their fields, who are still at Duke University; I had the opportunity to sit for two years on the University Judicial Board, the council of several students, deans, and faculty members which decided — in the Vietnam era when expulsion could mean an immediate trip to Southeast Asia — how to punish students who violated the integrity of the university by cheating, plagiarism, and other behavior unacceptable to the university community.

In my first two years at Duke, I enjoyed the privileged status of star player, chief player-recruiter, and probably "most favored" player by a coach I admired; in my final two years I played under a new coach whose ideas, philosophies, and personal style were anathema to me. Nevertheless, I learned to withhold many opinions, to do my best, to grit my teeth and to compete diligently in spite of circumstances I disliked intensely.

But I am not trying to dredge up the past or establish right from wrong in other decades. I am only laying out some of my diverse experiences, some of my good times and bad times, so that you can know the background from which I approach the present, big-time college athletics of today, which is my exclusive concern in this book.

In my college years, I became friends with women like Kate Fetterolf, who is quickly becoming one of the nation's best painters, though at the time she was merely an intelligent, attractive cheerleader. I played with and against many pro stars. I got to travel, to experience the respect of classmates, and to drive a new convertible each summer.

In other words, in many ways I enjoyed the privileges of being a star athlete, and I appreciated those privileges. I valued them then, and I value them now. But those privileges, and those good times, do not blind me to the realities that existed then or that exist now. There are some rotten things about big-time collegiate sports that don't need to be; and they are not those things which fans typically hear about — like scandals, cheating, and corruption.

It is my sincere view that big-time football and basketball players are being truly ripped off by the NCAA and the universities, which are justifying their theft and exploitation using noble-sounding concepts like amateurism and fair play.

"Look what the kids are getting: an education is a valuable thing," so many people are quick to say, in support of the theft and exploitation. Yes, I answer, so is a job. But no one wants to be underpaid.

Nor does anyone want to be disillusioned or embittered. Yet I am sure that even the knowledgeable fan has no awareness at all of the extent of unhappiness and pain that is caused by college football and basketball programs. I saw it as a player and as a coach, and I continue to see it each summer as director of the Prep Stars Invitational All-Star Basketball Camp. You may not believe how many kids get zapped. I'm not even talking about the ones who fail to get a college scholarship; I am talking about the ones who do. It is a continuous tale of human misery.

They aren't starving, or getting physically assaulted, so perhaps you think I am exaggerating my point. I don't think so. I see too many examples. I see an incredible psychological toll that leaves scars that never go away. And none of it is necessary. Maybe that's why I see it as truly tragic.

I began publishing a monthly newsletter, called "$TUDENT-ATH-LETE$," and I decided to write this book because it is my conviction that someone has to do something for the student-athletes — now. The players cannot effectively speak for themselves. They have no voice at NCAA meetings, no representation of any kind. They are like migrant farm workers before Cesar Chavez — too unorganized, too poor, too spread out, and too busy to do anything about their problems. The coaches are afraid to speak up. They have too much at stake, and making noise only draws attention that might end up putting their own heads in the noose. The atmosphere surrounding big-time sports is that tense, that paranoid. Administrators don't seem to truly understand, or don't dare speak up either.

Therefore, I think the task falls on someone like me, who has the background and the insight yet no vested interest, nothing really to lose and, a chance to usher in a great "new deal" for college athletes.

I consider myself a writer who will always have a close association with sports. My father was and still is a great coach, and my two brothers both played college basketball. Sports are in our blood. The things I say in this book should be said, even if they are unpleasant. It is my sincere hope that this book will be one of the forces which will influence public opinion sufficiently to bring about constructive, necessary change. The student-athlete truly deserves a better shake, and sports fans should understand precisely why that is.

PART I

THE RIP-OFF

of

Big-Time Student-Athletes

AN OVERVIEW

Over the next twelve months, a relatively small group of talented college students will generate more than a billion dollars in revenue. In return they will receive scholarships worth little more, and sometimes less, than classmates who generate no revenue at all. Many of the generators will spend four years of college penniless and unhappy, then leave without a pro contract and without a diploma. Instead of the revenue being returned to those who have produced it — either in cash or in more creative ways that would insure a better education — it will be squandered on bureaucratic overhead, needless national championships, and windfall allocations which schools can not plan on getting.

Presiding over the exploitation of today's revenue producing student-athlete is the NCAA, a cumbersome association of diverse schools which has grown rich, out of control, and irresponsible. Claiming it has the student-athletes' interests at heart, it allows them no representation, nor even participation at its conventions.

All of this will change as soon as the student-athletes realize their value and decide to end their subjugation. The time is near when one Rose Bowl football team, and perhaps two Final Four basketball teams, will make it clear to everyone that the theft of their money is over.

Football and basketball players have the power to usher in a new era of true scholar-athletes on college campuses. When they do, college athletics will be free of cheating, scandals, and corruption; and athletes will be graduating, going on to graduate school, and succeeding in non-athletic careers in record numbers.

Chapter 1

CHEATING, CORRUPTION, SCANDALS AND MORE . . .
public misconceptions

Always the universities and the NCAA get off unscathed. When the NCAA and the universities show a callous disregard for the United States Constitution, nothing happens. Their actions go unpunished. David Berst, the NCAA's investigator in the UNLV case was roundly criticized by Nevada District Judge Paul Goldman for his attitude, his lack of cooperation with the court, and with his pre-planned and orchestrated campaign to disparage Coach Jerry Tarkanian. But what happened to Berst? Today he is the NCAA's Director of Enforcement. He was actually rewarded for his lawless attitude and behavior.

CHEATING, CORRUPTION, SCANDALS AND MORE . . .

If a psychologist would give thousands of casual fans and "guys on the street" a series of word association tests, the first words that would come to many minds, upon hearing "college athletics," would be cheating, corruption, and scandal.

This is a tragedy. I believe the people involved in big-time collegiate athletics are probably at least as honest and as concerned with integrity and with following rules as people in any other major area. This is not to say that there aren't ANY bad people among college players and coaches, but the numbers are blown way out of proportion. In USA TODAY, 10-18-84, the sports editorial was entitled, "Don't Pay Athletes; Get Tough on Abuse." It began:

"It's quite a deal. You sign up for four years of free education, free room and board, and a chance to play football on one of the USA's most prestigious football teams.

"While an enthusiastic alumnus is slapping you on the back with one hand, he's greasing your amateur palm with a cool $20,000 with the other. Welcome to the lucrative world of college sports . . ."

I could not disagree more, and I have to believe that the person who wrote that editorial hasn't spent much time around locker rooms and playing fields. In the rare circumstances when a player does actually get some money, it hardly fits this picture. I can't say enough how wrong I believe that account is, as far as what is really going on.

I don't think I am naive on this subject. Something did happen at Tulane. And there have been violations of NCAA rules here and there — at Clemson, at Florida, at SMU and at other places where they have not been discovered. But before flinging words around like cheating and corruption, take a closer look at just what is going on. What is the nature of the cheating? Who is being corrupted? What is really happening?

Cheating, corruption, and scandal are strong words with connotations not too far removed from assault, rape, and murder.

Most fans, I think, have approximately the same response to both sets of words, even though they would be hard-pressed to define the cheating and corruption in sports that they roll their eyes and snicker at. Furthermore, I think most fans would be surprised to see the so-called cheating and corruption spelled out clearly in every detail, and to realize that **not much bad is actually happening**. A poor kid has gotten some new clothes, an undecided kid has received an extra paid-visit to a campus, some athletes have received some spending money.

If you take a close look at what these reporters are calling, "quite a deal" or a "daily bombardment" of big-time sports ills, you are likely to be surprised at how paltry the violations are. Even if NCAA activities were unquestionably fair and intelligent, how bad would the violations be? Nobody is getting killed, no one is getting physically assaulted, money is not being stolen by coaches or players — though the NCAA is stealing plenty — and no teams are conspiring to lose games on purpose.

The ranting and raving, the eye-rolling and snickering, ends up being caused by a plane ticket here or there, or a new suit to a kid who dresses poorly, or a few dollars to a kid with no money. Though USA TODAY claimed in the editorial that "outrageous payoffs . . . have been well documented," the paper listed as proof what an NCAA official SAID, even though he didn't name any names. Is that "well documented?"

Occasionally there is a report — and nearly all of them end up being unsubstantiated — that a kid has received the worst of all evils, a KHAR.

Do you need to see that word again? Or have it re-spelled? I spelled car with a "KH" to make it the four-letter word the media seem to want it to be. At times, the whole, hypocritical sports world seems to wretch over the ugliness of that word.

Did you hear what they did? They gave him a CAR!!!

It would spoil the whole context of evil and corruption if someone merely altered this terrible accusation slightly and asked, "Did you hear what they did? They provided him with some transportation."

For once and for all, can anyone explain what is so great about a car? At most colleges today, cars are necessary, especially for busy kids who have full course loads and daily practice schedules and not a lot of time to spend on hitchhiking or waiting for busses or walking across campuses.

As a matter of information, coaches don't flip the keys (to shiny new convertibles) to young seventeen-year-old super-recruits as inducements to come to their schools. Nor do many boosters. Even the stupid coaches and boosters are too smart for that. Cars are big, visible items. Everyone can see them. Everyone asks where they came from. Everyone suspects they came from some unscrupulous coach or alumnus who has a plaque on his wall engraved with the words **"win at any cost and to hell with rules and people."** (Presumably these guys are staunch, registered, anti-educationalists as well, if you believe the typical media accounts.) But more often the case, the coach requests that one of his players NOT make arrangements to get a new car — in order to avoid the possibility of attention.

Ignorant reporters are missing the proverbial forest through the trees.

The attention given to corruption, cheating and scandals in big-time collegiate sports is absurdly overrated and exaggerated. What problems do exist are easily solvable. But what is not so easily solvable is the present system of NCAA rule, which permits an annual theft of millions of dollars yet masquerades as integrity and leadership.

The real issue in big-time college sports — the issue which is hidden by the magnified attention given to cheating, corruption, and scandals among players — is the annual rip-off of big-time collegiate athletes while fat cats in gray suits, on the periphery of the action, line their pockets with gold. The NCAA bureaucrats enjoy comfortable salaries, generous expense accounts, and always plush accommodations and travel — and the wining and dining of colleagues — while sitting back and taking potshots at the evils their stupid, petty rules have created.

In the daily paper and on the nightly news, very little is said about the money that is being stolen and wasted by so-called leaders of big-time college sports. Instead the focus is on a player who got admitted to college with an SAT score of 470.

The kid did not admit himself. He did not forge papers to get in. Leaders of great American universities LET him in. But how many of THEM get fired? How many of them resign in disgrace?

A lot of coaches have resigned in disgrace, having been labeled cheaters, caught supposedly red-handed, accused of disregard for the rules, accused of trying to gain unfair advantage over their fellow competitors.

Always the universities and the NCAA get off unscathed. When the NCAA and the universities show a callous disregard for the United States Constitution, nothing happens. Their actions go unpunished. David Berst, the NCAA's investigator in the UNLV case was roundly criticized by U. S. District Judge Paul Goldman for his attitude, his lack of cooperation with the court, and with his pre-planned and orchestrated campaign to disparage Coach Jerry Tarkanian. But what happened to Berst? Today he is the NCAA's Director of Enforcement. He was actually rewarded for his lawless attitude and behavior.

The point is, the cards are stacked against the players. People all over the nation laugh at cartoons poking fun at stereotyped dumb jocks — big guys who can't read or write but who can run, block, tackle, or slam-dunk.

I have seen many people circulating a stapled group of papers with a cover, poorly printed, reading

"STATE UNIVERSITY ENTRANCE EXAM
FOR BASKETBALL AND FOOTBALL PROSPECTS."

Inside the exam are "tests." The first says "Connect the dots." There are only two dots on the page. Page two features a "Word Search" test, and asks "Can YOU find a word on this page? You may look across, up and down, forward or backwards." The page is covered with X's except for one word, "CAT," very clearly spelled out in the middle of the page. On page three it says "Which is bigger?" There are two pictures, one of a watermelon filling most of the page, the other of a lima bean in the lower right hand corner. At the bottom of the page, it says "Mark your answer in the correct box below" — and only one box is showing.

The test goes on. It's funny. Athletes are not furious at such jokes on themselves. They don't go yelling "Discrimination" or foul play. But maybe they should. Why are they saddled with this image? What can they do about it? What is anyone else doing about it? Who is trying to help them?

The NCAA and the college presidents are quick to jump in to keep their own images clean. But nowhere is it obvious that those in power are extending themselves to do anything for the athletes. What is clear is that most of them are covering their own behinds, quick to blame the problems on someone else.

It is time to change. Sure, athletes are not perfect. They are not all Einsteins, they are not all saints. Mostly, however, they are 17- and 18- and 20-year-olds able to be positively influenced by good leadership which they are not getting.

Instead, those who should be leading and helping them are making excuses and happily using their money.

The paranoia created by the NCAA, the finger-pointing, and the pettiness really aren't necessary at all. An economically-motivated concept of "unfair advantage" is directly responsible for a myriad of rules against human dignity and common sense.

Big-time collegiate sports today are diseased by a lack of leadership and vision, and an utter failure to respond to the changing times.

It is time for radical change. Time for an end to the paranoia, to the finger-pointing, to the charges of cheating and corruption.

Cheating and corruption? Who is cheating whom? Where is the corruption? The blame belongs squarely on the leadership of the universities and on the NCAA.

In this book, I want to lay out big-time sports as I see it and as I have experienced it, and let YOU be the judge. In my opinion, something is very rotten in the state of Denmark — you might be surprised to know how many student-athletes recognize that that comes from Shakespeare — and the rot has very little to do with the players. See for yourself. . . .

Chapter 2

"WHAT DO YOU WANT TO DO, PAY THOSE GUYS?"
the fallacy of the 'free ride'

There is no reason, even with establishment of player compensation, that college athletics need become "just like the pros." Lazy thinkers perceive a world of either-ors when there are all sorts of in-between alternatives and opportunities.

"WHAT DO YOU WANT TO DO, PAY THOSE GUYS?"

In nearly every discussion about major college sports, when the issue of compensation for players comes up, someone inevitably blurts out, "What do you want to do, PAY those guys?"

It is obvious from the tone of the question that the questioners believe it is clear to everyone that paying players would be among the worst of evils.

The answer is no. Don't PAY them. It is not necessary to pay them. It will be enough merely to stop the theft of their money. They generate huge amounts of money, and it makes common sense, in America, that those who generate money should participate in the distribution of it.

It is a strictly economic issue. No one is asking that they be compensated because they work hard or have it tough. A lot of people work harder and have even tougher lives. But we live in a capitalistic society. We believe, as a nation, that people should benefit from the fruits of their labors. There is nothing so dramatically different about college sports or college athletes that should cause this basic national belief to be suspended. Big time college athletes generate money. Big time college athletes should get some of that money.

One of the principal fears of those who ask "What do you want to do, PAY those guys?" is that "It will become just like the pros."

This question usually follows:

"Do you want college presidents suddenly bidding for high school athletes? Is that the business our universities should be in? Aren't you forgetting that the primary purpose of our universities is education?"

There is no reason, even with establishment of player compensation, that college athletics need become "just like the pros." Lazy thinkers perceive a world of either-ors when there are all sorts of in-between alternatives and opportunities.

First, no bidding wars need take place just because the players are to be compensated.

"Yeah, but what are you gonna do when the star starts asking for more than the third stringer?"

There is no need to compensate each player on a game by game performance basis. People throughout American society — even pro athletes — sign contracts for a period of years and get a certain amount of money over that period of time, regardless of whether they are first-rate at what they do or a bit slack. At the end of a contract period, a salesman or factory worker or secretary may make a case for getting a

23

raise, but nearly everyone agrees to a contract that pays a certain amount over a period of time, and does not reward or penalize them for a good or bad day (or week or month).

In the case of college athletes, they would sign a contract while in high school, stipulating the agreement. For instance, a student-athlete might be entitled to a degree — for however long it takes to get one — and to certain other benefits, like plane tickets, spending money, use of a car, and perhaps a grant upon graduation.

These would be the terms of their contract. Everyone who signed a grant-in-aid would get it. There would be no bidding war, since all major colleges would be limited — as they are now — to offering the same amount.

"Yeah, but what would stop some from sweetening the pot? If they are allowed to give $10,000, what would stop some from offering $20,000?"

When people are being fairly compensated for what they are doing, and when monies from a particular business or endeavor are being fairly distributed, people are much less inclined to look for ways to cheat. Naturally, no system can ever expect to stop ALL cheating. But bad rules make cheaters out of anyone. The collegiate sports situation now is similar to that which occurs with taxation. When people are asked to contribute ten percent of their income for taxes, MOST people willingly pay — in recognition that some taxes are necessary for things like national security, highways, social programs, etc. However, when a government at any time throughout history has raised taxes to the point of taking seventy or eighty percent of people's income, a nation of tax-evaders, tax-cheaters, and lawbreakers has usually been the result.

In businesses where profit-sharing is a reality, you have fewer people looking to rip-off the company, because they realize that they ARE the company. It is when people feel they are being taken advantage of that they feel JUSTIFIED in cheating and even stealing what they can.

In big-time collegiate sports, athletic departments are bending over backwards, daily, to follow rules they can have little respect for. Almost universally, the coaches who work with the kids day by day and who have access to the tremendous amount of money being made, know that the kids deserve more than they are getting. They see kids each day who not only do not have a car, but who do not have enough money to go out on dates, and who do not EVEN have enough money to get a hamburger at night.

This would be fine if everyone were poor, if everyone were suffering. But when, at the same time, a sports information director is making $30,000 (or more) just distributing information about these kids, and when a third (and unnecessary) assistant coach is making $30,000, it becomes difficult to understand the value system that keeps the generators of all that money penniless.

It becomes even more difficult to understand that value system when you read that the salaries of the NCAA bureaucrats in Mission, Kansas, totaled more than $2,500,000 in 1984 — just to run these staunchly AMATEUR sports.

A head coach can, and often does, send an assistant to the other side of the country to watch a high school basketball game because there is ONE kid playing there who they have a tiny chance to sign some day. The assistant coach will fly to the city, rent a car, stay in a nice motel, watch the game, eat a fine meal, and return the next day in time for practice.

How much money did that cost? And what value system, what NCAA rules, make THAT extravagant recruiting foray completely within the rules while the coach dare not give a penniless star a ten dollar bill after a long, tough week of practice?

To the people involved, it does not make sense that there can be SO much money available for recruiting and entertaining and equipment and social functions — do not forget social functions, the NCAA does not outlaw expenditures for them — yet no money available AT ALL for good, hard-working, academically-interested athletes.

Seen in context, from the inside, it is a wonder that the coaches have not yet made a secret agreement just to totally ignore all NCAA rules. Let the NCAA prosecute them all.

Unfortunately, for the players, the coaches spend their time trying to compete and win and handle their difficult jobs, and most of them are quite grateful to be coaches. They make good money, they live good lives. They work hard, yes, but they are able to benefit financially from doing something they love. Few of them are eager to get thrown out of the profession. It's a good profession. It could even be better, nearly all of them agree, if they did not have to walk a daily tightrope between following stupid NCAA rules and following the dictates of their consciences and their personal morality.

When **you can stick a thousand dollar bill in the hand of your assistant** for an admittedly non-essential trip, **but can NOT give your star player five dollars** — regardless of his degree of need or the circumstances surrounding him — you can hardly expect a reverence for the governing body which makes these rules, and you can hardly expect compliance with all of its regulations.

The penniless players are being exploited, ignored, and stolen from so dramatically, that the media accounts of slush funds and shoe boxes become almost comical. Athletes are generating huge sums of money, and everyone is benefitting from it but them.

The response to this kind of reasoning is often immediate and self-righteous.

"But they're getting an education! They're getting an education! That's worth a whole lot, isn't it? Or don't you know the value of an education?" they ask sarcastically.

THE VALUE OF AN EDUCATION

Critics of fair compensation for revenue producing student-athletes point out often how much the student-athletes are already getting.

A columnist, Gus Schrader, writing in the Cedar Rapids Gazette, offered this rather typical opinion:

"I'm so old-fashioned I was under the obviously mistaken notion the athletes were getting something for their participation: room, board, books, tuition, and, at least, the exposure to a college education.

"Maybe you don't think that last item is important. Maybe the athletes don't realize its value . . .

"I can't remember the exact figures mentioned, but it is estimated that over a lifetime, a man or woman would average several hundred thousand dollars more with a college education than without one . . .

"So do coaches really think they are robbing their players by forcing them to play college ball for room, board, books, and tuition?"

The columnist has a good point, and concerned student-athletes certainly will be quick to agree that it is wonderful to have the opportunity to get an education and it is wonderful to increase earning power over a lifetime by hundreds of thousands of dollars. However, **there is no reason why the NCAA should get credit for what students get BY VIRTUE OF BEING AMERICAN.**

Kenneth A. Kohl, the Associate Commissioner of Education in the Ford Administration, made this point perfectly clear with one statement:

"I am confident that any student . . . can go to college no matter what his or her family's financial resources."

Kohl did not say he was confident that any star ATHLETE could go to college; he said any American STUDENT. To support that contention, Kohl, one of the nation's top experts on education, wrote a book entitled, "Financing College Education." The book offers students information on Pell Grants, Supplemental Educational Opportunity Grants, the College Work-Study Program, the Guaranteed Student Loan Program, and many other sources of funding and methods of obtaining individual grants from charitable foundations and corporations, as well as from state and local governments.

Indeed, there is sufficient money available to non-athletic students to enable the Atlanta Constitution to carry the following small feature early in 1985 under the heading "Sign of the Times:"

"Tyrone Sorrells, the tight end/wide receiver who transferred from Georgia to Tech, is receiving more financial aid as a poverty-level regular student this year — while sitting out a year to become eligible to play football — than he will next year when he goes on full athletic scholarship."

So how much is Tyrone getting to play football? He is getting LESS money by playing than he would be getting if he had remained in a work-study program instead of going to football practice after classes each day. How much is any athlete getting?

Although it must be admitted that some schools cost more than others (for example a Duke or Stanford student is getting more than a UCLA or Pitt student), it is nevertheless true that most athletes are getting a very small amount of money. Certainly that amount is LESS than the actual cost of a scholarship.

For example, the National Institute of Education published a report for the 1984-85 academic year which indicates that the average cost per student for tuition, for the year, was $4,522. Of that amount, state and local tax payers footed an average bill of $3,467. The amount paid by students and their parents, on the average, was $1055.

In other words, the average REGULAR student had to pay $1055 to go to school. So that amount is what a student-ATHLETE is getting each year, over and above what the regular student is getting.

Even on the false assumption that regular students can get no money for room or board, it becomes clear that the average athlete gets only about three thousand dollars per year more than the average non-athlete. (At most state schools, the TOTAL cost for any student is $3000–$5000.)

Over a four year period, an athlete is going to get twelve to twenty thousand dollars — a dismal, paltry sum compared to his financial contribution to the school.

It is nevertheless necessary to re-emphasize that athletes are NOT disputing the value of an education. No athletes are discounting the privilege of living in America and having the opportunities accorded to Americans. But the NCAA cannot take credit for the efforts of the American people.

Athletes are getting full scholarships from the universities, but it is clear that nearly all of them could get a substantial amount of that money anyway through grants available to normal students. (Some students, as has been shown, actually get more money by NOT going on athletic scholarship.)

When all the figures are done being thrown around, one thing is apparent. In nearly every state, it is possible for ANY student to attend college for a total of less than $5,000. Certainly, then, it can not be said that the revenue producing athletes are getting anything near what they deserve. Five thousand dollars is indeed a paltry sum when you consider that the big schools regularly take in from $50,000 to more than $1,000,000 PER GAME on gate receipts alone.

A JOB IS VALUABLE!

Via the education-is-valuable argument, why not tell the professors to work for nothing, too? "Hey, guys, you're doing research, you're learning. Many of you have even been heard to say that you learned more from teaching a class than your students did. You learned more from them than they did from you. You said that yourselves. So why not work for nothing? Don't you know the value of an education?"

Of course this is being ridiculous — which is precisely the way any such arguments should be viewed. What does the value of an education have to do with whether or not someone is compensated fairly?

In cases where athletes are generating substantial revenues for their schools, the fact that they are getting an education at those schools in no way lessens their right to participate in some of the take.

Put simply, major college athletes would be happy to lay down their money for room, board, tuition, and books just like every other paying student — IF they were given a fair share of the revenue they bring in.

Now, what's the argument? If people think the "free ride" is so great, the athletes will happily forego it entirely — in exchange for a fair share of the income they generate.

Here's an example. It costs a kid from Louisville about $5000 to attend the University of Kentucky and pay for his room, board, tuition, and books for the year. Fine. Let everyone pay that — whether they are athletes or band members or French majors. Then give each member of the basketball team just half of the gate receipts — not TV revenue, not alumni contributions, just money collected at the door — from ONE game during their four years at Kentucky. HALF THE GATE FROM JUST ONE GAME IN A FOUR YEAR PERIOD. Doesn't seem too much to ask, does it? With about twelve home games per year, if each team has twelve players to compensate, the financing job could get done for the whole four year period by mid-season, and the next three and a half years would go for the coaches, the school, the sports program, expenses and whatever.

Of course each player, with his meager take of one-half the gate from one game, wouldn't be SO bad off. Twenty-four thousand people at ten dollars a head comes to $240 thousand, or $120 thousand for each player. That means, after plunking down four years of room, board, tuition, and book money, the kid would still have a cool hundred grand in the bank. If it were deposited for him in his freshman year, with the stipulation that he could not touch it until graduation, the interest would put his nest egg at somewhere near $150 thousand by the time he took his sheepskin to the local bank so he could pick up his jack!

There is no reason not to lay this out in something like sarcastic tones — when groups of so-called administrators are periodically getting together to ruminate over the PROBLEMS of big-time college sports. If the players were fairly compensated for their real economic value, we would be hard-pressed to find any problems.

Do you want to talk now about incentives to graduate? About academic advisors? About tutors? About counselors?

Stick a fair share, a 150 grand carrot in front of the rabbits' noses, and they'll all be Rhodes Scholars — or at least they will be a helluva lot closer than they are now.

All sorts of do-gooders will be quick to point out that Kentucky is an exception. Not ALL schools get 24,000 people per game. So big deal! So give the kids a **full** share of the gate for one game, or give them a 100,000 dollar carrot, not 150,000. The dollars are not the crucial issue here. This example is not what I propose for compensating college athletes. But it is a good illustration of the extent of the rip-off.

To try to couch the issue in terms of the value of an education is pure sophistry. It is justification for blatant theft.

MIGRANT WORKERS

Not surprisingly, many of the arguments against compensating athletes are similar to those used for years on grossly underpaid and badly-treated migrant workers. "A job is a valuable commodity." "It's a great privilege to be living in America." "Your time will come."

The similarities don't end with the lies of the establishment which is lining its pockets by the sweat of others' labors. Looking at the athletes' situation, the migrant worker analogy gains validity in many respects.

The athletes come eager to play — "Hey, THEY are the ones who want these jobs. Is anyone FORCING them to work?"

The athletes come and go so quickly, they are so transient, that by the time they realize their position, their value, they are already gone.

The athletes are so spread out, and so busy, and so poor, they can not begin to organize their collective power. Where are they going to get plane tickets to travel to meetings? Who is going to organize these meetings?

It is fully in the establishment's interests to keep the players unorganized, so the grand larceny can go merrily on.

And it does.

Chapter 3

SIGNING DAY AND BENCH SITTING
false promises, broken dreams

If a commitment to penniless amateurism is sincere and the good-old-days, win-one-for-the-gipper attitude is worth trying to achieve, then it MUST be accompanied by a situation where the kids recruited really are being brought into a wonderful situation — a situation where a school's best resources and human efforts are being put into the academic and athletic development of the players they recruit.

Some will claim this is already being done. But THAT is false.

No school with 15 basketball players on scholarship has a happy situation for its players. A basketball team does not contain enough happiness to distribute a good experience to fifteen people.

SIGNING DAY

Sports fans are aware of the ballyhoo associated with the signing of a high school athletic star. A press conference is often called so all the local TV and radio stations and newspapers can get the information at the same time. Local reporters will be upset if their deadlines are not considered.

When I was making a decision in 1967, I clearly remember national sports commentator Dick Stockton, who was then working as a sportscaster in Pittsburgh, reminding my father that he hoped to get the story first or, if a press conference were to be called, he "hoped" it would be called in the evening so he could be first to make the announcement on the Eleven O'clock News.

In any case, the announcement is usually accompanied by some sort of celebration — a gathering of family and friends — or it is made at a high school sports banquet where there will be people around to make a fuss over it. There will usually be sports fans around to confirm the wisdom of the choice and congratulate the young star and his parents.

Everything about the handshakes and congratulations gives the indication that something wonderful has happened. Certainly the coaches have contributed to this feeling. During the recruiting process, a real star will have received letters and calls from several important alumni, perhaps from the governor of the state where the school is, and from anyone else the coaches can mobilize to make their recruiting more impressive. —

With all this recruiting hoopla accompanied by telegrams of congratulations, to say nothing of the cigars and handshakes that might be passed around at the workplace of the star's father, it would indeed seem as though something wonderful has happened when a kid signs.

And something has — for the schools who sign the stars. They have just signed potentially big money-makers for the price of peanuts. They have gotten the signature of a kid who is essentially committed to play for them for four years. By helping to fill their arena with people, he will be responsible for bringing them many thousands of dollars in revenue, not just from gate receipts, but from increases in alumni contributions, in TV revenues, and in student applications. (The number of student applications — of non-athletes — at Georgetown, for example, increased by the THOUSANDS during the time Patrick Ewing was in school there.)

So, signing day is a big day FOR THE SCHOOLS. They get some big potential money makers — at almost no risk. Their commitment is a ONE year scholarship which can be revoked for various reasons during that year and simply not renewed after that year.

The NCAA reports that 4% of the athletic scholarships failed to get renewed in 1984. That is four players on every major football team. Or sixteen players off one football team if three schools renew all theirs.

Suddenly the percentages don't look so rosy. The threat of cancellation is always there. The renewal requirement has consequences. The player realizes that his scholarship is continuing at the grace of his coach. The PLAYER is the one with the pressure to perform up to expectations, and should he leave labeled an attitude problem, he will have difficulty finding another school willing to give him a scholarship while he sits out a year (the transfer rule requires sitting out a year) waiting to play.

The point of all this is that **the fanfare surrounding the signing is all one-sided. Only the school gets a great deal.** The handshakes, telegrams, and letters they pass out are easily enough obtained, and they create the illusion in the player's mind, and in the mind of his parents — AND IN THE MIND OF THE PUBLIC — that something wonderful has indeed happened.

Even sports reporters, who should know better, go on calling the contract "a free ride." It is anything but that.

At best, the kid will end up making the school many thousands of dollars **above** the cost of his room, board, books, and tuition, while preparing himself for a career in the pros. At worst, however, and a scenario which is more common, the kid will sit the bench and watch others get the praise — and the enjoyment — and he will feel like a failure, a second class citizen who did not pan out. His self-image will suffer. Every practice — daily, intense practices still, even though he's not playing in the games — will be a drudgery where he will be chided from time to time by coaches, mostly ignored (even worse), and often stung by comments not even directed at him.

"You guys aren't worth a damn," a coach will often tell his team at halftime of a game they are losing. "You aren't hustling, you're not hitting the boards, you're not playing with intensity," and so on and so on.

The coach thinks he is motivating. But often he is voicing the most damaging, humiliating criticism possible without even knowing it. When he tells the guys playing that they are playing THAT poorly, yet he doesn't opt to play the guys on his bench, he is saying loudly and clearly to the guys on the bench that THEY are even worse — much worse — than all that he has just said to the guys who are playing.

Don't under-estimate the extent of this devastation. Don't console yourself with some easy platitude like "That's all just part of the game."

It isn't. It is a totally unnecessary yet universal tragedy. It happens at every school all over the country, even at those schools with coaches who we look up to as character-developers and who supposedly have the interests of their kids at heart.

Don't let yourself believe that the kids sitting the benches at schools all over the nation aren't bitterly disillusioned, aren't aching inside, aren't suffering permanent psychological damage as a result.

Where did they go wrong? they wonder. They were high school stars. Everyone wanted them. Governors were calling. People with red blazers, or blue or orange, were shaking their hands and sending them telegrams. Coaches were sitting in their homes telling jokes to their parents and carefully remembering the names of their girlfriends, their family dogs, their favorite hangouts.

What happened to all the happy families they were being invited into? Isn't that what they were told during the recruiting process?

You will be hard-pressed to find a guy on the bench at any school in the nation who will be able to repeat to you, with feeling, the happy family concept that was so apparent back when he was being recruited. What happened to all the handshakes, the good feelings, the great new era the kid was supposed to help usher in?

"Some make it, some don't," the saying goes. "That's just the way it is."

No. Student-athletes don't have to buy that. 'Just the way it is' is not an adequate excuse.

Do you realize that even starters, the kids playing and receiving praise and newspaper coverage, get cynical about the collegiate sports experience which they aspired to so intensely? Do you think that even the stars can go through entire seasons with no awareness, no feeling, no resentment of the situation WHEN THEY HAVE TEAMMATES AND FRIENDS who they realize have been essentially ignored and permitted to fall by the wayside?

No players actually LIKE the present situation. They merely live with it because, yes, that's the way it is, and because they have not yet recognized that they have the power to change what they detest.

HYPOCRISY OR BLINDNESS?

So how do directors of athletics and administrators manage to tolerate and do nothing about the present system of penniless amateurism and excessive scholarship quotas?

The general public's ignorance can be understood. But those who are involved are either hypocrites or they are blind. How can a director of athletics claim he is doing what is best for the kids when he sees the universal bitterness and disillusionment that young athletes experience on every college campus?

How can any reasonable person support the present system of heavy recruitment followed by years of permanent bench warming? If the players were well paid, then it would be understandable. You can sit a pro down as long as you like. Pay him his hundred grand and he'll even do cartwheels for you at halftime.

But don't take a kid out of high school and make him and his parents think he is getting something wonderful, and then let him ride the bench for four years, disparaged by his coaches and clenching his teeth to get through one of the most unhappy experiences of his life.

If a commitment to penniless amateurism is sincere and the good-old-days, win-one-for-the-gipper attitude is worth trying to achieve, then it MUST be accompanied by a situation where the kids recruited really are being brought into a wonderful situation — a situation where a school's best resources and human efforts are being put into the academic and athletic development of the players they recruit.

Some will claim this is already being done. But THAT is false.

No school with 15 basketball players on scholarship has a happy situation for its players. **A basketball team does not contain enough happiness to distribute a good experience to fifteen people.**

Do you understand? Show me a college basketball team with fifteen recruited high school stars on scholarship, and I will show you some intensely unhappy kids. Can directors of athletics not know this fact of collegiate sports life?

Pro football teams carry 45 players on their rosters. How do you explain, within a staunch commitment to amateurism and providing a good experience "for the kids" (the most hypocritical prepositional phrase in collegiate sports today) college football teams having **95** kids on football scholarships at one time? How do you explain the **150** scholarships they are permitted by rule to give, in order to arrive at that ridiculously excessive, hate-producing number?

Please understand the implication. **There is not one major college in the nation with a complete team of happy players.**

The coaches can justify it to themselves by saying they do the best they can for their kids under the present system. They offer an opportunity, and it is up to the kids to make the most of it. (At least most coaches add that they would like to give their kids more — if they could — and some do anyway.) But what justification is there for faculty reps, directors of athletics, and college presidents who go annually to some convention/resort to cast their self-righteous NCAA votes for integrity and amateurism, yet permit a system to go on where there is no possibility of bringing satisfaction to large numbers of participants who they help recruit and therefore whose illusions they help to form?

You either have to give the kids what they are worth, and let them sink or swim on their own merits, or you have to be truly committed to providing for those kids who you go after, and whose abilities you exploit, the best possible situation you can construct. No one is coming even close to this effort.

BIG CUTS ARE NECESSARY

Since there aren't any basketball coaches who can give fifteen players a good experience, and since there aren't any football coaches who can give 95 kids a good experience, the obvious thing to do is to limit the total number of scholarships a school can give — to numbers like 12 and 68, which means giving a maximum of 3 basketball and 17 football scholarships per year for four years.

Academicians and critics of too-big athletic programs should welcome this proposal because, if for no other reason, it would save a lot of money on scholarships. (It would also save money by enabling football and basketball programs to cut down on the number of assistant coaches they employ. Two coaches is enough in basketball, and six or seven in football should be more than adequate.)

Many coaches will squawk at the suggestion that scholarship quotas be lowered. But that is merely because they have become accustomed to having a lot of bodies around. **Being one of a large number of available bodies was NEVER good for the players.** A large number of bodies allows a coach to treat players shoddily, with a what-the-hell attitude, "If you don't pan out, someone else will."

This is not theoretical. This is a fact of life. When there are a lot of extra players, coaches can afford to run a lot of gut drills to see "who really wants it," as the saying goes. Coaches can afford to run long, intense practices without worrying that someone will get hurt.

In fact, believe it or not, many coaches find themselves now in the position of actually HOPING someone will get hurt — not because they are sadists who want kids to feel pain, but because the competition for playing time is keen and their coaching decisions are often very difficult to justify to the kids they have recruited.

"Why aren't I playing?" a player will ask. And often there is no good answer. Several kids of about equal ability are around and all of them have a reasonable claim to a starting position or to playing time — and there just aren't enough starting positions or playing minutes to go around. An injury, especially a slight, not particularly painful one, is often just what a coach is hoping for. It will give him an excuse, a way to explain how one player got a headstart on another and simply managed to maintain that edge.

Of course coaches will deny this — and they should. But it is true nevertheless.

The system should not be set up in a way that an injury can ever be to a coach's benefit.

When you talk about reducing scholarship quotas, the quick rebuttal is, "What would we do if someone got hurt?"

Isn't that a wonderful question and concern? The answer should be obvious. The team will hurt when a player gets hurt — so you better do everything possible, if only from a selfish point of view, to reduce the chance of injuries. Perhaps practices should be shorter, less intense, and feature less "hitting in pads" and more explaining, more conditioning, stretching, and flexibility drills. Who knows? Who can say? Should a faculty rep tell a coach how to field a winning team? Of course not. But no one would have to legislate for shorter practices or safer practices or for a more intense search for better protective equipment — if the health of the players was paramount to success. The coaches would direct their intelligence and their resources to these matters, simply because it would lead to winning.

If people are trying to win at any cost, a common media accusation, then the task of administrators is to set up the system so that winning itself is facilitated by a regard for the health, education and welfare of the players.

If it is truly important to have a team of healthy players, a team of players who pass courses and graduate, and a team of players who truly benefit from and enjoy their collegiate athletic experience, then the present system is ridiculously, poorly constructed.

Chapter 4

TO ENHANCE THE EXPERIENCE
for the kids — a solution to the problems

To truly enhance the athletic atmosphere, the universities have to be willing to say what the coaches will not: if an athlete is recruited to play for State University, then indeed he will *play* for State University — just as a salesman hired to work for IBM indeed *works* for IBM.

"TO ENHANCE THE COLLEGIATE EXPERIENCE OF THE PARTICIPANTS . . . "

It is one of the NCAA's fundamental policies to attempt to enhance the collegiate experience of the people who accept athletic scholarships. The striking failure of the NCAA to do this is not surprising in view of the fact that the often-heard phrase "for the kids" is taken so seldomly into account when the NCAA is in the process of making rules and regulations.

A respected director of athletics told me that, during all of the years in which he has attended NCAA conventions and meetings, he has NEVER heard anyone even MENTION what would be best "for the kids" when decisions are being made.

The results of this neglect are obvious in the situation which exists. John Weistart, professor of Law at Duke University and a nationally recognized expert in sports law, has suggested that the NCAA might be taken to court for this failure which might be, in legal terms, a failure to live up to its "fiduciary responsibility." Just as a stock broker must in fact represent the best interests of his clients, the NCAA should represent the best interests of the people who fall under its jurisdiction.

The legal questions are covered to some degree in other parts of this book and, in any case, their ramifications are beyond the scope of this particular discussion. But just imagine, for a moment, the collegiate sports world — on signing day — if the NCAA did in fact take its "fiduciary responsibility" seriously, or if it simply made a real effort to make its rules with THE KIDS in mind.

SIGNING DAY WITH THE KIDS IN MIND: SOLUTIONS TO THE PROBLEMS

If the NCAA and the universities were sincere in their desire to enhance the experience of the student-athletes generating so much revenue for them, then signing day would indeed be a cause for family and friends of prospects to celebrate.

There are several ways to enhance the student-athlete's collegiate experience. Any of the following ways would be acceptable and far superior to the present, totally unacceptable circumstances of the student-athlete's life on campus.

First, and simplest, the NCAA and the universities could pay the athletes a fair share of what they generate, and let them fend for themselves both academically and athletically. With the incentive to make fifty to a hundred thousand dollars a year, and with the only requirement being that the athlete be a student in good standing at the university he represented, the universities would be free to devote their full attention to academic matters. The players, on their own, could provide for tutors, remedial help, counseling, and whatever else they might need to stay in school, maintain certain grade levels, and make steady progress toward graduation — whatever the colleges required of regular students or decided to require of those representing them.

Given the profit motive, the players would find a way to make it themselves and, in any case, the universities would have no responsibility for their failures when they did not make it.

LESS RADICAL STEPS

If a less radical departure from the past seems desirable, which no doubt it would to most lovers of college athletics, there are three basic issues to deal with: the athletic, academic, and financial atmospheres. If the universities insist on taking a large portion of athletes' money, they must provide an atmosphere fostering development, self-pride, and success. To do this in the athletic sphere is simple.

ENHANCING THE ATHLETIC ATMOSPHERE

The athletic atmosphere for student-athletes could be enhanced tremendously with four simple rules:

1. Cut scholarship quotas of football teams to 17 per year, and of basketball teams to 3 per year.

2. Allow a cummulative total of 12 scholarships for basketball and 68 for football.

3. Do not permit freshmen to play varsity.

4. Call defections, transfers, and drop-offs "coaching failures" and do not permit transfers of those scholarships until those players would have completed their eligibility.

The first step, to cut scholarship quotas, would enhance the student-athletes' athletic experience tremendously. Playing time, THE crucial ingredient to any athlete's happiness, would virtually be assured for each recruited athlete.

To truly enhance the athletic atmosphere, the universities have to be willing to say what the coaches will not: if an athlete is recruited to play for State University, then indeed he will PLAY for State University — just as a salesman hired to work for IBM indeed WORKS for IBM. If that salesman does poorly, then for the period of time he is under contract, IBM does not do as well. In the same way, if the recruited player plays poorly, the university team would suffer accordingly.

If the coaches are experts in judging people and talent, this should present no great hardship and, in any case, the ability to judge people and talent should be rewarded. (A rule like this would be of little consequence to coaches like Dean Smith and Mike Krzyzewski who keep —

and see graduate — nearly all the players they recruit at the University of North Carolina and at Duke.)

In any business it is the responsibility of the personnel department to locate, recruit, and hire people who are going to be able to do their jobs well.

The universities should be comfortable with this approach. It is generally the approach they take with regard to graduate admissions. They admit students who have demonstrated their ability, and the graduate schools make an effort to see that these students are successful.

[Fans and undergraduate students, in many cases, will be surprised to know that it is generally easier to get good grades in graduate school than it is in undergraduate school. At most graduate schools, there is little, if any, weeding out process. Selection is considered the screening process — just as it should be for high school athletes who are identified, located and recruited — selected — to come to a university.]

By limiting scholarship quotas to 3 per year for basketball and 17 per year for football, it would be clear that the schools would have to select carefully, and then nurture intelligently, each of the players they recruit.

There would be few cases of athletes feeling disillusioned, bitter, or deceived — as is so incredibly common today.

FRESHMAN INELIGIBILITY

With just 3 basketball scholarships per year and 17 football scholarships per year, and Freshmen not permitted to play on the varsity teams, there would normally be just 9 basketball players and 51 football players available to play. Yet there would be 12 basketball players, and 68 football players, to practice.

This rule would satisfy those who favor the idea of making a kid demonstrate academic prowess before permitting him to play ball, and more importantly, from the standpoint of the athlete, it would limit the competition for playing time.

RED-SHIRTING

What if a school wanted to 'red-shirt' a kid? Fine, it would be welcome to do that, although it would have to offer one less scholarship to an incoming Freshman that year, so that the total number of scholarships would never exceed 12 or 68.

FOR THE KIDS

What a tremendous, positive change for the personal experience of each athlete. Suddenly, all of them would feel justifiably important. Each would be a valued member of the team, and all of them would have to be treated that way even after arriving at school, and even after demonstrating in their first year of competition that they weren't as good as the coaches had hoped.

With just 9, or 51, eligible players, a coach couldn't out-recruit his mistakes. He would have to work to DEVELOP his players and to turn his mistakes into successes.

Presently a mistake is of little consequence — as long as there aren't too many. If one player doesn't pan out, so what? Get someone else. Let the mistake transfer or drop off the team or sit far down the bench. No big deal.

DEFECTIONS

If defecting, transferring, or disinterested players could not be replaced by offering new scholarships, the coaches would be certain to value the kids recruited and to do their very best to give them a great experience. The last man on the team, now so routinely forgotten, would have to be treated well and continuously developed. Who could know when a few injuries or transfers might make him a sudden starter?

DRASTIC CHANGES?

Are these drastic changes? They are changes, but not ones that would alter significantly the product turned out by the top coaches. They would, however, render ineffective the mediocre coaches and the coaches with inadequate people skills. But that should be desired anyway if anyone cares to keep THE KIDS in mind.

ENHANCING THE ACADEMIC ENVIRONMENT

In order to enhance the student-athletes' academic life, several changes must be made.

1. ALLOW FINANCIAL AID FOR REMEDIAL STUDIES

. . . and do not begin a student-athlete's eligibility until he enters college, regardless of his age.

Borderline and ill-prepared students should be encouraged to prepare themselves academically to enter college, and they should not be penalized if remedial efforts take extra time.

If the coaches of an athletic team have sufficient interest in a student-athlete to want to arrange to pay for his remedial studies, they should be permitted to do so.

2. GIVE SCHOLARSHIPS FOR INDEFINITE PERIODS OF TIME

The present "one year renewable" scholarship, which is the only one the NCAA permits, is — as Woody Allen would say — "a travesty of a mockery of a sham." What justification is there for letting colleges own a player — and have to give their permission to another school in order for the school to talk to him about transferring — when the players get only a one year scholarship which can be revoked for a variety of reasons and not renewed at all after each year?

The schools have to be willing to fulfill their part of the bargain. The athlete contributes his athletic ability but the schools don't educate. To alter that record, the schools have to be willing to say, "We want to use YOUR athletic talents in our behalf, and in return you can use OUR resources to get an education. If you don't get a degree in four years, we will keep trying, because we are betting on you."

If the school has to try extra long or work extra hard or spend extra money, then it should. It was the school's decision to recruit that particular athlete. The school was not required to select him. It put a premium on HIS particular skills and abilities, so it should be the school's responsibility to see to it that he succeeds in the mission it has selected him for. Administrators cannot pretend to be naive. They know what kind of people are likely to succeed, and they are free to recruit those people — just as they are free NOT to recruit those who are likely to become a drag on their treasury.

Traditionally, the universities with dismal graduation rates among their student-athletes have justified their shoddy performance with the reasoning that they have provided the athletes with an OPPORTUNITY, but the athletes have failed to take advantage of it. This is not acceptable reasoning when coming from educated, university representatives and used against uneducated seventeen-year-olds. The percentages tell the story. When some seventy percent of the major college student-athletes are annually failing to get a degree, it becomes necessary to quit blaming them and to start blaming the process. Many of those seventy percent are not adequately prepared when they are admitted and their eventual failure, therefore, is easily predictable. Put any group of borderline students into a competitive academic environment, and then give them some other time-consuming activity unrelated to their academic success and they will fail every time.

Only after the colleges start admitting kids who are prepared to succeed in college, and after they start helping financially to prepare the athletic stars who are not prepared, can they use the "failed to seize the opportunity" argument.

3. **LINK SCHOLARSHIPS TO SHEEPSKINS**

Finally, let's look at the implications of linking the scholarship rate to the graduation rate: No players graduating, then no scholarships to give. Basically, this would do little more than make education an integral part of winning. With direct linkage, it would PAY coaches to be the educator-counselors they are supposed to be, **even if their selfish intent were merely to win at any cost.**

The COST, you see, would be sheepskins. You couldn't win consistently without them. Try building a team with no scholarships to give. It isn't easy. But that is exactly what would be required if a coach recruited a group of borderline students who didn't make it in the classroom.

A basketball player who flunked out in his first year would leave his team with only eight players on scholarship for FIVE years. THAT would make coaches very wary of recruiting a kid who could not make it in the classroom, and it would make coaches work with the kid and counsel the kid and help him reach his potential — even if that were the last thing the coach cared about.

The desire to win, not basic human goodness, is all that would be required to turn nearly all coaches into caring, attentive leaders and counselors — presumably what higher education wants them to be.

It doesn't take an Einstein to realize that a whole group of failures-to-graduate in a particular class — not an uncommon occurrence today — would leave a coach and athletic program devastated, which would not be bad at all if academics are truly deemed to be important.

The win-at-any-cost type of coach, at worst, would be staying up at night writing papers for his kids while trying to keep the professors from learning his style of writing! At best, and most often, athletes would be graduating in numbers not now even hoped for by most colleges.

ENHANCING THE STUDENT-ATHLETE'S LIFE FINANCIALLY

In consideration of the amount of money generated by revenue producing major college basketball and football players, there can be no disputing the fact that they are entitled to benefits beyond room, board, tuition, and books.

There can be no legitimate rationale for keeping their scholarships at the current level while $96 million TV contracts are being signed for basketball playoffs, while the Rose Bowl is returning $12,000,000 to the Big-10 and Pac-10 conferences for ONE game, and while many football and basketball programs are paying for the entire sports budgets at their universities.

Reasonable, minimum benefits to be added to the current room, board, books, and tuition should include the following:

1. Spending money of $200 per month.

2. Plane tickets for travel to and from home at vacations and before and after the school year.

3. Plane tickets and lodging for parents to watch a couple of games during the season.

4. Use of a car during the time school is in session.

These benefits are basic. Spending money in a world of ten dollar pizzas is essential. Critics claim that dollar amounts of this nature won't cure ALL cheating, but it WILL make a lot of players more comfortable;

people generating millions of dollars do deserve to be comfortable. They will also be less inclined to look for ways to get a buck.

The need for some travel expenses should be obvious in view of the national recruiting carried on in recent years by nearly all of the large, money-making programs.

Providing for parents of players to watch games is not necessary, but it certainly is something the players want very much, and it is an area that often invites cheating. Why shouldn't a wealthy alumnus be permitted to treat a kid's parents to a free trip — on him — to watch their son play?

The schools need not be forced to provide these benefits. They should merely be PERMITTED BY RULE to provide them.

Finally, the use of a car might be handled similarly. Courtesy cars now given routinely to coaches and athletic directors would go to players who, of course, need them more. It would not be necessary for every player to get a new car. Players could share cars. Seniors could get new ones, Freshmen the oldest ones, and so forth. It is not important that each kid get a shiny, new Mercedes 450SL — only that the ridiculous rule be ended so that kids can benefit from the transportation opportunities available to big-time sports programs.

INCENTIVES

Finally, the possibility of cash incentives — FOR GOOD STUDENTS — may be the best idea of all. This program is not one that student-athletes are even likely themselves to fight for. But what is stopping the universities from taking the initiative?

Why not let student-athletes enter college WITHOUT THE REQUIREMENT to take full course loads and without the need to search for easy courses or 'get-by' courses while they concentrate on athletics?

Why not let each athlete progress academically AT HIS OWN PACE? This might mean he would take just one course per semester — if that were all he felt capable of handling. But ADD to that non-requirement the INCENTIVE of cash rewards for academic performance.

CASH FOR S. A. T. SCORES

What would be the effect of an offer that every player, upon signing a grant-in-aid could be permitted to accept — from the school or from alumni — $10 for every point he scored on the Scholastic Aptitude Test above 470?

Do you think we would have athletes getting into school with 470's? With or without a Proposition 48 or other rules establishing minimum standards, the kids would strive on their own to raise their scores — if they knew immediate monetary rewards awaited. The kid with a rather low SAT score of 670 would have 200 points over a 470, and thus could receive $2000 in spending money. The kid with a score of 1200 would have 730 points above 470 and therefore would be eligible to receive $7300. Nobody would be REQUIRED to give him $7300, but they would be permitted by rule to do that.

Why NOT reward academic achievement through the athletic program? Can you imagine all the kids who would WANT to take SAT preparation courses if they knew that just 50 extra points could mean $500 extra dollars?

CASH FOR GRADES

Why not allow schools to reward players in proportion to their legitimate 'quality points' earned, at perhaps $100 for each point over twenty-four, which would be a "C" average in four major, 3 hour courses? Twelve course hours [4 × 3] times 2.0, the score for a C, would give 24 points, the break even point. A "D" average would cut into the kid's normal expense money, whereas a "B" average in four courses (12 × 3.0) would give a 36, and a $1200 bonus payoff.

Strange? Complicated? Unnecessary? Radical?

What is the argument? Why shouldn't a university reward academic excellence with cash? Must there be a pretense that no one has any interest in cash? Is it feared that all the intelligent kids would suddenly become drug addicts and gamblers with SO much money?

There is probably only one real reason that cash incentives and rewards will meet with disapproval by those in power. It is not really that they couldn't muster up some creative proposals. It is because, up to now, they have gotten away with stealing ALL the players' money, and they see no reason to part with any of it under any circumstances.

For many years, the universities and the NCAA have presided over sports programs that have not been any more responsive to the psychological needs of many of the participants than they have been to their financial rights.

Clearly, there are methods and dollars available to enhance tremendously the lives of revenue producing major college student-athletes, but no one in the NCAA is even talking about making any real positive changes.

A NOTE ON PURE AMATEURISM

The colleges must either pay a fair share, or change their system. If the colleges are indeed for a pure form of amateurism, they need to demonstrate this by NOT charging admission to the games, by NOT recruiting players from out of state, by NOT paying coaches more than their physical education instructors, by NOT traveling across the nation to play games, by NOT giving scholarships for athletic excellence, and by NOT engaging in contracts to televise the games.

The principles of amateurism are not upheld as long as these common practices continue.

Chapter 5

STANDING IN THE WAY: THE NCAA
structured collusion

The NCAA is perpetrating a daily theft of athletes' earnings, and it is exploiting athletes' bodies. With a smooth self-righteousness, the NCAA makes studied claims of innocence, preaches the virtues of amateurism and academic priorities, and lines its own pockets with gold.

STANDING IN THE WAY: THE NCAA
carefully orchestrated collusion

The NCAA stands firmly in the way of fair compensation for revenue producing student-athletes. A history of exploitation, as well as a smugly simplistic position-statement from NCAA president, John R. Davis, makes this abundantly clear.

"It's not in the philosophy of institutions to hire a bunch of pro athletes to represent them. Institutions are providing a means for an education for those students they recruit and that's all. They are not going beyond that."

Constant references to "the membership" and "the will of the member institutions" is the NCAA's Catch-22. The leadership is quick to point out, at any stage of discussion, that the NCAA is not a group of besieged bureaucrats holed up in Mission, Kansas who occasionally lash out at this or that renegade school but instead are just some good citizens carrying out the will of the member institutions. Any personal communication reveals the smugness of that position and belies Judge Paul Goldman's observation (in 1984):

"The NCAA has numerous, very distinguished individuals on its various committees and its Council, for public consumption, but the real power is in the hands of the bureaucrats who are unknown to, and unelected by, the membership of the NCAA."

Indeed, it is often difficult to know what anyone is talking about when he refers to the NCAA. Is he referring to the group of bureaucrats who run the show between conventions? Is he referring to the group of 800 schools which make up the entire association? Or is he referring to the 650 "little" schools that are basically responsible for the NCAA's rule book and for so much legislation detrimental to the schools with revenue producing athletic programs?

The meanings run together because, regardless of which group is specifically being referred to, there is without doubt an organized collusion, a structured collusion you might call it, which assures that the players will lose out again and again in any legislation proposed and voted on by the members. For an obvious example, look at the comment by the NCAA Select Committee on Athletic Problems and Concerns in Higher Education.

"Many of the existing rules . . . [limiting player benefits] are intended to protect institutional treasuries . . ."

What is best for the bureaucrats and what is best for the schools is seldom what is best for the players. But the players have no voice. The players have no representation of any kind. They do not appear at NCAA conventions. They propose no legislation. The players go out on the courts and fields and generate money while the schools and the NCAA sit back and decide how to use it.

This is the history of the NCAA, regardless of what you are referring to, and there is no foreseeable change in the future. The NCAA bureaucrats themselves are enjoying the best of times. Their numbers are growing, their salaries are growing, and their expense accounts are growing. Furthermore, they are even gaining more power, as mandated by the Special Presidents' Convention in New Orleans in February, 1985.

The college presidents, themselves, are proud of their new role, their stand of becoming active participants in the regulation of college athletics. That they have had to make a point of doing this at all demonstrates their long history of failure in this regard. Passing NCAA legislation to bring about institutional control of athletic programs is almost comical. What president did NOT feel in control of his athletic program?

Obviously, the presidents are in control. At San Francisco, and more recently at Tulane, the presidents wiped out entire programs. So what's the problem? Why all the fuss?

The presidents, at their special convention, were not truly after control, not truly out to regulate collegiate athletics. They were there to make a statement to the public in behalf of the integrity of higher education. They wanted to go on record as saying things that should have been obvious without saying anything. But they went ahead and did it up right, and the result is more rules, more regulations, more exploitation of student-athletes and a continuation and enlargement of the cancerous atmosphere of paranoia that pervades big-time sports.

The presidents put even coaches and directors of athletics on the run, so strong were their actions in behalf of integrity. Therefore, the few noises formerly being made in behalf of the players have been silenced by the rap of the NCAA gavel.

INCREDIBLE EVIL

What happened? How did things get to the point where universities are in collusion with a group of powerful bureaucrats to suppress the rights of a group of young athletes just wanting to play some ball and get an education? From where did all the evil arise that must be so zealously pursued and attacked? Whoever could have guessed that the university presidents would permit millions of THEIR dollars to be spent on legal fees and investigations into the actions of their own members? Are these kinds of expenditures (and the associated paranoia which that pursuit engenders) really what the presidents want?

A look back provides some help in understanding the absurd situation which is big-time collegiate athletics today.

HISTORICAL PERSPECTIVE

It is not necessary to over-dramatize the cause of major college athletes by claiming that the NCAA was originally staffed with Ali Baba and forty thieves. In the beginning, there was no intention to steal from the revenue producers, because there wasn't revenue to steal.

In other words, the big money generated in recent years by major college basketball and football generally took everyone by surprise. The profits got gradually larger and larger, and the NCAA found itself in the enviable position of having more money to distribute than anyone was asking for.

Basketball teams and the universities they represented were not accustomed to getting big payoffs for participation in the NCAA basketball tournament. So when they got some money back, everyone was grateful. The university president was grateful to the basketball coach for winning, and certainly there was impetus for the president to return the money the basketball program generated to the basketball program — for a larger recruiting budget, new equipment, perhaps renovation of gym or locker rooms or coaches' offices.

Everyone was grateful to the NCAA, the dispersers of the cash, and lo and behold, there was still more money in the coffers, still more money to give out. So why not invite the swimming teams to California for a championship? Why not bring the top golf teams to Florida? Why not present trophies? Why not give scholarships? Why not bring some special friends out to the Final Four for a weekend — on us?

The NCAA was able to make a lot of friends by distributing a lot of money to people who hadn't earned it. Under usual circumstances, the earners would raise hell. But in this case they didn't. The coaches were too busy thanking the NCAA, too busy being congratulated by their presidents, and too worried about next year to start even thinking about fair distributions.

Initially, only conference winners were invited to the NCAA playoffs. So, a coach could hardly count on getting there to receive some of that money. In the Atlantic Coast Conference, for example, to get to the NCAA Tournament, a team had to be sharp during one, three-game tournament, had to win all three games on that weekend in March in order to be invited at all.

What coach would make noise about NCAA distributions when his own participation was so tenuous? It was all any coach could do just to make sure his own team would be participating. So, what developed was the unusual situation where the generators of all the revenue weren't squawking at all. The huge TV contracts signed by the NCAA with the major networks had hardly been foreseen a few years earlier. College basketball was struggling for acceptance, and all of a sudden it had arrived.

The NCAA didn't plan and probably never intended any grand theft. The directors of the NCAA had to have been as surprised as anyone else by the sudden popularity of big time sports.

Once understanding this history, the NCAA can be seen in a different light. The NCAA is simply an organization that grew so fast, with so much good fortune, that it hardly had time to evaluate itself. The member institutions had never felt the need to establish an organization that could effectively deal with the problems and opportunities that came up, because no one had anticipated those problems and those opportunities.

Thirty years ago it made sense to put hundreds of big and little schools under the collective roof of the NCAA. Big or little, the sports programs at the member schools were not essentially different in nature. But, of course, times changed.

The NCAA, now, clearly needs to be re-constituted but there is not a mechanism in place to handle such a task.

College presidents have a lot more to worry about than the running of athletic programs. They hardly have time to oversee the NCAA, let alone roll up their sleeves and change it.

The NCAA is like a runaway truck; control has been lost. No one ever planned for it to be so big. No one ever realized it would have so much money and so much power, and apparently no one had the foresight to structure it in a way that change would be readily possible.

Legal counsels at the major universities uniformly throw their hands in the air when talking about the NCAA. "You'll never get anything done through the NCAA," one told me.

President Edward Foote of Miami (FL) University has said publicly that the NCAA is simply too big and too unwieldy to be effective. He says the NCAA needs to be totally re-organized, but he also said he is not optimistic it can be done. Having failed in some special efforts to bring about change, he is now himself (after the Special Convention) endorsing the company line.

If a university president feels as though HE is powerless to do anything about the NCAA, WHO CAN?

A coach is one tiny part of a university. His voice is only as loud as his last season. Throw a chair across a court and even if you've won the Olympics and a couple of national championships, your opinion becomes suspect.

Clearly the migrant workers, the players, are not in an ideal position to organize and change the NCAA. So, with no one really having the time or being in a position to oversee and provide controlled, steady growth, the bureaucrats, on the scene, assumed the power without contention.

Changes, as a result, require a grand effort. Wisdom, logic, and common sense have little to do with the process. Just to get a proposal up for a vote at an NCAA convention takes a prodigious effort for someone not accustomed to doing such things.

Let's take a realistic example. Say a player like Mark Price at Georgia Tech sincerely believes he deserves some of the money which he obviously generates for his university, for the Atlantic Coast Conference, and for the NCAA. He will have to take his feelings to his head coach, Bobby Cremins, who will have to be convinced of the intelligence and sincerity of Price's feelings, and then the two of them will have to talk it over with the team. If it seems the team generally feels the same way, Cremins MAY go along with them and make an appointment with the university's faculty representative, who generally attends NCAA meetings.

Of course, Cremins has dozens of things to do, games to worry about, recruiting, appearances, endorsement contracts, and summer camps — and Price has to hit the books in addition to playing ball. But an appointment can be made, and the faculty rep will likely tell them that, to get a proposal before the NCAA convention, they will need the agreement of five other schools.

Who will take the time to call five other schools? Will Cremins do that in behalf of his players? (What if he doesn't really agree with them?) Will the faculty rep suddenly start calling around? How will they bring five other schools together to talk about what they want, so that some action can be taken? And how soon can all of this get done? Can something like that come to a vote before Price graduates?

Obviously, **the nature of the system stifles any notion of participants taking initiative**. People not accustomed to dealing in these things rightly see the procedures as mighty obstacles in their path. Tennessee football player Charles Davis expressed these sentiments precisely to a Knoxville reporter, when asked what he thought of a proposal to get athletes more benefits:

"Present players won't be able to benefit [from the proposed changes] but future players might."

How many players, how many human beings, are likely to stick their necks out to bring about changes which they feel they will have no opportunity to benefit from?

It is a cleverly rigged system.

Clearly, it is in the interest of the NCAA to make it difficult for players — and even coaches and universities — to make changes. In the special New Orleans convention, it was no surprise, as the NCAA News reported, that the only properly submitted proposals on the agenda were ones proposed by the NCAA Presidents' Commission and the NCAA Council.

Doesn't it seem strange that in the history of the NCAA there has never been a player-initiated proposal brought before an NCAA convention? Are there even any coach-initiated proposals? The people directly involved are usually either too busy or too in the dark to even know what to do. And those who do KNOW, have become frustrated by the unwieldy nature of the process.

If you ask some players how to make a change in NCAA rules — the things that govern them and steal from them and unfairly restrict their whole lives — most of them will have no idea. MOST of them have no idea who their faculty rep is. MOST of them have never even considered the possibility of changing a rule that negatively affects them, and no one is doing it for them. With many university legal departments and presidents concluding that effective action within the NCAA is impossible, it is small wonder that the players have felt powerless themselves.

THE "LITTLE" SCHOOLS

Despite all the moralizing about corruption in big-time college sports, the single most important factor that prevents a solution to the problems is not unscrupulous coaches, is not players looking for handouts, and is not zealous alumni butting in and giving out benefits.

THE factor that most influences big-time college sports and prevents the one hundred or so big-time schools from policing themselves are the NCAA's "little" schools.

The NCAA, though careful to claim at every juncture that they merely carry out the will of the member institutions, is made up of more than 800 schools, each one with one vote on all essential matters.

The facts of NCAA life are that **the little schools are constantly lined up against the one hundred or so big schools with revenue producing athletic programs**.

Proposals calling for increased aid to student-athletes, for example, are voted down routinely because the little schools do not have money to pay. Although they cannot carry their weight at the turnstyles, they do not want to be considered inferior. As long as everyone can give the same, poverty-level scholarships, the little schools can run competitive programs, retain the illusion of (artificially imposed) parity, and benefit from NCAA revenue distributions — available because of the money generated by the big schools.

Needless to belabor, this is a totally ridiculous situation that has had the effect of stymying most serious efforts by the revenue-producing schools to propose legislation.

The smaller schools take pride in the purity of their philosophy and in their seemingly untainted commitment to education. But it is a pride based more on lack of opportunity rather than on greater self-discipline or vision.

It is easy for the small schools to rail against the abuses of major college sports. Non-revenue sports are not subject to the same kind of alumni involvement nor the same kind of pressures as are revenue-producing sports. Common sense tells you the two are different. But again, the structure of the NCAA does not account for this.

For another example, consider the recent, tough sanctions approved by the NCAA Special Convention regarding the enforcement measures in "Proposal 3." If a school is found guilty of two so-called "major" violations in a five year period, they can be penalized with a suspended program for a two year period.

This is nothing for a Division III school to weather. A Division III football program, for example, costs a lot of money. So a Division III school might actually save money by not having to field a team for two years.

On the other hand, if a major football program were penalized in the same way, not only would millions of dollars be lost, but many other sports programs would have to be suspended as well — or paid for out of general funds usually used on education — because the football programs at major schools typically fund the entire minor sports budgets.

To levy the same punishment on the big schools as on the little schools is absurd. Little schools rarely have such abuses or even the temptation to commit them, while major schools have these possibilities as daily concerns, and sometimes, despite a concerted, sincere effort by coaches and administrators, enthusiastic booster club members may cause violations anyway.

It is not so simple as to claim that the schools must be able to control their booster clubs. Everyone knows that no one can guarantee the control of other individuals, especially not those individuals who have their own jobs and businesses and who can function totally outside the institutions they support in sports.

To make one rule which governs both the situation as it relates to the revenue-losers and the situation as it relates to the million-dollar producers is patently crazy. But it is done. It is indeed a fact of NCAA governing life.

There can be no question that the big schools would be much better off by being members of a Revenue Producing Major College Athletic Association (RPMCAA) rather than by being members of the NCAA. But any attempt to change the present structure will be met with violent opposition. The political intricacies are myriad. The people-networks are carefully orchestrated by the NCAA bureaucrats. Fear is ever-present among individual institutions, especially among those making noises about making change.

The NCAA bureaucratic high brass has a good thing going. They exist on money generated by others' efforts, and they stroke each others' egos — especially the representatives of the little schools who have no other claim to media attention and public renown.

The NCAA could not exist in the high fashion it has become accustomed to if basketball championship revenues were removed from its operating budget.

So the NCAA will not let go of its power easily. What people with power ever do?

The NCAA clings to and cultivates its power carefully, and in the process makes a farce of athletes' rights, a subject which goes, year after year, totally unacknowledged. No one in the NCAA stands to benefit from an athlete's bill of rights. If the athletes achieve greater benefits, the coffers of the NCAA are proportionately depleted. Don't think for a moment the NCAA is not fully aware of that. And don't be misled by the claims that the NCAA is merely carrying out the will of the member institutions.

The NCAA is perpetrating a daily theft of athletes' rightful earnings, and it is exploiting athletes' bodies. With a smooth self-righteousness, the NCAA makes studied claims of innocence, preaches the virtues of amateurism and academic priorities, and lines its own pockets with gold.

It is blatant theft and hypocrisy, but in the NCAA's defense, many of them don't even know it. They have so thoroughly learned their roles, or so long ago quit thinking, that many of them seem truly to be convinced that what they are doing is "for the kids."

A CLIMATE OF PARANOIA

It is curious that the NCAA, being as it is an association of universities, would have taken on a life of its own in such a way as to produce so much fear, paranoia, and ill-feeling among those who are subject to its power. In theory, of course, this is not the case. The NCAA supposedly has a cooperative relationship with its member institutions. In matters related to possible rules violations, procedure calls for a member school to call up the local friendly NCAA representative in Mission, Kansas and ask for an interpretation. Everyone is a good friend, all working together, of course, for quality sports programs. Confidentiality is assured on all such matters, but no one makes a point of noting that a request by a university may actually tip off the NCAA Enforcement Department that some wrong-doing is going on. The notion of "cooperative association" is a farce, and the coaches are fully aware of that. As a result, their athletic programs often have more secrecy, and certainly fewer leaks, than the White House. The best policy is to keep everything quiet. Don't leak any information to the public about anything. Don't say a word. Control what the players say. Control the people working in the athletic department.

Ask any reporter about the seige mentality within big-time sports programs. It is a necessary ingredient to uninvestigated success. But is it what we want? Is it what the university presidents want? Do the coaches want it? Do the players want it? Who wants such secrecy and fear to be an integral part of big-time college sports?

It would be healthier to have a group of black-hatted gamblers snooping around athletic programs than to have the present fear and secrecy festering always like a cancer from within. When you speak of corrupting influences on young athletes, forget about the occasional gambler or drug-dealer. MOST athletes can spot them and put them off in a second. But what do they do when their coaches feed them a daily diet of antidotes for openness and free expression?

A MONUMENT TO NARROW-MINDED LEADERSHIP

Perhaps more than any other single ingredient, the factor most standing in the way of progress for players is the mentality of those who hold positions of power within the NCAA. That there would be differences of opinion in certain matters is, of course, to be expected. But what exists are not just differences of opinion but a monumental narrow-mindedness which has to make players wonder whether their leaders even understand the questions.

The president of the NCAA himself, in response to a question about compensation for revenue producing athletes said:

"But what about the wrestlers? They'll want money too. And how are the wrestling coaches gonna like that? All of their wrestlers will be going out for football."

What realistic hope is there for change within the system when the leaders are making inane comments like that? What about the wrestlers? Yes, really! And what about the band, the rugby club and the Little Sisters of the Poor? What about Biafra, Ethiopia, and Outer Mongolia? What possible reason could there be for giving the producers of millions of dollars of revenue some return — as long as there is poverty in the world? Is THAT Mr. Davis' question?

The NCAA president is hardly alone in expressing such viewpoints.

John Bridgers, the director of athletics at the University of New Mexico, (whose basketball program netted 1.2 million during the 1984-85 season) has pointed out often that . . .

" . . . only ten percent of the athletics programs in the nation make money . . . What about programs that lose money? . . . What about swimmers, or wrestlers, or athletes in track and field? Should they be paid?"

Said Coach Abe Lemons, whose basketball program at The University of Texas went six years without a graduation:

"I keep seeing articles . . . about some football coaches wanting to give football players $50 or $100 a month . . . How about . . . players [in] baseball, tennis, golf, volleyball, water polo, squash, track, cross country, swimming — in both men's and women's sports?

"Put a pencil to that amount and see what you come up with . . ."

Where did these people study economics — Siberia? Revenue PRODUCING student-athletes are not asking to be GIVEN anything. They should merely benefit from the money they EARN. Is that too complex to understand?

It is difficult to know, when the NCAA leaders are offering arguments that avoid the primary ECONOMIC issue, whether they are truly that narrow-minded, or whether they are intentionally offering smoke screens and sophistry in order to maintain the present system as it is.

The "education-is-valuable" argument falls in the same category. It is difficult to ascertain whether such arguments are meant to keep revenue producing student-athletes thinking, like slaves, that they are actually happy with the exploitation they are enduring. Or, do the promulgators of such arguments really not know that what they are saying is a totally unenlightened, unacceptable answer to the question of just compensation?

The NCAA leadership, similarly, uses the amateurism argument in defense of their annual theft — as though Carl Lewis weren't making hundreds of thousands of dollars as an amateur, as though every European country does not have wealthy "amateurs" competing in the Olympic Games, and as though they have no awareness of the original snobbish connotation of amateurism, and no awareness that their own rules and allowable grants-in-aid for athletics repudiate even their own definition of amateurism.

The NCAA leadership claims the right to do whatever it wishes and needs no intelligent, rational position from which to operate. By its way of thinking, the athletes generating millions of dollars will remain penniless amateurs forever, they will glory in their privilege of receiving a valuable education from the United States government, and they will never seek to benefit from the public's special interest in them, as all other Americans do. To the NCAA leadership, this group of ridiculous assumptions makes perfectly good sense.

THE "WAR VETERAN" INTANGIBLE

One factor which can NOT be under-estimated in dealing with the NCAA bureaucrats is the war veteran mentality which cements their people into a collective unit and infuses their actions with a sense of mission and purpose. The NCAA bureaucrats, led by Walter Byers, their leader of more than a third of a century, have been through a lot. They have battled. They have withstood a million threats. They have sat in dozens of courts. And they are still there, in Mission, Kansas, in bright new buildings, sitting on nice new furniture, and traveling here and there in style. They have arrived. Despite hundreds of detractors down through the years, they have survived and flourished, and they are proud of it.

As a result, they will dream up whatever rationales are necessary to support the turf they are holding. In their minds, they have worked very hard for what they have. Never mind that what they have is a result of the labors of others. They may say that what they do is merely the will of the member institutions, but clearly they have taken on a life of their own, and they support that life and uphold it with any power they can muster.

Not unlike plantation owners in 1860, they will find seemingly rational explanations for blatant exploitation, because their very existence and way of life is at stake. If the money from the NCAA basketball championships were removed from the coffers of the NCAA, the house would come tumbling down.

Therefore, the relationship between the NCAA and schools or players seeking change can hardly be looked upon as cooperative in nature. Rather, there is a very obvious US-AGAINST-THEM mentality which exists. It shows itself in a variety of ways:

**At a Los Angeles rules interpretation meeting, which I attended (in April, 1985), the NCAA 'interpreter' several times warned his constituents using the phrase, "If you do THAT, WE'll come after you."

**At the Prep Stars Invitational All-Star Basketball Camp, which I direct, an NCAA representative's arrogant tones were heard by two hundred-plus prospects. "If you have enough brains in your head to know how to make a telephone call, there is no excuse for violating an NCAA rule." The athletes were treated to that statement no less than seven times in a twenty-minute delivery.

Perhaps the best illustration of the non-cooperative nature of the association can be seen in the extreme interpretations of the "unfair advantage" concept, which is extended to go far beyond advantages that any schools are actually worried about, and which gets the NCAA involved in case after case of nitpicking and pettiness that coaches, players, and fans universally roll their eyes at.

A cooperative association? How do you explain the annual, million dollar expenditures for legal fees to carry on litigation against its own members?

The NCAA is, at times, an association of some 800 schools working together; at times, the NCAA is some 650 little schools working against the schools with revenue producing athletic programs; and at other times, the NCAA is the bureaucrats in Mission, Kansas, acting alone. ALWAYS, it is a group of people whose basic philosophies and financial interests run counter to those of revenue producing major college athletes. And ALWAYS, the unrepresented athletes lose out when they clash.

Chapter 6

THE BIG RIP-OFFS
squandering millions

If money being made by major college sports were put back into major sports problems — put back, figuratively speaking, into the beautification of the land — there would be no outcry against them. But rules are made preventing the money from going back to the major sports. The money is earmarked — more by creeping custom than by philosophical constructs — for supporting minor sport athletes and programs, and for paying the way for NCAA officials to spread money around arbitrarily, again with little expressed gratitude for the source of their funds.

Most any business or profession would have devastating cheating and corruption if their earned profits were not permitted to be used to solve their problems and to accrue to the benefit of those who generate the profits.

THE BIG RIP-OFFS

The biggest rip-offs of revenue producing student-athletes come in four major areas: (1) minor sports, (2) NCAA salaries and operating expenses, (3) legal fees, and (4) the football bowl system. Even a brief look at each of these four areas can leave a sports fan appalled. It is difficult to understand how anyone can rail against the abuses of big-time sports when the extent of the NCAA rip-off of revenue producing football and basketball players is seen. Let's take these rip-offs one by one.

THE "TRUE" STUDENT-ATHLETES AND THE MINOR SPORT RIP-OFF

One of the curious developments on college campuses in recent times has been the evolution in the public mind of the minor sport athlete as the true student-athlete. The golfer or tennis player, or volleyballer or soccer player, is the guy who has his priorities in line. He works hard in the classroom, or so the thinking goes, because he realizes that sports don't last forever. He has his total self-development in perspective.

Of course. What fails to be spoken is the fact that his uniform and equipment, as well as his coaches, are being paid for from revenues generated by those misplaced-priority-behemoths who hulk and sulk in the back of classrooms and intimidate the rest of the student body because they are bigger or (in many cases) blacker than the student body at large.

The golfers, tennis players, and soccer players, are not bigger, not blacker in most cases, and do not stand out in any crowds of students. Nor are they likely to develop any unrealistic notions about their value as athletes because few of them have ten thousand people flocking to their weekly games, nor nationwide television audiences to play in front of.

In my years of being associated with college athletics, I have never witnessed any minor sport athletes thanking major sport athletes for the scholarships they are on or for the equipment they are using. Nor am I

63

aware of widespread gratitude being directed by minor sport coaches to major sport coaches.

I am aware, though, of resentment among minor sport athletes and coaches, and sometimes by female athletes and coaches because the major sports "get everything." The major sports use the courts and fields when they want to, and they get the best lockerooms, the best dorms, and the best of this and that. That is a common accusation which is no doubt true in some cases, and false in many others. But regardless of how often it is true, it SHOULD be true — and then some.

Why have so many people been allowed to forget that the major sports support, in many cases, the entire minor sports budget of a university? Why isn't a grateful attitude obvious?

Isn't it strange? A pole vaulter may look down on "some big dumb football player who doesn't even belong in college." In a majority of cases, that same pole vaulter, in a job interview, has a better chance to land a job than the football player. Yet that football player is paying the pole vaulter's way through school!

Wouldn't it be fairer if NO football-generated money were given to minor sports programs but instead was used to make sure that football players get the best education possible, the best job preparation, and a substantial cash award upon graduation? Wouldn't things be fairer if NO basketball-generated money were used by the NCAA to pay legal fees, fund minor sport championships or cover operating expenses?

It has become natural to assume that two sports will carry all of the others as well as pay for a highly professional sports association. Is this a proper assumption now that so many problems in the major sports have apparently been identified by college presidents and administrators?

STRIP-MINING

The major sport athletes seem something like coal miners, providing energy to run the households of thousands, even while they are being condemned for disfiguring the land from which they are taking the coal.

If money being made by major college sports were put back into major sports problems — put back, figuratively speaking, into the beautification of the land — there would be no outcry against them. But rules are made preventing the money from going back to the major sports. The money is earmarked — more by creeping custom than by philosophical constructs — for supporting minor sport athletes and programs, and for paying the way for NCAA officials to spread money around arbitrarily, again with little expressed gratitude for the source of their funds.

Most any business or profession would have devastating cheating and corruption if their earned profits were not permitted to be used to solve their problems and to accrue to the benefit of those who generate the profits.

MINOR SPORT NATIONAL CHAMPIONSHIPS —
A WASTE OF MONEY

National championships are the biggest cause of problems in big-time sports, because enormous sums of money are being used to fund unnecessary championships. The money should be going back to the basketball players who generate it.

The NCAA ran 73 different national championships in three divisions during the 83-84 season, and only a dozen or so of them made money (and four of those were basketball and football championships).

The NCAA paid for 21,578 trips to national championships sites, at an average cost of $290 per trip. What an incredible waste of money.

How can so many revenue-losing national championships be justified when we do not even have a national championship in Division I football?

Take a look at **the 1983-84 national championships that lost money.** They were staged, basically, with money generated by the Division I Basketball national championship tournament, which in 1984 generated a $24 million dollar profit and made considerably more in 1985. (The numbers below, from the "NCAA Annual Reports, 1984" are rounded to the nearest thousands and are net dollars lost.)

Men's Division I Sports:

Fencing	−28,000
Indoor Track	−171,000
Water Polo	−39,000
Cross Country	−81,000
Golf	−59,000
Soccer	−44,000
Swimming & Diving	−114,000
Tennis	−22,000

Women's Division I Sports:

Fencing	−22,000
Golf	−52,000
Lacrosse	−57,000
Soccer	−82,000
Indoor Track & Field	−133,000
Cross Country	−76,000
Field Hockey	−57,000
Softball	−88,000
Swimming & Diving	−128,000
Tennis	−65,000
Volleyball	−146,000

Men's Division II Sports:

Baseball	−159,000
Cross Country	−55,000
Golf	−44,000
Gymnastics	−28,000
Ice Hockey	−28,000
Soccer	−71,000
Swimming & Diving	−78,000
Tennis	−50,000
Outdoor Track & Field	−157,000
Wrestling	−64,000

Women's Division II Sports:

Basketball	−74,000
Gymnastics	−37,000
Cross Country	−45,000
Field Hockey	−17,000
Outdoor Track & Field	−150,000
Tennis	−38,000
Volleyball	−87,000

Men's Division III Sports:

Basketball	−87,000
Cross Country	−71,000
Football	− 6,000
Golf	−47,000
Ice Hockey	−24,000
Lacrosse	−16,000
Soccer	−98,000
Swimming & Diving	−138,000
Tennis	−45,000
Wrestling	−79,000

Women's Division III Sports:

Basketball	−106,000
Cross Country	−53,000
Field Hockey	−44,000
Softball	−72,000
Swimming & Diving	−127,000
Tennis	−53,000
Outdoor Track & Field	−144,000
Volleyball	−94,000

Men's and Women's (Coed) Sports:

Rifle	−27,000
Skiing	−103,000

Down through the years, Walter Byers and his cronies at the NCAA have undoubtedly made a lot of friends by disbursing this kind of money to minor sports for the purpose of staging their championships.

When you consider the productive, educational use that all of this money could be put to, the thoughts stagger the imagination.

If the Division III schools truly believe these championships are worthwhile educational experiences for their athletes, they will find funds to send their athletes, or they will find ways to stage their championships more economically.

Small wonder, with so much of their money being squandered on non-essential title games, that Division I basketball and football players are confused to find themselves the object of so much scorn and ridicule.

How many basketball and football doctors and professionals would we have now if all of that money were being put into a scholarship fund, not into needless national championships?

How can this kind of disbursement of funds be called anything but blatant theft when hundreds of Division I basketball players are leaving school without diplomas, in need of tutoring, counseling, and further education?

How can this disbursement of funds inspire anything but bitterness and cynicism in Division I players?

How can the NCAA and the universities get away with this un-American kind of welfare system?

LEGAL FEES

The amount of money spent each year by the NCAA on legal fees is not an amount that would feed the hungry on two continents or provide peace for all nations. But it would provide full scholarships for about two hundred basketball and football players each year — something that seems to be a much better use of more than a million dollars annually than using it to try to hound Jerry Tarkanian out of the coaching business or to prevent universities in Oklahoma and Georgia from arranging their own contracts for televising football games.

The money spent would not be an issue if it were not for the fact that those funds came basically from the funds that basketball players generate. Therefore, when a basketball player like Albert Butts of LaSalle University takes the NCAA to court over an ineligibility ruling, he must fight them knowing that they are using money HE helped to generate to fight him back.

Because the NCAA uses basketball players' money for legal expenses, their funds are virtually unlimited. This is not just unfair, it is an absurd waste of money when you consider the fact that all they really need to do is point out the violation to the member-presidents and swift, decisive action can be taken which requires no court ruling at all.

If a university president can wipe out a whole athletic program by mere decree, certainly he can declare a particular player ineligible to participate.

Why does it take a whole association of representatives to accomplish such an action? Why must the NCAA spend millions of dollars of basketball players' money to do what could be done more efficiently, at no cost, by one university president himself, acting perhaps at the recommendation of a board of eligibility experts?

Is it really necessary for the major schools to have an adversary in Mission, Kansas to keep them in line with annual court cases? Wouldn't a yearly convention of the top hundred or so schools be adequate to police their big-time sports programs — at a fraction of the present cost?

Let's look at that cost.

NCAA SALARIES AND OPERATING EXPENSES

Nearly everyone acknowledges — or screams out — that the problems in collegiate sports occur almost exclusively in the programs of a hundred or so schools.

Doesn't this make it ridiculous, then, to have an annual convention of over a thousand people to deal with problems pertaining mainly to a few dozen schools? The NCAA pays over $100,000 in expenses for its annual convention. The enforcement department alone — whose activities deal almost exclusively with fifty schools — needs some $1,250,000 annual dollars to operate. This includes more than $450,000 in salaries.

The Administration Department needs some $1,300,000 dollars annually to operate, which includes more than $860,000 in salaries.

Add the costs of running the departments of Championships ($826,000), Communications ($2,500,000) and Publishing ($1,200,000), and the cost of supporting the various committees ($1,100,000) and you begin to see AMATEUR sports in perspective.

Do you begin to understand why these people in Mission, Kansas do not want to disband the NCAA? Do you see what a fat life they have, spending so much basketball player-generated money for so little return?

There is no reason that it should take millions of dollars to run the sports programs of a hundred or so schools. Does that begin to make it understandable why the NCAA has worked so diligently to bring more than 800 schools under its wing? And why it has so zealously supported Division III schools' national championships with complete funding and transportation guarantees while giving their athletes scholarship awards?

It is a very nice little racket — steal from the rich, give to the poor, and come back and rail against the abuses of the rich while stealing still more money the next year. The theft goes on and on, and nothing about the historic, Special Convention on integrity and economics did a thing to stem the flow of this preverted system of Robin Hood Welfare.

THE FOOTBALL BOWL SYSTEM

Presumably, the bowl system has been good for college football in the past, and certainly many good people have worked diligently in volunteer capacities over the years to enable the system to achieve what success it has had. However, there is little evidence to support the conclusion that the bowl system now is anything other than a rip-off of football players' money, with the booty being shared by a great deal of people.

Let's take a close look at the expenditures of the Orange Bowl, as listed in its 1983 Federal Income Tax return.

It might be interesting to note, before doing that, that although the income tax returns for bowl committees are open to public examination — as they are for any non-profit corporation — the directors of some of the bowls seemed to indicate they had some secret to protect. While the Rose Bowl gave out the public information without so much as a question, the director of the Orange Bowl, Dan McNamera, when asked by phone for the Committee's federal tax identification number, responded with an immediate "No way. Under no circumstances."

Makes you wonder what the Orange bowl has to hide, or why the secrecy and lack of cooperation in a matter that is clearly, by law, a public right. Nevertheless, if the motivation for a total lack of cooperation was secrecy, it makes sense. It cannot but damage the case of continued existence for the bowl system, once the facts are out on the table.

The Orange Bowl, for example, according to its tax return of 1983, paid slightly more than 3.6 million dollars to the participating universities. This is in accord with the NCAA rule requiring that seventy-five percent of the profits from the bowl games go to the participating schools. Initially, this sounds like a great deal of money for the universities, until you begin to see what other money was spent on, reducing the profit.

Non-profit corporations have no particular reputation for being spendthrifts, and the Orange Bowl appears to be no exception.

The Orange Bowl spent **$308,248 on salaries and wages.** It gave grants totaling $41,000 to groups like Junior Achievement of Greater Miami, Miami Senior High School band, Miami Central High School band, City of Miami Folklore Festival, Easter Seal Society, and the Museum of Science Around the World Fair. It paid $17,600 in expenses for "Fiesta By the Bay," and the list goes on . . .

$15,000   marathon,
$288,603   King George Parade,

69

$132,105	tennis tournament,
$29,909	Orange Bowl Queen and Court,
$10,129	"Great Bands of the Orange Bowl,"
$6,952	sailing regatta,
$6,000	prayer breakfast,
$67,513	"General Festival Expenses,"
$48,882	selecting one team to participate,
$221,650	"Pre-Game and Half-Time Pageantry,"
$33,651	awards,
$34,282	"Entertaining Participants,"
$28,171	"Team Party,"
$103,535	coronation ball,
$19,278	"officials, gatemen, ushers, etc.,"
$19,435	"Coaches' Luncheon,"
$10,317	courtesy cars,
$25,472	"labor, materials, misc.,"
$11,145	"News Media Relations,"
$7,216	press party (which presumably had nothing to do with news media relations),
$31,503	"Press-Other,"
$219,490	public relations,
$188,327	publicity,
$26,493	"General Committee,"
$4,851	"President's Gift,"
$15,409	"Miscellaneous Expenses."

Forget the pension plan contribution of some $94,858. Forget the fact that nearly all of these figures would be much higher, had we examined the figures for 1985 when the payoff to the universities was over a million dollars more.

The point is, the expenditures are absolutely profligate. Did you note the $48,000 for team selection? **The Orange Bowl spent $48,000 to find one team.** (They have a commitment each year from the champion of the Big Eight Conference.) So what could they possibly waste $48,000 on?

I am certain that my brother Dave, an avid sports fan, armed with a subscription to USA TODAY, could get the Orange Bowl a good participant for not a dollar over $24,000 — half the cost!

What DOES take $48,000 in selection expenses? According to the Assistant Director of the Sun Bowl, Jeff Jenkins:

"The [11 man] Selection Committee travels each week during the football season to talk to representatives of the various universities and to scout prospective teams."

Eleven men, traveling EACH WEEK OF THE FOOTBALL SEASON, watching games, and wining and dining their administrative cronies. Think about that, and multiply by sixteen — and start thinking about how much money is spent each year on selecting about 27 teams to compete in post-season bowl games. How much MORE do the bowls have to spend on selection when they need to find, not one but, TWO teams to participate?

If each bowl needing to select a team or two has an eleven man selection committee, that means 176 men are traveling the nation each football season seeking out teams. It also means, at fifty thousand dollars a committee, that nearly a million dollars is spent each year on selection alone — when my brother could get it done for two or three hundred grand, tops!

No apologies for the tone. How can an examination of these practices lead to anything but frivolity and sarcasm? The bowls waste football money unconscionably, money that could be going for scholarships and remedial help and counseling, and all of the other things that might prevent the abuses that the university presidents, the NCAA, and the media are so fond of calling attention to.

If football players had a voice in the process, do you think they would vote thousands of their dollars for sailing regattas, festivals by the sea, and coronation balls? Do you think they would vote $308,000 for Orange bowl salaries — or would they rather show up on the day before the game, play the game and leave with full lifetime scholarships and grants going directly into trust funds they could use upon graduation?

The coaches themselves will admit the bowl appearances are largely treated as rewards to the players and, for their efforts and extra practice and because of the realization that they are incredibly exploited, some rather wasteful spending seems warranted during the weeklong activities preceeding New Year's Day.

The problem is, the cummulative waste goes into the millions, to say nothing of the distributions which do go back to the universities but which the football players themselves never see.

Short of a strike or some such radical measure, there is no reason to suspect that the waste might stop and the players might begin benefiting from the public interest in their sport. Too many people are enjoying that weekend traveling. Too many people are enjoying part of that $300,000 chunk of cash doled out in salaries to parade-makers and festival organizers. You can make a lot of friends spending $219,000 in public relations and another $188,000 in publicity, to say nothing of the millions which the committees so graciously give back to the universities themselves.

Chapter 7

A POT OF GOLD FOR EDUCATION
a generation of athlete-surgeons

To talk about free, all-expense paid EDUCATIONS
FOR LIFE for all RPMCAA student-athletes seems
initially to be the stuff of dream worlds and fantasylands . . .

A POT OF GOLD FOR EDUCATION

On the assumption that new leadership will change the course of the NCAA — or that players will organize and put an end to the exploitation — let's look at the truly wonderful EDUCATIONAL objectives that could be accomplished once revenues are distributed to the players, instead of wasted on national championships, pageantry, and unnecessary bureaucratic expenses.

With the 32,000,000 annual dollars received from CBS alone for televising rights to the championship basketball playoff games, it would be possible, indeed, to do no less than educate a generation of athlete-surgeons. The phrase sounds almost comical in this day of dumb jocks widely disparaged for their inability to speak coherently or read or write. But the phrase would not be comical at all — if basketball and football players were permitted to enjoy the rewards associated with the tremendous public interest in basketball and football national championships.

In the following example, the 32,000,000 annual, basketball dollars (one-third of the three year, 96 million dollar contract the NCAA signed with CBS) are used to explore the benefits that could accrue to basketball players.

It is reasonable to conclude that a similar deal could be arranged for football players. Although there are many more football players to provide for, a football national championship could be expected to generate many times the revenue generated by the annual basketball tournament.

A Generation of Athlete-Surgeons

By figuring on three basketball players graduating per year (the maximum possible under the "Athlete-Enhancement" program (explained in Chapter 4), the following programs could be fully paid for:

PLAYERS' SCHOLARSHIP FUND — $11.25 Million

A players' scholarship fund would be responsible for distributing full scholarships to EVERY RPMCAA (Revenue Producing Major College Athletic Association) basketball player who wanted one — for as long as he wished to continue his education. If a player wished to stay in school for two extra years to complete his education, The Fund would pay for it. If a player wished to go on to become a lawyer-doctor specializing in outer space exploration, The Fund would pay for it.

Incredibly, it would take just 11.25 million dollars per year to permit such an incredible educational program. Eleven and a quarter million dollars would give EACH graduating player THREE years of a totally free education — with expenses and spending money and traveling allowances.

The math is simple. Three players per school, at approximately 125 schools (the ones with revenue producing programs), is 375 players per year to be funded. Even if each one of them decided to go on to school for the three years, each would still get $10,000 per year to cover the costs of his education.

Naturally, many would decide not to go on at all, others would decide to go for one or two more years. Certainly the assumption of a three year average would be more than enough to cover the actual amount of additional education the athletes would opt for, and of course the money left over each year would stay in the fund and continue to increase the principal sum annually by the millions.

To talk about a fund of this sort, and free, ALL expense-paid educations FOR LIFE for ALL RPMCAA basketball players, seems initially to be the stuff of dream worlds and fantasylands. Which makes the tragedy of the current waste stand out all the more dramatically.

The "Pot of Gold" concept could end here, except for the fact that only a third of the annual TV dollars have so far been used up. What about the other two-thirds?

A GRAND REMEDIAL PROGRAM — $4.75 Million

One of the chief criticisms of universities accused of exploiting athletes is their willingness to admit athletes who are not prepared for college. Then, of course, the athletes leave without an education — they fail — because they were in most cases not capable of succeeding from the start. As a result, a grand remedial program seems to be an excellent place to use a portion of the money that basketball players generate through their national tournament.

A grand remedial program might include the opportunity for each RPMCAA school to designate two players per year for entrance into "special remedial studies." That would be 250 players per year. At a cost of $10,000 per player, the total amount of money to fund the program would be a paltry two and half million dollars annually.

Would a special school for 250 basketball player-students be advisable? Wow, what a great basketball league they could have, while preparing themselves academically for college. Let a group of Harvard, Yale and Princeton academicians run the school — and let THEM decide when, or if, the students were ready to do college work. Keep the coaches and individual schools entirely out of it. Make it truly remedial, and give the students as much time as they need, without taking away any of their collegiate eligibility in the process.

75

Would it cost another two million to get this school going and keep it running each year? Okay. And let's throw in another quarter of a million to pay the people at Harvard, Yale, and Princeton. (They are willing to accept money readily for academic purposes.) That would give us 4.75 million dollars for a spectacular, dream world, fantasyland remedial program, and it would bring our total expenditure of basketball tournament TV money to an even $16,000,000 — ONLY HALF THE ANNUAL TOTAL COLLECTED FROM CBS.

Let's look at what could be done with the other half.

RETROACTIVE SCHOLARSHIP FUND — $4.75 Million

It would be a tragedy to leave nothing at all for the many great athletes who blazed the trail for the athletes of today. Besides, it would make sense, especially, to reward present Juniors and Seniors who may have to stick their necks out to bring about change, yet who would have to fear getting nothing but problems and criticism — and perhaps bills for college — in return.

Therefore, as a practical matter, and in recognition of the contribution of past athletes, it would make sense to establish a retroactive scholarship fund, offering money to past athletes to complete their education or to go on to graduate school.

A fund of 4.75 million dollars would enable 475 athletes to get full, annual scholarships valued at $10,000 apiece — enough at most state universities to provide for tuition, room, board, books, travel expenses, spending money, and an occasional pizza. That would still leave the total program with $11,250,000 — just the amount needed to fund the last dream world, fantasyland program.

THE "SECOND CAREER" PROGRAM — $11.25 Million

One of the ironic things about the current system of NCAA rule is that the players generating money for their universities and for the NCAA inevitably start out behind regular students in the job market and in the struggle for achievement outside the university environment. Indeed, this situation causes many serious students to look with a strange curiosity upon people (not destined for pro careers) who concentrate an abundance of time and energy on athletic endeavors — for so little return — while letting their futures remain virtually on hold.

To assure that the effort expended on sports is no longer a wasteful one as far as the athlete's future is concerned, the Second Career Fund is established.

The Second Career Fund provides for each player who graduates from an RPMCAA school to have the opportunity to apply for a $30,000 grant. This money may be used to start a business, help a family, or for any other worthwhile project, as determined by the panel of athletes making the grants.

There would be no reason to be particularly strict about this grant-giving, since **each graduating player could receive $30,000** before depleting the 11.25 million dollar fund. However, it would naturally be wise to establish some guidelines, so that graduates would be encouraged to make the most of their good fortune. In fact, wouldn't this be a perfect subject for a college course? "How To Use $30,000 Wisely," or "How to Start a Small Business." Senior athletes would be flocking to such classes, sitting in front rows, and paying careful attention, taking pages of notes.

With these four special funds, no one would again have to question why any kid was spending an inordinate amount of time on basketball or football, and no kid would have to look back and wonder if it was worth it — in case his dream to sign an NBA or NFL contract did not materialize.

When you take a good, long look at the tremendous opportunities and rewards which can be afforded to basketball players — and to football players through revenues generated by a national football championship — the extent of the rip-off perpetrated by the universities and the NCAA becomes all the more heinous.

Weighing their present circumstances against future possibilities, basketball and football players can be nothing but cynical, and angry with the people responsible for the blatant theft and exploitation which they are enduring.

In the laying out of facts and figures above, there was not even an attempt to have players participate in the revenue gathered at individual schools from regular season gate receipts, TV contracts, and alumni contributions.

For players to enjoy the benefits of the above dream worlds and fantasylands, it would only take a national football championship which we do not now have, and a re-distribution of the funds now collected — via TV contracts alone — from the national basketball championships.

CURRENT WASTE OF FUNDS

Even after so many years of having a national basketball championship, no one is quite sure how to use the funds. Currently they are used primarily to fund minor sport national championships, NCAA legal fees, etc., and the rest — nearly twenty million dollars — is distributed back to the schools.

The schools themselves, however, don't even have a good use for the money, since they don't know in advance how much they can count on. They can't include it in thought-out budgets. If their teams do well, then they get funds. Some end up using the money for other sports, some use it to give raises and more incentives to the winning programs, and some use it for academic and other discretionary purposes.

There is even a movement afoot to share the money with ALL Division I schools, or in some way to disburse it so that the successful schools are not rewarded financially in such a way as to encourage cheating. Distributing economic rewards to the winners naturally does promote the very win-at-all-costs attitude that the NCAA leadership claims to detest.

No one within the NCAA, incidentally, has made a case for distributing the money to the players. The players, as always, are left out of the discussions.

University of Kentucky President, Otis Singletary, made the statement at the NCAA Special Convention in New Orleans that "you can not just wave a magic wand and solve all the problems." But with a proper distribution of basketball championship funds, and the establishment of a national football championship — with the revenue going to the football players — a wand wouldn't even be necessary. Graduations would be taking place in record numbers. Potential "cheaters" would not want to jeopardize their good fortune. And we might very well have, before all of the dumb jock graffiti could be washed off the locker room walls, a generation of athlete-surgeons.

Chapter 8

MAKING THE DREAM COME TRUE
a union, a strike, whatever it takes

ONE DAY in Pasadena brings a payoff of some $6,000,000 to each of the participating teams (and their conferences) in the Rose Bowl. Now, what if just one of those teams, shortly before game time, decides it is feeling sick?

A UNION, A STRIKE, WHATEVER IT TAKES

Unfortunately, the NCAA and the universities are not likely to change dramatically the way things are, even after seeing in black and white the errors of their ways and the incredible EDUCATIONAL benefits that could be realized by letting money go back to those who earn it.

Players have to explore the possibilities, therefore, of bringing about rapid change through legislation, while being prepared to act in their own behalf on the assumption that the NCAA and the universities will balk at their attempts to be compensated justly.

NEWSWEEK Magazine probably summed up the situation as succinctly as it can be done, in an article called "2001: A Union Odyssey," which appeared August 5, 1985.

". . . a union seems to be the only practical way to give voice to the wishes and air the grievances of masses [of people] who do essentially the same job."

In the case of revenue producing basketball and football players, this makes utter good sense, since no one is listening to their wishes and grievances and since they currently have no representation at all.

A warning to players is in order here. You will certainly encounter opposition in your attempt to unionize. People opposed to you for whatever reason will dream up every sort of subterfuge and platitude possible to disparage your effort. They will accuse you of greed, ignorance, selfishness and anything else that sounds at all plausible.

It does not take a soothsayer to forecast these events. This is replete throughout the history of American labor, in all its recurring, recapitulating glory.

In fact, it is not even necessary to wait, to see this happening in the sports world. In July of 1985, the Denver Post took a poll of coaches and players in the Western Athletic Conference. Associated Press reports showed that "six of the nine players [who were polled] agreed that forming a national union of college athletes would be a good idea. The coaches were unanimously opposed to the union prospect."

Unfortunately, the poll did not end there. It gave Brigham Young football coach LaVell Edwards the opportunity to say that he would "quit coaching if players ever unionized."

Air Force football coach Fisher DeBerry added, "If it comes to needing a union, then we ought to abolish college football."

These are wild, uninformed, almost un-American statements that "molders of young men" should not be disposed to make. The United States Constitution guarantees workers the right to peaceably assemble — to unionize, and history has taught over and over again that people just don't get what they deserve UNTIL they unionize.

Coach DeBerry said, in that same Denver Post poll, "Students ought to trust the institution that they signed to go to. They ought to trust the integrity of that institution and its coaches to do the very best for them."

(Really Coach?)

It would be incredible how much those statements sound like others made in 1965 by grape farmers who opposed the efforts of Cesar Chavez to organize migrant farm workers — except that those statements sound just like statements made by factory owners and big business to the groups that eventually became the Teamsters Union, the United Auto Workers, the AFL-CIO, and nearly every other union ever formed in America.

Chavez was told in '65 . . .

"[we] have a wonderful relationship . . . and any problem we might face can be discussed and resolved. The laborers have been able to do this with their employers on an individual basis . . . The result of this harmonious living is that we are happy here." (Chavez, p. 152)

Another grower . . .

"It is without fear of contradiction it can be said that Mexican American groups, along with Filipinos, should feel very proud of their standing in our . . . community for their accomplishments individually and collectively. These groups work in an area where the finest labor and management relations have existed for many years and we certainly hope to maintain this basis of communication and agreement for many years to come, without outside harassment." (p. 156)

The grower went on to point out how the workers in California were making, on the average, $1.43 an hour, the highest in the nation! (He did not bother to add that this 'generous' wage was far below that of any union in the country.)

Somehow, things just never seem as good to the exploited as they seem to the exploiters; and in any case, student-athletes must realize that all of the great unions in the history of the nation have faced much, MUCH more difficult circumstances than student-athletes are facing — yet within a short time, people became accustomed to the new order of things, even after rioting and bitter struggles.

Today, union leaders literally walk with presidents, they dine at the White House, and they are courted by governors, senators, and big business. Yet each new union must struggle for recognition. Seldom is recognition offered willingly.

At times student-athletes may feel like it is you-against-the-world. In many cases, for other unions, it was indeed just that. People fought and died on the streets to gain their rights. But, fortunately, student-athletes exist within a much more benign environment, and many many people believe already in the student-athlete cause.

Ernest Chambers, a legislator from Nebraska, has proposed bills in the Nebraska state legislature since 1980, trying to get University of Nebraska football players put on the state payroll. Athletic boosters — wealthy, influential people at every university — have often tried to give student-athletes money and have supported their favorite teams with large financial contributions. Many of them, not all of course, believe that student-athletes are entitled to much more than the NCAA and the universities permit. In fact, many coaches, though they may initially disagree with the idea of a union, nevertheless agree that student-athletes are being ripped off and are entitled to more than they are getting.

Said Dale Brown, the head basketball coach at Louisiana State University:

"Just because something is an NCAA rule doesn't make it right. I think we're a group of hypocrites and are cheating the kids out of money. Mark my words: Someday there will be a revolution among players."

There are sports fans, coaches, and even administrators throughout the nation who recognize the phoney concept of amateurism that is keeping student-athletes from achieving a fair share of what they earn.

Penn State football coach Joe Paterno has said:

"It is very difficult to tell a kid he can't take a $10 bill from an alumnus or sell a complimentary ticket, when Carl Lewis lives like a millionaire and is still declared an amateur."

Many people understand that a self-serving bureaucracy is responsible for keeping student-athletes from benefitting from their true economic value.

Said Happy Fine, a columnist in "Eastern Basketball," (6-10-85):

"The athletes generating all that money are . . . limited to tuition, room, board, books . . . Every conceivable perk beyond that, even the borrowing of a car or accepting a free dinner, is — in many situations — a violation of one of the NCAA's myriad rules. Now that bureaucracy wants to make more rules . . ."

ESPECIALLY TO STUDENT-ATHLETES

When you consider all that you have going for you, especially in comparison with the history of nearly any other union's struggle, the picture begins to look very bright. Cesar Chavez, for example, in trying to organize the farm workers, was faced with rampant illiteracy. Many of those who could read and write did not speak English. There was immense poverty, the work force was scattered in two countries and forced to migrate from harvest to harvest throughout the West. There was cultural bias to hurdle, as well as powerful interests, such as the Nixon White House, standing in the way of a national farm workers' union. Compare your own situation with that described by Ronald B. Taylor in "CHAVEZ:"

"To a young farm worker like Cesar Chavez the power of the growers appeared awesome. They could summon congressmen to do their bidding, their politicians passed laws favoring agribusiness and blocked legislation that could benefit farm workers . . . when farmers needed a supply of water . . . they asked for and received BILLIONS of federal and state dollars for dams . . ." (p. 75)

You, on the other hand, have intelligence, you are easy to reach, the names and addresses of every one of you are readily available to all. You are actually a very closed group — players on a hundred or so basketball teams, a hundred or so football teams. You will be carried to meetings (games) with other players, so you can meet without effort or planning; and after games you can interact, exchange ideas freely, and spread the word.

You have no need of secrecy. This is an issue of obvious interest — and of potentially great benefit — to all of you.

Additionally, when you decide the time is right to act, you need no one's help. You can stop games and interfere with million dollar contracts immediately — the next day, any day — just by refusing to play.

You don't have to urge outsiders to boycott this or that, you don't need to form picket lines or march in the streets. Your NON-actions will be loud and clear. It won't even take TWO teams. If just one team walks into a filled stadium and decides not to play, the world will know of it. In basketball, if just eleven players act together, 30,000 fans at a Carrier Dome could be left sitting, wanting some $300,000 back.

The point should be abundantly clear to you. You can have immediate economic clout. Once you have decided to act in concert, your ability to demand your fair share will be easy — especially because you are demanding nothing other that what YOU generate. You are demanding only what should be already yours. This will be especially true if you wait and sit out of NCAA playoff games.

Holding a players' convention may be wise, before refusing to play games, so that all of you, or at least a great majority of you, can be sure to act together and stand together.

There may be some negative consequences to your actions. Certainly there will be threats to that effect. But those threats will be more scare tactics than anything else. Because you indeed have clout that no one really wants to consider.

NEW YEAR'S DAY: PARADES ONLY!

Imagine the consequences of four particular football teams deciding on New Year's Day to attend parades but not to play in bowl games. Millions of dollars are spent and committed throughout the year which depend on the enormous profits to be collected on New Year's Day.

ONE DAY in Pasadena brings a payoff of some $6,000,000 to each of the participating teams (and their conferences) in the Rose Bowl. Now, what if just one of those teams, shortly before game time, decides it is feeling sick?

What attempts would be made to negotiate? What realizations would the big-time powers be forced to come to?

YOU, as revenue producing major college football and basketball players have great economic value to the NCAA and to the universities. If the NCAA and the universities will not acknowledge this value and make plans to see to it that you get a fair portion of it, then they can expect to suffer accordingly. They can NOT expect to exploit you indefinitely without consequence.

The bowls would do well to buy strike insurance from Lloyds of London. How much would it cost? What are the odds?

Remember the prophetic words?

We shall overcome.

PART II

STUDENT-ATHLETES'

ENCYCLOPEDIA

STUDENT-ATHLETES' ENCYCLOPEDIA

"The N.C.A.A. may want us to be reassured by a mound of signed affidavits. But problems as fundamental as those in college sports are not that easily resolved."
—John Weistart
Professor of Law
Duke University

"The leaders are the responsible parties, not the troops ... don't punish the troops. Punish the leaders. Student-athletes are very impressionable. When you haven't had much and you are offered what seems like a truckload, we ALL have a tendency to break."
—Roman Gabriel
former pro quarterback

AFFIDAVITS AND ACCOUNTABILITY

The voters at the NCAA Special Convention in New Orleans passed Proposition Number 5, which holds student-athletes responsible for violations of NCAA rules, and Proposition Number 9, calling for all of the member institutions to administer affidavits to all players, so that student-athletes can affirm — again — that they are not receiving benefits in violation of NCAA rules.

This is typical of the NCAA. There already is a statement which players must sign each year, stating the same things, but the NCAA has added this affidavit in order to make its message of 'cleaning up college sports' more emphatic to the public.

The affidavit is little more than extra, irritating paper work for the schools, and it sounds initially innocuous. But it does harm the players. It requires an additional "lie" from the players who are right now receiving some added benefits.

It is inconceivable that players who have been receiving added benefits will suddenly turn them down now that they are being asked to sign a paper indicating they are not receiving anything.

Why force a player into a lie? Morally, it makes perfect sense that players, especially poor ones, get more than NCAA rules permit. So a player who is getting some extra money or benefits, and who has been getting them without incident, will now continue to do so despite the affidavit, just like he has been doing despite the annual, signed statement.

The ONLY reason for having the affidavits and statements is to enable the NCAA and the media to label kids "liars" who before would have just been "cheaters."

The NCAA steadfastly includes this kind of fraud ("knowingly did misrepresent . . .") each time it lists the violations of member schools.

There are those who will say, if players are receiving more than is allowed by NCAA rules, then they are liars and cheaters anyway, so what is one more lie to them? But it is not that simple. There are a lot of good, moral kids who are getting more than NCAA rules allow. It is moral for them to side-step stupid rules, and to accept added benefits for their parents and families.

But it's too bad they have to become inured to constant lying, in order to receive what they are entitled to.

Almost to a man, it is the poor kids who are getting extra benefits; and they both need them and deserve them. Why hold THEM accountable if they make a choice to help their families and accept some money that they become convinced they deserve?

How can the NCAA justify taking away their eligibility permanently, as a punishment for accepting benefits beyond the NCAA standard scholarship? That is what Proposition #5 requires.

For a young athlete who has just four years to play college sports, taking away even one year is an enormous punishment. To take away all four years is cruel, grossly unfair, and ridiculous. Surely, even the NCAA realizes that a seventeen-year-old may do something he will regret, yet be quite capable of having changed considerably by age 20. So how could a permanent loss of eligibility ever be contemplated as a penalty for a seventeen-year-old who has not even broken a law?

Remember, a student-athlete can violate NCAA rules easily without breaking even the slightest law. That is usually the case. Yet, most young athletes would probably rather go to PRISON for a year than be denied eligibility permanently.

To think that the NCAA would ban a kid permanently for accepting a hundred dollars, for example, as a Senior in high school is inconceivable, yet they have done it. The rule is on the books, ready to be enforced.

The rule goes on to say emphatically that eligibility will be restored only in cases "when circumstances clearly warrant restoration." In other words, the penalty for a violation is on the books calling for permanent ineligibility.

There is no justification whatever for holding players accountable for violations of NCAA rules as long as their money is being stolen by the NCAA. Once the players are properly compensated, then accountability and affidavits make sense. Right now, both propositions merely make it easier for NCAA theft and exploitation to continue.

'YELLOW DOG' STATEMENTS

By requiring the players to sign these papers, the NCAA is exacting from the players — who have no other real alternative as a place to ply their trade — a complicity, an agreement so to speak, to follow rules which they do not believe in.

This is similar to forcing workers to sign no-union agreements as a condition for being hired, a requirement which is illegal. People cannot be forced to sign contracts and agreements which deny them Constitutionally-guaranteed rights, even if they are willing to sign them because they need the money and the job. The NCAA is doing this same thing — again — with regard to drug-testing. Current plans call for the NCAA to include a consent statement in the annual student-athlete's statement, acknowledging "the right of the student's institution, if it so elects, to conduct regular drug-testing on its campus for its student-athletes."

FOR its student-athletes? How is this FOR them?

It would be advisable for ALL basketball and football players to refuse to sign both the annual statements and the affidavits, actions which would call for the automatic disqualification from NCAA championships of every school and the automatic disqualification from all NCAA competition of every student-athlete.

This action would effectively nullify these forced affirmations, but it won't happen this year. The coaches will present these statements and affidavits as formalities and the players, unorganized as they are right now, will sign them, realizing that lies are sometimes necessary when you're dealing with bandits.

If the NCAA and college presidents are sincere in their desire to clean up college sports and educate their students, they should feel no need to exact promises from those who they intend and purport to educate. Nor should they feel a need to punish those who, at seventeen, may have been tempted by the colleges' own representatives to accept some benefits not provided for by the rules.

The affidavit and accountability rules will have little effect beyond that of permanently harming the lives of a few unlucky individuals who are gleefully made examples of, and of teaching a whole group of student-athletes (who never get caught) that lying may be a good method of operating.

In the current situation, at the present time, many student-athletes feel they have little choice but to pay deference to the whims of their arbitrary, capricious, and all-powerful rulers.

"Students who are non-athletes shop around their junior and senior years to secure the best deal they can for themselves after leaving school. To deny athletes the same privilege is unjust discrimination."

—Joe Marcin
Sports Columnist
The Sporting News 11-12-84

"(Barring athletes from signing with an agent during their Senior year) is a self-serving rule predicated on protecting the school while it wrings its four years worth out of the athletes."

—Ed Fowler
Houston Chroncle

AGENTS

The problem of agents is often talked about in connection with big-time college sports, and almost always in a negative vein. NCAA rules do not permit players to sign with an agent before their seasons are completed and, should any agent identify himself and attempt to establish a relationship with any players on a major college team, he would be run off campus.

Small wonder agents are forced to do things secretly.

If agents were permitted to act in the open, to identify themselves, and to introduce their services in a competitive manner with other agents, everyone would benefit.

The only reason that players' agents are commonly identified with unsavory characters, underworld figures, and gangsters is that even the good ones must go underground to ply their trade.

Why should they have to?

On every college campus it is standard procedure for representatives of big companies to come onto the campuses and to interview prospective employees. At that time they lay out what the company has to offer, what it is looking for, and what a student's chances are of landing a job after graduation.

Only representatives of pro teams, or agents hoping to sign players to pro contracts, are not permitted on campus.

A Ralph Sampson or a Patrick Ewing coming out of college will learn soon enough of their value, through the grapevine if nowhere else, and their future will be no worse off for having waited.

However, there is a large pool of players — especially borderline NBA prospects — who have no idea of what the future may bring. Some hear rumors that they will be drafted late in the first round, which could mean a lucrative and perhaps a no-cut contract, yet they will not be drafted at all. It happens every year.

If their coach has not had an abundance of players who have played NBA or who have at least been good enough to try out and make it through a rookie camp, the players may get no solid advice at all about what is in store for them, what their chances are at rookie camp, who they might best try out for, and so forth.

Equally at a disadvantage is a player who did not have an outstanding relationship with his coach. Where is HE supposed to go to get help?

Players coming out of college, for whatever reason, typically have dozens of unanswered questions.

In 1984 — finally — the NCAA adopted legislation allowing a three person, "career counseling panel" to be established to aid athletes on each campus. This was a step in the right direction, but one which has not gone nearly far enough. The people on these panels often do not know the first thing about athletic opportunities outside the country — probably **the** primary interest of the majority of players. Presumably, the NCAA is making an effort to gather information from a variety of pro sports (and other) organizations, in order to make this information available to the career counseling panels, but as usual, they have not put a great deal of effort or money into this program. (This program merely benefits the players, a low priority group.)

A good recent example would be the case of the University of Florida's Eugene McDowell. He left Florida prior to his Senior year, on the advice that he would be a late First Round draft choice in the 1985 NBA Draft. But his advisors were mistaken. McDowell was taken so late, his chances of making the NBA were very slim, and he settled for a contract in Europe. Had he known his real position, he very likely would have remained in school another year — and very possibly would have become a First Round choice after the 1986 season.

The NCAA is so fearful that a bit of professionalism may rub off on a player, that they make rules which hurt his future.

Why couldn't McDowell declare himself eligible for the pro draft, find out his value accordingly, and then decide to remain in college after seeing that he was drafted late? He had gotten no money. He had merely been drafted. But nevertheless, NCAA rules do not permit a player to find out his worth and then decide. Players are **required by rule to make their choice before knowing their value**. Once McDowell or any other player declares himself available for the draft, he becomes a pro in the eyes of the NCAA right then and there.

If a player like McDowell finds the NBA has little interest in him, then what? Why isn't there a special committee which helps players find the best teams for their skills, or which helps players get places to play in Europe, in South America, or in Australia? — where people are paying money for good basketball players.

It is absurd that such a necessary function is not now performed. That no such committee now exists is attributable to the thieves who annually steal millions of dollars of football- and basketball-generated money with hardly a thought for the needs of the football and basketball players who bring that money in.

My personal experience for seven years as a player and coach in Europe and in the Caribbean has shown me that many players could land attractive opportunities in other countries if the NCAA would put some money to the purpose of locating those opportunities. But the NCAA, instead, spends its time railing against the abuses of unscrupulous agents who sign kids early — against the rules.

"What would you nominate as the most profitable, but still legitimate, business in the U.S. these days? Round up the usual suspects — broadcasters, cosmetics producers, cigarette companies and maybe a hot technology venture — and you would be hard put to find a business pocketing more than 15 cents of every sales dollar after taxes. What if we could show you a business likely to bring 75 cents of every revenue dollar to the bottom line this year? Interested?

"Our candidate, it is true, doesn't pay taxes. But even if it did, at the full 46% corporate tax rate it still would net 40 cents on the dollar, putting IBM to shame. Our nominee: big-time college basketball."

—John Merwin
Forbes Magazine

ALUMNI RELATIONS

One of the major areas of NCAA exploitation of football and basketball players involves the climate the NCAA rules create with regard to player relations with alumni and booster club members.

This prime source of future job offers, business contacts, capital lenders or business partners is all but shut off entirely by NCAA rules and fear of NCAA rules. The thinking is, if players are permitted to associate freely with alumni or booster club members then, oh-the-worst-of-all-evils, a player may end up getting a car to drive or have a loan co-signed, and then the ax of the NCAA will fall on the program and everyone will be on suspension.

Of course, this is not mere paranoia in view of the absurd, anti-American NCAA rules. These atrocities — the use of a car or the co-signing of a loan — may indeed occur between two friends, one with money and one without; and the present NCAA rules, fully supported, reconfirmed and then some, by the college presidents, will assure the death of programs that allow this to happen.

The result is a generation of protective coaches, and a wall of silence and non-association among people with similar interests who should, within a free-market society, be forming valuable alliances and networks that would be useful for the remainder of their lives.

By preventing open communication and association between players and the very people most anxious to know them and help them, the NCAA restricts the players' future earning power and their success in non-athletic careers.

In their zeal to make sure that no one gets an extra penny, the NCAA effectively cuts off what should be one of the major benefits of being an athlete.

———————

"College football and basketball are out of control for the fundamental reason that the people who run college athletics insist on enacting amateur rules to govern what fundamentally are professional sports . . .

"In a sport where coaches earn $250,000 a year and colleges are fighting each other in court over television money, the athlete has justifiable reason to feel that he should get his fair share. And one way or another, he will.

"The NCAA is swimming against the tide of history; and in the end, it will lose."

—Joe McGuff
Kansas City Star

AMATEURISM

The NCAA pretends to take great pride in upholding the principles of amateurism.

An amateur athlete is one who plays without compensation, who plays for fun, for social benefits, for exercise, as a hobby.

Applying this concept to revenue producing major college athletes brings snickers from even the casual, uninformed fan. Everyone knows that major college revenue producing athletes are compensated with scholarships. They play with sprained ankles heavily taped, they attend physically-demanding, daily practice sessions, they lift weights and workout throughout the off-season, and they pursue excellence in a manner that goes far beyond fun.

In this pursuit, they make many sacrifices. They lose many social benefits on the campus because they have little time for pursuits other than studies and their sport. Often they are segregated from the rest of the campus — by necessity — because their meals must be eaten at a later time than the school cafeterias are open; and their important games require that they be in a quiet sleeping environment on Friday nights when regular college students are likely to be whooping it up.

Big-time athletes are not out there playing for fun. They play long after the fun has gone. They sit in whirlpools, they get ultra-sound treatment on injuries, and they are expected to learn to play with pain.

They are not a group of guys who gather for social benefits and enjoy some cold beers with the other team after some friendly strife on the field. They fly to games, people pay big money to watch them play, and their coaches and directors of athletics are paid extremely well to see to it that they win.

Revenue producing major college athletes simply are not amateurs in any sense of that word, even by the NCAA's own definition.

The only attempt to make them amateurs is to try to make sure that they have no money.

It is unclear how the NCAA has continued to maintain its belief that the principles of amateurism can be upheld by steadfastly holding to one archaic idea.

Amateurism, truly, is exemplified by the collegiate rugby clubs. Many of them, without any support at all from their universities, gather teams and bunch into cars and go to play other teams. When the match is completed, both teams typically get together — with a keg of beer normally the main attraction — and they sit and talk and tell stories and often sing bawdy songs.

Rugby club parties have long been known as some of the best on any campus.

These players practice when they can, they wrap their own ankles, and they generally take a few weeks off and let time heal their injuries. Many of the teams have no coach, or one of the students functions as a coach. They don't have anything like a training rule. For the most part, they admire the athlete who can stay up all night drinking and still turn in a gutty performance on the field the next day.

Naturally, there are rugby clubs that do not put any emphasis on drinking; and there are amateur teams in other sports, some even in football and basketball at small colleges, which adhere fairly closely to the NCAA's definition of amateur — playing for exercise, social benefits, and as an avocation.

Revenue producing major college athletes have no qualms with this form of athletics. If the colleges are indeed for this form, they need to demonstrate this by NOT charging admission to the games, by NOT recruiting players from out of state, by NOT paying coaches more than their physical education instructors, by NOT traveling across the nation to play games, by NOT giving scholarships for athletic excellence, and by NOT engaging in contracts to televise the games.

The principles of amateurism are not upheld as long as these common practices continue.

The colleges must decide. Either uphold the true principles of amateurism, or recognize the very different status of their non-amateur athletes and compensate them proportionately to their economic value. The present system can be looked upon with nothing but cynicism and contempt by the athletes who are stolen from and exploited via a rationale which even the casual fan recognizes as a farce.

EXCESSIVE ASSISTANT COACHES

Basketball and football teams have many more assistant coaches than they need.

If you take two coaches and their expense accounts out of the basketball programs, and six or seven coaches and their expense accounts out of the football programs, you have a significant savings in the overall sports budget.

If pressed, head coaches will admit that the reason they hire as many assistants as the Joneses is not to assure themselves of more or better strategies, nor even to get more individual teaching during practices. The primary reason why so many assistants cling to the major sports programs is for recruiting — probably the major area in which critics claim abuses. So, cut down on the number of assistants, and automatically you are going to cut down on the number of recruiting abuses. There is simply no compelling reason to have as many basketball and football assistants as there are now, and there will be even less reason for so many when the scholarship quotas get trimmed to where they should be.

———————

"The former blue chipper who completes his eligibility but is not drafted and is not within reasonable reach of a degree is no longer perceived as a big gun. Rather, he tends to be seen as a smoking gun, a potential embarrassment to the athletic program. Because of his academic circumstances and his failure to secure a pro contract, he constitutes a loose cannon on the deck, a potential source of disenchantment and dissension within the ranks of new recruits and athletes with remaining sports eligibility."

> —Harry Edwards
> Professor
> University of California-Berkeley

ATTRITION

Attrition is an ugly word that administrators, coaches, and college presidents all like to avoid when talking about the wonderful opportunities they offer to student-athletes.

Nearly all of the major schools offer roughly thirty football scholarships and five basketball scholarships per year to student-athletes. The athletes have five years in which to complete their eligibility. This means that, in any five year period, approximately 150 football scholarships and 25 basketball scholarships have been awarded.

The problem is that only 95 football players and 15 basketball players — many more than are needed in both cases — can even make their team rosters.

Where are the other 55 football players? Where are the other 10 basketball players. Where do they transfer to? Why do they transfer? How many drop out? How many flunk out?

This attrition rate is similar at nearly all of the large schools, and it is an atrocity. It is also vivid illustration of the expendability of each student-athlete who signs a grant-in-aid. Over one-third of those who sign will not be on the roster at any given time. Some are run off, some are injured, some merely fall by the wayside. "Everyone can't be a star," say the hypocrites.

Presumably, a similar justification is used with the line "Everyone can't graduate." How many schools do you think graduate two-thirds of their athletes? With their contribution to their schools considered, they ALL ought, at the very least, to graduate. The schools rightfully owe them more than that. But you have to look long and hard to find ANY schools that graduate that percentage. There may not be even one major state university that does it. Even the University of North Carolina, where Dean Smith's basketball players nearly all graduate, had only four football players graduating in 1985. What happened to the others?

Atrocious attrition rates. They are all over — monuments to blatant exploitation, monuments to a system perpetuated by precisely those who claim such a commitment to integrity, education, and doing what they do "for the kids."

AVOCATION

The amateur athlete, according to the fundamental policy of the NCAA, as stated in the NCAA Manual, plays his sport as an avocation — as a hobby, for fun, in addition to his regular employment.

Can you imagine a major college revenue producing football player telling his coach he'll be missing much of spring practice because he has gotten a bit behind in his "regular employment." It is standard fare for hobbies to suffer, or to get put off awhile, when a person gets behind in his regular work.

"I'm sorry, Coach Bryant, Mr. Bear, Sir, but I have to go to the city library in Tuscaloosa to do some extra research for this paper I have due in a few weeks. I need to put off this here avocation on the field, Sir."

Enough said.

"Ten years ago there was a commitment, an approval of us . . . There's a good deal less of that attitude today."

—William Hunt
NCAA Enforcement

AYATOLLAH

This word means holy man and is a title of respect in the Islam religion. Of course, it is a word most often associated in the minds of Americans with the Ayatollah Khomeini and the abuse of power.

The Ayatollah Khomeini's name, not coincidentally, was brought up in association with the NCAA when Judge Paul Goldman was presiding over the court case involving the NCAA and UNLV basketball coach Jerry Tarkanian.

Judge Goldman, in rebuttal to the claim that the NCAA's enforcement methods were efficient, said, "so were those of Adolph Eichmann and the Ayatollah Khomeini."

This is not to say that every NCAA official should be equated with the Ayatollah Khomeini, but it is to emphasize the point that the NCAA, like the Ayatollah, has abused its power and now fails to represent the very people for whom it was formed.

"The thing fans and announcers and administrators rarely acknowledge is that basketball and football players are the most unhappy groups of athletes on every large campus. To say that HALF the scholarship football and basketball players at big schools are unhappy is being conservative."

—Dave DeVenzio
Former scholarship basketball player
Kent State University

BENCH-SITTING

One of the most ridiculous, intolerable hypocrisies in collegiate sports involves the players on the bench at each major college in the nation.

"Hey, that's the way it goes," some athletic directors or coaches may argue, "everyone can't be a star."

But that is not an adequate response. Everyone can PLAY. Each recruited player SHOULD be an important part of the team. That is what each recruited player believes he is going to be when he signs with a particular college, and that is certainly what he is LED to believe.

No one tells high school prospects that a high percentage of big time college players are not happy at all.

Athletics directors and administrators brush this enormous problem under the rug. The stated goal of their athletics programs is to provide an enriching experience to the participants. But they fail miserably on that account. Some athletes have an enriching experience, sure, but many do not THROUGH NO FAULT OF THEIR OWN. They are brought into a program where everyone knows they cannot all succeed. The percentages dictate that MANY of them must fail.

Each individual, it is true, has an opportunity for success. But it will not be possible for each of the recruited athletes to succeed. Why do athletics administrators tolerate this system? Why do NCAA rules guarantee its continuation?

When a basketball coach, for example, needs a point guard — someone who can run his team and handle the ball — it would be nice if the coach would go out and get a point guard to do just that. But few coaches operate that way. The normal thing to do is to go out and recruit several point guards and sign three of them. One of the three is likely to develop into the kind of player the coach is looking for and, since only one point guard plays at a time, the other two recruited players become back-ups. They are expected to work hard everyday in practice, to learn all of the team's plays and know what is going on at all times, so in case the starting point guard gets hurt, they can fill in.

The problem is, no one prepared them for life as a major college back-up. No one let them know how "un-fun" daily practice is when you are not getting a chance to play in the games.

If a kid has spent so much time on basketball or football in his years between thirteen and seventeen that he becomes a recruited, sought-after athlete, then he is likely — and everyone knows this in advance — to be miserable sitting the bench at a college. The fact that he is getting an education for which he is supposed to be grateful is small consolation to him. He dreamed of PLAYING, and he was recruited TO PLAY.

Kids all over the country who are sitting on benches are just barely getting by psychologically. During national anthems and locker room pep talks and at times when TV commentators are giving fans the impression that an exciting, wonderful, rah-rah event is about to take place on the field, at least as many players as are planning to play are planning to sit there feeling unhappy.

People don't talk much about the feelings of players on the bench. It is too ugly.

Commentators don't take viewers into locker rooms to watch some disenchanted high school star pick at pimples or pull out hairs on his face WHILE THE COACH IS GIVING THE PRE-GAME TALK. Players are incredibly adept at subtly and at times not-so-subtly showing their displeasure at their plight as back-ups. But little is said directly.

The players themselves don't even know they have a right to rebel. They are fed a steady diet of grin-and-bear-it, never give up, always do your best, what is said in the clubhouse stays in the clubhouse, and your-time-will-come. The problem is, for many, their times do not come. What promised to be four exciting college years of being part of a major college team turned into four years of frustration, four years of feeling like an outcast, four years of silent smoldering, trying to sort out the situation and pick up the pieces. How, where, when did things go so wrong, they ask themselves, and they usually, broodingly, fear they are themselves to blame for what has happened to them. Athletes learn these things early and hear them over and over again — look to yourself for the problem and solution. Don't go looking for excuses. Don't go blaming things on others.

For coaches and administrators, these cherished philosophies are perfect for keeping their hypocrisy under wraps.

They can NOT get away with saying they never thought of these things nor with saying it isn't like this at their school. IT IS LIKE THIS AT EVERY MAJOR COLLEGE. But no one is doing a thing about it. Few even want to talk about he problem. And players, of course, have no power. So the problem, the enormous, hypocritical problem remains, debasing many human lives each year.

They are quick, those who are responsible, to tell you that the kids are getting an education and a wonderful opportunity for travel and for making lifelong associations. That merely shows you how hypocritical they are. The fact that sports in America offer good opportunities and potentially good experiences to young athletes in no way absolves administrators of responsibility for turning those experiences so sour.

Be sure that the miserable players would be happy to travel less and meet less people in order to be truly part of the happy family they were invited into during the recruiting process.

For someone who has been there and has seen it first hand and who notices it on the bench and in the team program at every game, it is difficult not to be totally cynical. The misery on the field makes a mockery of announcers' excited comments, a joke of every coach's pre-game forecasts.

It isn't easy to love sports and to know how much joy and enrichment they can offer a person, and then to watch the present system go on and on without regard for the daily dehumanizing of so many participants.

Critics will step in to say that the extent of this problem is over-stated. But I have to differ. If anything, I have understated it, not wanting to resort to ugly words nor to naming names.

But you can check for yourself. Hang around a locker room or just watch the benches during games. There is misery out there lurking just beneath the surface. When players finally get some power and finally get a chance to voice this widespread misery, fans will be shocked. So far though, the disillusioned players have been able to be painted as isolated cases who didn't pan out, had bad attitudes or a bit of bad luck. But football players, for example, don't need bad luck when 150 are signed, when only 95 make the roster — and only half of those get to play.

The tragedy of it is that this annual dehumanization is totally preventable. Big-time sports COULD be just what the TV commentators lead us to believe. But right now it isn't even close.

If only newspapers began reporting the games accurately, headlines across the nation would read:

"Flutie Spectacular
as Fifty Indifferent Teammates Look On."

"Something is wrong. It is obvious that we are not looking to protect the student-athlete's interests. We are not looking out for that student's economic, psychological, or family interests. We are simply not addressing the realities of the world we live in."

—Cecil Mackey
President
Michigan State University

BENEFITS

Benefits are what revenue producing major college student-athletes are in pursuit of, INCREASED benefits.

In taking surveys related to big-time college sports, most people indicate that they are not in favor of PAYING college athletes. However, many of those same people are under the mistaken impression that athletes get many more BENEFITS than they actually do.

Student-athletes are not hung up on terminology. Few student-athletes feel that just compensation must come in the form of cash payments. Additional benefits — plane tickets, spending money, use of automobiles, extended scholarships, and special incentive grants — will be fine. Cash up front is not necessary, but increased compensation is.

"... there is not a single NCAA rule specifying athletes' rights in any regard, only his obligations and prohibitions.

"For at least two decades, then, a contract has been struck between 17- to 19-year-old athletes and universities: An education in return for athletic performance. The athletes have kept their part of the bargain, the universities have not."

—Harry Edwards
Professor
University of California-Berkeley

BIDDING WARS

When the subject of compensation for players comes up in any conversation, one point is usually brought up immediately, the fear of "bidding wars." Once the dam is cracked, the feeling goes, there will be a flood to follow. Colleges, say the fearful, will become like pros, trying to out-bid each other for players until the situation gets out of hand.

"Do you want the colleges in the business of bidding for players?" ask the critics.

The answer is no. There is no reason that the colleges need to get in bidding wars. In fact, there are two simple alternatives, neither of which would cause bidding wars.

The first alternative is not my personal choice but it has merit never-

101

theless. The colleges can get out of the bidding entirely, giving no scholarships but letting their alumni and booster clubs do whatever bidding they feel moved to do. Proponents of this idea ask why any organization should be able to tell some individual what he can and can not do with his money. If there are booster club members and alumni willing to put money into the effort of getting players for their schools, what harm would it do to the colleges? They would need to allot no money for recruiting budgets, something which costs them considerably now, and they could turn their full attention to education, giving athletes no special privileges at all. If some of their students got rich in the process of playing for them, so what? Aren't colleges normally happy to have rich students who become future alumni contributors?

If athletes got no scholarships, the colleges would be free to treat them like all other students, letting them sink or swim on their own merits, and letting them pay for their own tutors for any extra help they might need.

This is the view supported by people like Ernest Chambers, the Nebraska legislator who believes in "athletic Darwinism," or letting the strong programs survive and the weaker ones drop into lower divisions. This view makes some sense, although I believe a second alternative is better.

The second alternative is to establish clearly the benefits which are included in an athlete's scholarship — just as is already done. The difference would be simply in increasing the benefits dramatically, in proportion to the economic value of the athletes. This would be in keeping with the idea of complete institutional control of athletics programs, but giving the athletes a share of the money which they generate.

The system could be very similar to what we have today, as long as the athletes were given things like plane tickets for travel to and from home, spending money each month, use of automobiles, and assured scholarships for as long as they wish to continue their education.

Players will be grateful for scholarships of this nature and will not be tempted to cheat or to try to get more benefits on the side. Naturally, not all cheating can be stopped. But there will be very little temptation to cheat once the bulk of the money generated by athletes is returned to athletes.

The best example of this is in pro sports, where it is very difficult to fix a game or entice a player into a relationship with an underworld figure with money. It can happen. But people who are fairly compensated are certainly less vulnerable.

The chief fear of people against fair compensation for players — that college presidents would have to engage in the business of bidding for players — is simply not realistic. Once the money is distributed proportionate to economic value, the problems of cheating and corruption will vanish. Fair rules will be gladly followed and therefore will be much more easily enforcible.

" . . . figures show the NCAA made more than $20 million in 1980 and spent only about $19,000 on education-related matters."

—Bruce Landeck
Assistant Legal Counsel
for Johnson County (Kansas)

BLATANT THEFT

It has been suggested by various people that the use of the word "theft" is primarily for shock value and is not meant to be taken literally.

But the theft on the part of the universities and the NCAA, at the expense of major college revenue producing players, is blatant and should indeed be taken literally.

The proof, as the saying goes, is in the pudding. The players will be happy to pay for their own educations — like other students — in return for a share of TV contract revenue and gate receipts. If what the universities are giving the players is so generous, the universities should be happy to make this offer to the athletes.

They don't, because they are making big money off the players, and they will use any means possible to protect what they have come to look upon as theirs.

It is not unusual that people become blind when their economic interests are threatened; and certainly the universities and the NCAA perceive that their economic interests are threatened when people begin talking about fair compensation for players.

A lot of people are living off the fat of the athletes' land, spending unearned money that they have no right to. Of course they will put up all sorts of spurious arguments as to why things should remain as they are. They will pretend to be committed to upholding high-sounding concepts like amateurism, Americanism, and so forth.

But in the end, those most against fair compensation are those who have become accustomed to living off others' money, and to being praised for distributing handouts to grateful, undeserving recipients.

There is truly no other name for this but theft. Blatant theft. People who are earning large sums of money are being deprived of any legitimate share of their earnings.

There is no reason why revenue producing major college athletes should not fall under the capitalistic system. That they are diligently being kept out of the mainstream of American society is, however, not unusual. History teaches that factory workers and migrant farm workers, as well as professional athletes, teachers and most public servants have had to organize, protest, and strike before they were "given" their fair share. Not often do people in power "give" other people what they are worth. Like the early American industrialists, the big farm owners, and the professional sports club owners, the NCAA and the universities will cry foul and accuse those fighting for their rights of greed, of being spoiled and selfish. They will try to maintain their theft for as long as they can get away with it. That too has been a lesson of history. It is just that student-athletes have trusted in and hoped for better from college presidents who should have read history and learned from it. Why are college presidents seemingly requiring a strike before they admit that their revenue producing athletes have a special value to their universities? Why are they taking a chance on messing up a good thing that the public genuinely loves and which adds much to the universities as well?

"I will stay away from the coaches in the offices, but saying I can't have dinner with someone on their own time is ridiculous . . . "

"I was not recruiting players illegally. I have never written a player or visited one. I witnessed an accident and I tried to help a kid."

　　　　　—John Appleton
　　　　　Dallas Businessman
　　　　　(Who gave an SMU player $900 to pay for a traffic accident)

A BOOSTER'S GIFT

When I was at Duke, a well-to-do Duke alumnus once let me drive his car to Fort Lauderdale over spring break. He took the time to replace his Frank Sinatra and Tony Bennett tapes with the Rolling Stones and the Beatles, and he delivered the car to me with a full tank of gas.

I was overjoyed with that offer. I didn't have a car, I had no thoughts of driving to Fort Lauderdale, and I appreciated more than I was ever able to express that he took the time to replace those tapes and help me in every way he could to have an enjoyable time in Florida.

It NEVER occurred to me at any time while I was in school that either of us was breaking a rule. He didn't lend me that car to keep me at Duke, nor because any coach had promised me that I would get any such thing. I was merely a college student who wanted to go to Florida over spring break, just like any other student.

His gift of the car for a week was an act of friendship, nothing more, and I am still grateful for it. I am glad I did not know at the time that it was a violation of a rule. And I think it is appalling that it remains a violation now. What was so bad about it?

I don't remember ever playing in the Duke Indoor Stadium when the seats weren't filled with people. A lot of people paid a lot of money.

Getting a car to drive to Florida for a week wasn't such a terrible thing, though the lender, Duke University, and the player would all be called cheaters if it happened today.

"With all the money we help bring in, I think we should be compensated."
—Keith Byars
Football Star
Ohio State University

BOWL GAMES

The bowl games played over the holidays by college football teams are no longer an essential part of college football. Fans want a real national championship, and players want a real national championship.

It is impossible to say that the bowl games are entirely useless. A lot of good people work hard and volunteer their services to make the bowl games a success. Nevertheless, the also-ran bowls simply aren't necessary. Even the Rose Bowl, the famous "granddaddy of them all," has been rather inconsequential for the past few years. There is no special aura when Ohio State plays Washington and neither of them is even ranked in the top five.

It just doesn't make sense to continue the bowl system from the players' standpoint — when so much more money could be generated, and so much good could be done through a national championship where the profits would be earmarked for a Football Players' Fund.

The continuation of the bowl system can only be looked upon as exploitive, a tribute to cronyism, and as a waste of money. It is time this system dies or, at the least, gets incorporated into a national championship playoff which benefits the players.

BRIBERY

A newspaper headline during the past year read "Memphis State Coach Denies Bribing Lee."

The article explained that Dana Kirk, the head basketball coach of Memphis State University, denied that he had given Keith Lee money for signing with Memphis State back in 1981.

Whether or not Kirk had given Lee any money was unknown. Nevertheless, the newspaper felt comfortable calling the alledged money a "bribe," which it in no way could be. Even if a coach does give a player money, there is no bribery involved, and it is wrong to lead the public to believe that some sort of law has been broken.

It is against no law to give a player money to attend a particular school. Indeed, in the case of Memphis State and Keith Lee, Lee certainly deserved much more than room, board, books and tuition. If all Lee got in four years at Memphis State was room, board, books and tuition, Lee was the victim of theft. During Lee's career, he was responsible for generating millions of dollars for Memphis State, and it is safe to say that the revenue generated would have been significantly less without him.

To call the act of giving Lee some deserved money a "bribery" is both morally, as well as semantically, wrong.

Without an NCAA to sanction such theft, the headline would properly read, **Memphis State Coach denies giving Lee just compensation.**

Any way you look at it, a shoebox-gift containing ten thousand dollars is not a bribe. It may properly be called an "inducement."

If such an inducement existed, Keith Lee was certainly entitled to more than ten thousand dollars by any standard of fairness and Americanism — other than that of the NCAA.

"We, as players, are not blind to the large amounts of dollars being made by the NCAA and the universities because of our talented basketball skills and desires."
—Billy Thompson
Basketball Star
University of Louisville

ATHLETICS BUDGETS

It would have been possible to name this section "Pressure for Profits Fuels Cheating in College Sports." That is precisely the title which USA TODAY gave to a March 6, 1985 article primarily showing the revenues and expenditures of the University of Michigan's department of athletics.

Despite USA TODAY's title, there was little that explained how the profit motive fueled cheating, except in the most obvious way. Naturally, coaches want to keep their jobs, so they have to win; and directors of athletics who are trying to run programs with 21 sports, like the University of Michigan, have to make money to do that.

But coaches and directors of athletics are middle men. Do the top men, the presidents, make it clear that their coaches are there, tenured and all, regardless of the won-loss record? Do the presidents make it clear that the minor sports program can be paid for from the general fund — if the major sports show no profits?

Of course not. Universities are businesses — a fact they often try to conceal. They have limited funds to work with. Presidents have professional reputations to uphold, just as coaches and athletics directors do. A president does not want to cut out the volleyball team any more than he wants to dismantle an engineering program. Cuts are never popular. It is easier to keep generating money through the athletics program, and then go occasionally to a New Orleans convention to cry 'Wolf' to reassure the public.

A look at the University of Michigan athletics budget SHOULD have called for a title like "Football Funds the World." USA TODAY claimed that Don Canham, Michigan's director of athletics, "oversees a budget that is bigger than many corporations."

So what? What's so great about a corporation? Any person can incorporate. But the implication is that bigness is bad and somehow almost in itself connected with cheating. USA TODAY entitled the box which explained Michigan's athletics revenues and expenditures "The cost of success."

Why? The headline should have been "The Benefits of Football."

Here is the **University of Michigan's athletics budget** for the year ending June, 1984. How can it truly be called anything but the "benefits of football?"

REVENUES — $12,121,013

Football $4,483,301

Other Sports. . . . . $ 958,933
(Among these, only basketball and hockey make money.)

Investment Income (There is investment income
because of the surpluses generated by football.) $1,279,242

TV and Radio (almost entirely from football and basketball). $1,495,072

"Other" (includes "programs, concessions, schools and clinics,
use of school facilities and other miscellaneous revenue"
which is largely a result of football and basketball) $3,904,465

EXPENDITURES — $11,876,262

Football (including all the financial aid to football players) $2,448,500

Operation, Maintenance. $1,321,191

Salaries, Wages, Benefits (Including those going to
coaches in ALL of the other sports and added
personnel needed to run other sports). $3,424,599

Other Sports. $2,230,457

OTHER (includes "merchandizing, administrative and
operating costs and miscellaneous expenditures"). $2,451,514

Pressure for profits fuels cheating? There was no evidence that the University of Michigan cheats. In fact, said USA TODAY, Michigan enjoys the respect of its competitors. "The Michigan athletic teams win championships, make money, and stay free of NCAA infractions."

What that means is that the Michigan FOOTBALL TEAM makes so much money that athletes in eighteen other sports can compete on a high level, under the direction of well-paid coaches, using the finest equipment, and win championships — all to the greater glory and prestige of the University and the President and the Board of Trustees.

Michigan football is a tremendous gift to the University. It enables all sorts of people to ply their own trades successfully. The university does not have to dip into its general fund to provide first-rate athletic experiences for prospective students, so there is money available for academic purposes that otherwise would be directed, as it is at Harvard, Rutgers, Duke and Colorado, to athletics. The alumni can be proud of the athletic teams and of course keep their contributions coming in. Everyone's job at the University of Michigan — from the President to the head of the Chemistry Department — is facilitated because each Michigan football game in Ann Arbor brings in more than a million dollars.

Is anyone even vaguely referring to the University of Michigan when talking of the evils of big-time college sports or the way that sports corrupt our institutions of higher learning?

Do you think the NCAA dares to FIND two major violations in the Michigan football program — and give IT the "death penalty?"

Big-time football is doing a lot for the University of Michigan — just as it is for most of the large universities. It's just that people forget. They take it for granted.

They need to start thinking again.

"Byers and his key NCAA people have built the organization into a strong business enterprise to serve their own self-interest by rewarding the small schools with equal vote and classifying them with the large schools . . . so [the small schools through their votes] will back the NCAA's foolish philosophies."
—Roger Stanton
Publisher
Basketball Weekly

BUREAUCRATS

Few office and staff workers in any organization like to think of themselves as "bureaucrats," or "the petty officials that make up a rigid, administrative hierarchy characterized by excessive red tape and routine." But that is an excellent definition for the one hundred-plus staff members of the NCAA in Mission, Kansas, who put a great deal of time and effort into petty matters, while losing sight completely of what a national collegiate athletic association really ought to do.

For just one example, the NCAA is excellent at keeping copious records on what coaches have given away T-shirts, or offered five-mile drives to prospects back in 1973. But they have, supposedly, no power, no ability, no insight at all to enable them to deal with an issue like providing rules for athletes in multi-million dollar athletics programs in order to allow them to accept funds in true emergency situations.

Petty. Rigid. Narrow. Red tape. These words have real meaning in the NCAA context.

———————

"What were all the big guys (the top hundred schools) even doing in the same room with those other social climbers? Maybe they thought that Walter Byers, the Ghengis Khan of the N.C.A.A., didn't have enough paperwork to keep all his stoolies busy . . . "

—Dan Jenkins (11-85)
National Sports Columnist

BYERS, WALTER

Walter Byers has power. Walter Byers is the executive director of the NCAA. Walter Byers has been executive director of the NCAA for more than a third of a century.

Many changes have taken place in major college sports during that time. The growth in public interest has been as phenomenal as the growth in TV revenues.

During these years, Mr. Byers has undoubtedly rendered many valuable services to the NCAA and to the member institutions which form the association. Nevertheless, he is currently at odds with many people, including most notably the very athletes whose revenues enable Mr. Byers' job to be so expansive and lucrative.

It does not make sense for Mr. Byers to go through the final years before his retirement in a basically adversary relationship with athletes.

Wouldn't it be much better to have him preside over the affairs of the minor sports, where his experience and expertise would be welcome — as the minor sports struggle to fund their own national championships and to justify their continuation on college campuses?

The major sports clearly have a new set of problems to face and to solve in the Nineties and in the 21st Century; and for major college athletes who produce revenue, Mr. Byers is a thorn in the side, not an aid to their development.

Ironically, few people in big-time sports have an answer to the following questions:

How long is Mr. Byers' term of office?

Who decides when Mr. Byers gets removed?

Is there some graceful way to move him from executive director of the NCAA to the position of executive director of an NCAA-MS (National Collegiate Athletic Association for Minor Sports)?

Is there some way to prevent, in the future, any one person from becoming so powerful in collegiate sports?

109

Too often, when people have offered outstanding public service but have become ineffective or out of tune with the times — as was the case with Willy Loman in Arthur Miller's famous play, DEATH OF A SALESMAN, they are left behind and are unappreciated in their later years. This should not happen to Mr. Byers. He has done a lot for collegiate sports, and he should be recognized and rewarded for his years of service. His experience and expertise should be used to the fullest extent possible to help minor sports establish themselves and build up fan support in the coming decade, as basketball and football have done during the past decade.

Mr. Byers is clearly at odds with the just concerns of revenue producing athletes, and there is no reason why he needs to grapple with the changes that must inevitably come. It is unrealistic to think that a man who has spent so much time in college sports is going to be able to change with the times. He has presided over the NCAA that has prided itself on tough investigations, that has declared its own war on "cheating" and "corruption," and that has enjoyed the benefits of giving hand-outs to the undeserving.

No one can expect Mr. Byers to like the changes that must come. But why is it necessary that he be dragged into dealing with them at all? He has served a long time and has done his job to the best of his ability and as he has seen fit to do it.

He has done his job in many ways that have been anathema to players; and his leadership has certainly been responsible for the arrogance so often exhibited by NCAA officials; but that can be put into the past. Changes were rapid, running the NCAA was never an easy job, and everyone deserves the benefit of the doubt. It is not necessary for players to condemn anyone for the injustices of the past. The past can be forgotten — as long as the present situation is corrected. Certainly, Mr. Byers himself will admit that he is not the best person for the job of ushering in a future which provides fair compensation for major college revenue producing student-athletes.

It is time for new directions and new leadership in big-time college sports — for new faces, with new enthusiasm, to implement new ideas with an excited sense of accomplishment, not with a begrudging sense of defeat.

"Other sports are not generating the kind of income that football and basketball do, and it's time we recognized that. People are not filling up a stadium of 60,000 people to watch a lacrosse game. It's time to give sports what they earn themselves. That's the way of life in this country. That's competition."
—Digger Phelps
Head Basketball Coach
Notre Dame University

CAPITALISM

Capitalism is the system of economics that Americans believe in. It is a system that calls for free enterprise, for material incentives in return for productive work. In America, we believe that people who generate money deserve to benefit proportionately — not with an amount of money equal to their needs, but with an amount equal to their production.

In America, we applaud the songs of a Bruce Springsteen, and pay $20 to watch him perform, not begrudging the fact that he may take in over a million dollars for just one concert. We are as free not to attend his concerts and not to listen to his albums as we are free to make him a millionaire through our interest and willingness to spend our money to avail ourselves of his ability.

We call this a market system, and our laws attempt to provide equal opportunity so that anyone may make his or her best attempt to get whatever share of the economic pie that his or her abilities will enable.

We permit musical groups from England, as well as artists from Japan and authors from Australia, to compete for the favor of the American people who may spend their dollars as they wish.

It may not be a perfect system, but it IS the American way, and it has worked reasonably well for our nation as a whole.

In view of this, it is difficult to understand why our institutions of higher learning, which naturally support and encourage the American economic system (and are supported in turn by it) are so reluctant to let revenue producing athletes benefit from the fruits of their labors.

What revenue producing athletes want is NOT special treatment nor special favors nor special dormitories nor special food. Revenue producing athletes do NOT want special treatment, nor do they feel entitled to anything extra because they are athletes who work hard.

What revenue producing athletes want is tied only to what all Americans have come to expect — that they will benefit in proportion to their worth in the market system in which we live.

Revenue producing athletes wish to be part of the American capitalistic system. That's all.

Basketball and football players should expect nothing at schools where the basketball and football teams generate no revenue. But players who are responsible for generating huge sums of money should be proportionately compensated. It is un-American to do it any other way.

CAR

See KHAR — a four letter word.

CFA

The forming of the College Football Association was the first major step taken by a group of schools to reduce the power of the NCAA. The CFA consists of the top football powers in the nation, except for the schools in the PAC-10 and Big-10 conferences.

The CFA was responsible for taking the NCAA to court in the Oklahoma-Georgia TV case.

The formation of the CFA was the first substantial act of a large number of NCAA member schools that demonstrated the common view that NCAA rule was detrimental to the major universities.

A College Basketball Association would be useful too, in the same way as the CFA has been, but an RPMCAA (Revenue Producing Major College Athletic Association) — an association completely detached from the NCAA, would be even better.

"The recent incident of Knight of Indiana throwing a chair across the court was, in his own words, 'to fire up the crowd.'

"Is this really what we want?"

—Dixon L. Riggs
Faculty Athletics Representative
University of Northern Iowa

WHY NOT BAN FOR LIFE ALL CHAIR THROWERS?

One of the disappointments in the quest to get players fair compensation is Indiana coach Bobby Knight. In his typical fashion, he has strong views. He is on a sort of crusade against "cheaters," which makes one wonder about his own narrowly defined morality.

Knight claims he hasn't heard of a college president yet who has come forward to say he has had enough "cheating," he won't have any more of it, and he will fire a coach who does it.

Knight proposes taking away all of a player's eligibility should he be found accepting more than the standard NCAA scholarship. He proposes firing the coach, and taking away all of the school's home games, so they could produce no revenue.

112

This is a typical over-reaction of a person caught up in his own sense of self-righteousness. Of course, it says loud and clear that Knight does not offer kids added inducements, but what is so noble about that? Why not offer inducements to needy kids?

Why shouldn't a wealthy coach like Bobby Knight be permitted to provide spending money to players out of his own pocket?

There has been talk around the NCAA of putting a cap on coaches' salaries. That is another intolerable abridgement of personal freedom. The NCAA is so used to doing such things, people can throw out such constitutionally absurd proposals without batting an eye.

But if they want to limit coaches' take home pay, why not enable them to contribute to a players' fund?

Why doesn't a so-called moralist like Knight sense an immorality in the fact that he has become wealthy coaching basketball while players each year leave the game penniless? If there is some real substance to the concept of amateurism, does it extend so far that a kid has to be kept poor in order to maintain it?

Hasn't Bobby Knight ever had the urge to give twenty or a hundred dollars to a needy player on his team? Doesn't it bother him to walk around with a wallet full of cash while a kid on his team has no father, five little brothers and sisters, and a mother working day and night to keep them fed?

Is it adequate justification to say the kid must be patient. "Just wait until you get out of college and get a job, just wait until we get a new track built, just wait until the NCAA takes a hundred flights, stays a thousand nights in big hotels, and eats ten thousand steaks." Just wait. Just wait.

What concept of amateurism would be smashed if a needy player's brothers and sisters were assured guaranteed scholarships — with the money that lines the NCAA's pockets and lines Bobby Knight's pockets? What concept of amateurism would be compromised if every player were guaranteed a full scholarship as long as he wished to continue to educate himself?

When looking at what COULD be done with the money players generated versus what IS done with it, it is difficult not to be cynical about a narrowly-defined morality like that of Bobby Knight. Since he is all for the idea of removing eligibility PERMANENTLY from any SEVENTEEN year old who does what is natural and human and accepts some inducements for his family, **what penalty would Knight propose for a coach who tosses chairs on the court?**

Wouldn't it be better to ban for life any chair-tossing coaches than to ban a seventeen-year-old kid who tries to get something more for his family?

There will be critics who step forward to paint a seemy side of recruiting — as though coaches are giving out tainted money for drugs and fancy cars. But the money is only tainted because the NCAA says it is tainted. And there aren't many young, poor basketball and football players driving fancy convertibles while their little brothers and sisters starve in the projects.

What would be wrong with the creation of a Players Super Fund, so that money could be distributed to players and their families according to some agreed upon principles that would apply to all scholarship athletes regardless of what school they attend?

Why isn't Knight politicking for something like this, instead of announcing to the world that he doesn't break NCAA rules? What is so good about not-breaking some rules that ensure an annual theft of millions of dollars? And how is Knight so blind as to think there is no need? Why does he support the present expenditures of NCAA dollars? Certainly he is one benefitting enormously from the status quo.

NO HOME GAMES?

Under the views of Bobby Knight, if one kid accepts inducements (regardless of how much he and his family need them) the coach gets fired, the kid loses his eligibility permanently — no second chances — and the school plays no more home games.

With that loss in revenue, of course, the minor sport program would necessarily and SUDDENLY shut down for the year, presumably the minor sport athletes on scholarship would all be suspended from school — or their money would be taken from other general funds, taken away from other educational purposes.

A typical example of the over-reaction of the self-righteous. What is the attraction of such far-reaching punishments? Why punish innocent victims at all? Why not be intelligent and creative enough to hand out punishments fitting the infractions in each individual circumstance? Why punish an entire team and university because one kid got an against-the-rules inducement?

It is not sufficient to say that this is the only way to stop the problem. Even Knight would not be so presumptuous as to say that he had thought up every possible way, and that only HIS methods would work. Why not appoint a kind of blue ribbon committee composed of players, coaches and administrators, and let them STUDY the situation and come up with realistic, intelligent proposals — rather than relying on moralists popping off?

Giving a seventeen-year-old player no second chance is stupid. Firing a coach could be right, but more often, considering the extenuating circumstances, it would not be right or moral to do it. And removing all home games from the schedule and taking away all that revenue is a thoughtless joke.

—CBS Nightwatch

ERNEST CHAMBERS

A state legislator from Nebraska, Ernest Chambers deserves a lot of credit. He was one of the first people to speak out on behalf of student-athletes. He recognized the exploitation of student-athletes and introduced, as early as 1980, a bill into the Nebraska state legislature to put Nebraska football players on the state payroll. He stated clearly, "they make millions of dollars for the University of Nebraska, they should get some reward for that." He proposed $500 per month.

He was laughed at, back then, but he had the courage and persistence to speak out when the rest of the world was turning its back to reality.

The concept of "athletic Darwinism" comes from Mr. Chambers. It means, according to Mr. Chambers, "the strong, which supports itself through its own revenues, will survive, and the others will be weeded out. Then we will have a natural breaking out of a superleague based on competition instead of artificial barriers set up by the NCAA."

Not a bad idea at all.

"No matter how much the athletes have been slipped on the sly, they have been underpaid."

—John Schulian
Playboy Magazine

"CHEATING"

Whenever the word "cheating" appears in this book, referring to inducements and offers to student-athletes, it is enclosed by quotation marks to indicate that this word is usually employed erroneously in contemporary usage. The word's common definition is typically applied to student-athletes, and to coaches or boosters who give "extra" aid to student-athletes.

The standard interpretation of "cheating" by the media and the NCAA is that some student-athlete has gotten something (from a coach or a sports fan or an alumnus of some school or from a friend of some school) which the NCAA has prohibited — a benefit not permitted under NCAA rules. This may be, for example, anything from an empty shoe box to a shoe box containing ten thousand dollars, from a ride home from practice to a free hamburger at McDonalds.

The NCAA and the universities have put everything beyond room, board, tuition and books on the "not entitled to" list. It does not matter to them that many academic scholarship winners get more than "room, board, tuition, and books" as part of their scholarships. It does not matter to them that many poverty level students get more benefits than these by simply applying for state and federal student grants.

What matters to the NCAA and to the universities who support this prohibition is that they try to catch and punish severely any athlete who realizes that he is entitled to more than he is getting and who may therefore accept some money or a ride or a plane ticket (or a free T-shirt) from a school he may or may not attend.

THE REAL CHEATERS

Clearly, the NCAA and the universities are CHEATING revenue producing athletes out of millions of dollars each year by diligently and ruthlessly enforcing their unjustifiable prohibitions.

It is a patent absurdity that a player who is robbed of thousands of dollars can be denied his scholarship and the right to participate in his sport — by his robbers — because he has accepted a ten dollar gift from a friend associated with his school.

In view of the outrageous annual robbery (of revenue producing student-athletes) being perpetrated by the universities and the NCAA, **no so-called "cheating" violation of the past twenty years has been a legitimate claim.** The only cheaters have been the NCAA and the universities.

Ten thousand dollars does not nearly compensate a big-time basketball or football player in proportion to his economic worth to a revenue producing program.

How can a player be called a "cheater" for making an attempt to recover some of the money that is stolen from him?

The NCAA and the universities who exploit star athletes are clearly the cheaters. Their cheating needs no quotations. It is dramatic, consistent, and especially outrageous in view of the effort made to disguise the theft with noble-sounding rationales. The universities continually make big money on athletes who they often fail to provide with even a diploma in return.

"If I'm a coach and I get penalized, my attorney is going to be saying this is a group boycott, and illegal refusal to deal, a violation of antitrust laws."
      —Charles Alan Wright
      Law Professor
      (Former Chairman of NCAA Infractions Committee)
      University of Texas

COACHES

Coaches in the major sports are in a delicate position. First, they are paid extremely well and they therefore have no desire to rock any boats to the extent that their own positions will be jeopardized.

Second, they work and live every day with the athletes they coach, and they are intensely aware of the athletes' problems and needs, and they usually are sympathetic to these problems and needs.

Third, they stand in a delicate balance between participant and administrator. In some ways they are on the side of the university — as a representative and an employee of the university — yet in other ways they are on the side of the players, trying to get the players more benefits, searching for loopholes by which to do this legally, or at least discreetly and quietly.

Philosophically, they may be for amateur sports, yet they realize they are benefitting handsomely from the rewards of the essentially professional sports which they are coaching on the college level. Philosophically, they may agree with the president of the university that an education is a wonderful thing and a substantial reward, yet they will hope to keep certain of their ideas and actions from the president because they believe their players need and deserve more benefits than they are getting.

The coach may be further torn by a personal need to win — therefore to entice good players to come to his school with a promise of added benefits — yet he may believe that a player should want to come without need of added benefits.

COACHES' DAILY DILEMMAS

Not only are there philosophical conflicts, but daily practical matters that make philosophies ridiculous.

A high school kid may be recruited, flown to the campus, taken out to dinner in a rented car, and be given money for a movie. But the star player, already on the team, already averaging twenty points or two touchdowns a game, may not by rule be flown home for Christmas, may not have enough to go to a movie (and may not by rule be given any money for such purposes — not even directly from a coach's personal funds), and may not be lent even an old wreck for transportation.

The coach is aware constantly that many of his players have very little, if any, money. He knows their families cannot be sending money from home — he recruited them and knows their home situations well —

117

and he may have promised the parents that he would do his best to take care of their son during college.

What does "take care of" mean? Should the coach give some of his players money from his own pocket? The coach may make more than a hundred thousand dollars a year from basketball coaching, but that doesn't matter. By NCAA rule, the coach is not permitted to give money even from his own pocket. If he does it, he knows he is breaking a rule. He is a "cheater." If he is caught, he can lose his job. If the player is caught accepting money from his coach (or from anyone even vaguely connected with the school) he can lose all his eligibility and his scholarship.

In most cases like this, the coach simply gives the needy player some money. The player knows to say nothing, and the coach says nothing. No one ever finds out. Everything is fine. Except that they are "cheaters," and most coaches don't want to be in the position of being called "cheaters," so they find other ways — loopholes — through which to funnel some money to their players.

"CHEATERS" OR HUMANITARIANS?

So who is right — the coach who gives his players some needed money or the coach who ignores their needs and just hopes nothing happens?

Nearly every one of the top coaches in the nation has, at one time or another, either given money to players or enabled players to get money in ways that were against the rules — or at least they KNEW that their players were getting some money in ways outside the rules, but they did not report it, did nothing about it.

Few big-time coaches believe that the present system is just, but they are afraid to speak out and alienate the minor sport coaches with whom they work, or the athletics directors, administrators, and presidents on whom their own jobs depend. The easy way out is to find means to alter the situation discreetly, finding trusted alumni and friends here and there who are wealthy enough and intelligent enough to be discreet and therefore are never caught in any wrongdoing.

But isn't it a shame that nearly everyone agrees that a certain amount of wrongdoing simply goes with the terrain? Why can't a business like college sports be made clean enough (and the rules be made realistic enough) that people can simply admit what is going on? Do college sports programs have to exist under a veil of secrecy in a climate of general paranoia?

This IS the case right now. Anyone who does not believe this needs merely to go snooping around any big-time athletic department and see how many straightforward answers he gets to his questions.

Where do the coaches stand? They are the leaders, the example-setters, the bastions of integrity, and the public spokesmen on the one hand; and they are the regular guys, the understanding fathers, and the sneak-it-by-em-and-don't-say-anything cloak and dagger men on the other. What position should coaches take?

With the college presidents making their recent, hypocritical pitch for integrity in New Orleans, the coaches have little choice but to keep a low profile and just hope the whole thing blows over.

HOW COACHES ARE TO BLAME

The coaches are in their present bind largely because of their own failure to speak out when they had the chance — before the recent public concern over collegiate athletics became so great.

Coaches know they have too many scholarships to give, they know they have more people on their teams than they have the ability to keep happy, and they know their players deserve compensation they are not getting. They have known for a long time that the situation wasn't right, but they were enjoying their own increasing success too much to stand up and make their feelings known.

Face it, some of them are just grown up dumb jocks who never have given a great deal of thought to sports' place in society and on the college campus. They govern their teams via a constant reference to what they did when they played. Many of them are much more concerned with diagramming plays or signing this or that prospect than they are with any larger perspective on things.

In fairness to coaches though, their jobs are for the most part so dependent on their won-lost records that it is small wonder they pass up the opportunities they have, to try to bring about meaningful changes. It makes more sense right now to concentrate on winning and keeping certain borderline students eligible. These other considerations can be put on the back burner, or they can be raised by the John Woodens, the Al McGuires, and the Ray Meyers — retired coaches who should have time for such things.

For whatever reasons, it is clear that most big-time coaches do not speak out, do not make a crusade of changing the way things are. Win now, talk later, seems to be the most intelligent course to follow. It is unfortunate, yet understandable.

"[The NCAA legislation to place a cap on coaches' salaries] is about as close to being communistic as you can get."

—Hayden Fry
Head Football Coach
University of Iowa

119

COMMUNISM

Communism is a word normally associated with Russia. The word, though, actually comes from the word "commune," and "communism" is the set of economic principles that normally govern life in a commune — whether it be a group of hippies in California or a group of socialist republics in the Soviet Union.

In a communist system of economics the total accummulated wealth of the state (or of the group of people belonging to the commune) is shared equally by all the people, regardless of what they produce.

This is precisely what is done, at least in theory, in the Soviet Union and on American college campuses where sports are concerned. Basketball and football players generate all the money, and the scholarships which they receive are precisely the same as those going to the athletes in other sports which generate no money and in fact lose many thousands of dollars each year.

In America, it makes little sense for universities to support a communist system of economics.

"It's ridiculous to take a kid out of the ghetto, send him 100 miles from his home and give him books, tuition and board and not give him spending money."
—Marshall Criser
President
University of Florida

COMMON SENSE

One of the most noteworthy aspects of NCAA rules is that they continually defy common sense. There are periods of time, for example, called "Quiet Periods," when coaches are not allowed to say a word to high school prospects. As a result, there are, from time to time, extremely uneasy situations arising when coaches run into prospects by accident and are at a loss to explain their predicament.

They do their best with "I'm sorry, but NCAA rules prohibit me from talking with you right now," but this is hardly an adequate explanation when the high school kid in question is not even a real prospect.

This percise situation occurred a couple of years ago when I, momentarily forgetting the rule, tried to introduce a young athlete to Dean Smith. To the kid, only 5'9" and hardly a prospect for the University of North Carolina, it was a real thrill to meet an almost legendary figure face to face. But the kid didn't get the benefit of Smith's usual charm and personal interest. He got instead a cursory "I'm sorry . . ." and that was the end of the introduction.

A rule like that doesn't ruin anyone's life, and it doesn't exploit anyone or deny anyone crucial rights. It merely defies common sense. Is it really so important to police the hundred-plus revenue producing schools so carefully that there must be required periods of total silence even when a simple introduction is being made?

If all the examples of NCAA rules defying common sense were limited to introductions and thrills for young athletes, it would not be necessary to mention anything about NCAA rules and common sense. But often the rules extend absurdly, with implications bordering on the tragic.

Dale Brown, the head basketball coach of Louisiana State University tells the story of an LSU basketball player who was dying and asked that three of his best friends on the team join him at his bedside before he died. The governor of Louisiana learned of the player's wish and offered a private jet to pick up the LSU basketball team and deliver them to the kid's side.

The NCAA, however, learned of the offer and ruled that such a free trip would be against an NCAA rule and would constitute a major violation.

The governor's jet therefore was recalled, and the team did not go.

A couple of team members finally did manage to get to their friend's side, but without the slightest help from the NCAA.

Nearly every coach can site similar situations where players have been prevented from receiving expense money to visit sick or dying loved ones at home — because NCAA rules prohibit such free trips while they make no exceptions for exceptional circumstances.

"Though they are in the pro sports business, college players are not paid. Coaches get rich. Schools make millions. Sports writers buy new cars on money they make writing about kids who make no money. Everyone turns a buck, and that's fine, it's the American way — everyone except the players, who are told it is against the rules, it is cheating if they make a buck, it is corrupt."
　　　　　　　　　　　　—Dave Kindred
　　　　　　　　　　　　Columnist
　　　　　　　　　　　　Atlanta Constitution

"CORRUPTION"

"Corruption" is another word requiring quotations — because it is a media word and a word largely spread around by the NCAA. It is associated with student-athletes who accept (and athletic programs which offer) inducements that are against NCAA rules.

"Corruption" is a harsh word to be bandied about as carelessly as the NCAA is prone to do. "Corruption," prior to this new, prevalent usage pertaining to collegiate sports, was a word reserved for politicians and financial officials who embezzled public funds and committed crimes against the state and the people.

It is tragic that the NCAA and the media have been allowed to use this word in association with athletes, whose infractions very rarely have anything at all to do with criminal offenses.

It is against no law to accept money for playing sports, nor is it against any law for an athlete to accept a plane ticket or a free meal for his parents or a T-shirt for his little brother.

In the vast majority of cases in which athletes or athletic programs are accused of "corruption," no law of any kind has been violated. The word "corruption" therefore is misused, and it should be dropped from the national sports vocabulary.

It is difficult to understand why the NCAA, which is supposed to exist in behalf of collegiate sports, seems so often to be responsible for the negative public image which has come to be associated with collegiate sports.

Why isn't the NCAA currently involved in a public relations campaign to explain to sports fans and to the general public that infractions and violations of NCAA rules are not crimes, and that athletes who violate NCAA rules are hardly criminals?

WHO IS CORRUPT?

If you are looking for corruption in college sports, you need to look to the people who are flying first class to resort conventions — with the money being generated by others.

When have athletes had the opportunity to vote for the salaries of the NCAA officials?

How is it that a group of people can feel at ease while voting themselves comfortable salaries and sizeable expense accounts to be paid with other people's money?

The next time you hear talk of "corruption" in college sports, you will do well to give careful consideration to just who is fostering the corruption.

"We need to apply strict penalties to those who violate NCAA rules. But to bar a school from participation . . . for one or two years is wrong. If one part of the body is found to have cancer, you cut out the cancer; you don't kill the body . . . too many innocent people would suffer."

—Dave Hart
Director of Athletics
University of Missouri

THE "DEATH PENALTY"

The death penalty is the name given to the new rule, adopted at the NCAA's 1985 Special Convention, which can result in the complete suspension of an athletic program caught with two major violations in a five year period.

Oddly, the two major violations do not even have to be attributed to the same program. If the golf team gets the first probation, then the tennis team is found guilty of a major violation, the tennis program — the second offender — can be suspended for two years.

It will certainly be interesting to see what happens if schools like Michigan or Ohio State have their entire football programs suspended for two years. Would they drop all minor sports suddenly and layoff all sports personnel? Or would these schools dip into the general educational fund for the millions of dollars necessary to run these programs?

Look for some new court battles when the first "death penalty" suspension hits a major program.

Seems a lot wiser to cut out all of the extra, money-losing sport programs right now, and put ALL football money back into football so these programs can indeed be the exemplary, shining lights of virtue that the university presidents want them to be.

It doesn't make much sense to steal from them and encourage them to cheat on the one hand, and then let their demise bring down everyone else on the other. Might as well have one great program from the start, if it's a choice between that and none.

"The NCAA is living in the Dark Ages. It's idiotic. They've got so many rules they don't understand them themselves."

—Jim Bush
Former Head Track & Field Coach
UCLA

DIVISION I

The NCAA has certain requirements for schools wishing to call themselves "Division I" competitors. Among these is the requirement of a "broad-based" sports program with a minimum of fourteen sports (16 by 1988) for men and women.

This seemingly innocuous concept assures that all university athletic programs will be strapped financially or at least under constant financial pressure. It also assures that the welfare system of subsidizing 11 or 12 other sports goes merrily on; and it enables directors of athletics to continue to justify the annual theft of football and basketball players by saying "We are just following NCAA rules."

There is no inherent reason why 'broad-based' sports programs must be a requirement for admission into Division I competition.

"[Donors] are the life blood . . . to exist in major college sports, there has to be money from the outside."

—Gene Hooks
Director of Athletics
Wake Forest University

DONORS

How much money do donors give annually to major college athletics programs? A former NCAA president estimated at least $100,000,000. That number seems low, when matched against the money contributed during the 1984-85 season to the athletic programs at six schools in the Carolinas.

In an article appearing in the Charlotte Observer in November of 1984, the following contributions were projected by each school for the 1984-1985 year:

Clemson University	$5,000,000
Duke University	$1,000,000
North Carolina State University	$2,000,000
University of North Carolina	$5,000,000
University of South Carolina	$3,000,000
Wake Forest University	$1,400,000

These figures, as the Charlotte Observer pointed out, did not include the money raised for the new 22,500-seat Student Activities Center at the University of North Carolina, paid for entirely by private pledges amounting to $38 million.

Similarly, each of the other schools had recent athletic projects financed largely by private funds. Duke renovated its football stadium at a cost of $5.1 million (which included construction of a sports-health building); Clemson added seats to its football stadium at a cost of $15 million; Wake Forest added a $1.5 million athletic dorm; NC State added a $3.3 million general athletic facility with new offices, weight rooms and training rooms; and South Carolina gave its football stadium a $1 million facelift.

Figure on a conservative $60 million for facilities, along with $17.5 million in annual contributions, and you have a glimpse of big-time AMATEUR sports.

At each of the four state-supported schools above, a full scholarship costs about $5,000 per year. That's fifty thousand dollars to put a whole basketball team on the court, and a quarter of a million dollars for a football team. Put all six teams together, basketball and football, and it would still cost less than a couple of million dollars a year in scholarships to run high quality programs. Balance that against the $17.5 million annual contributions — which of course do not include gate receipts, concessions, or TV contracts — and then wait for the inevitable question . . .

"But where are we going to get money to pay the players?"

"I am only for drug-testing if the entire population is tested. That might seem far-fetched, but you can bet me, corporate officers at GM and Chrysler, actors, and people in all walks of life use drugs and nobody is calling for them to be tested . . . "

—Ron Davis
Baseball Player
Minnesota Twins

"To me, random drug testing is against the First Amendment. The right to privacy is definitely being threatened."

—Chris Chambliss
Pro Baseball Player
Atlanta Braves

"I resent the idea of using athletes as examples as if they are the only ones that use drugs. A lot of students use drugs that aren't athletes, but most of the time people single athletes out for drug testing as though they are [the only ones using drugs]."

—Clarence 'Big House' Gaines
Head Basketball Coach
Winston-Salem (NC) State College

"I'm a physician; I oppose this (the NCAA drug-testing proposal). I spoke with our team doctor, and he opposes it vehemently.
"It is bad legislation. It's not going to accomplish what it intends to accomplish. The drug problem is a major public health problem. This is not the way to attack it."

—Dr. Paul Gikas (in the
Washington Post, 1-15-85)
Professor of Pathology
University of Michigan

DRUG TESTING

No one is FOR the use of harmful drugs. But some coaches use them, some athletic administrators use them, and so do some college presidents and some college athletes.

But effective drug education programs need to be the focus of NCAA attention, not drug testing.

At this point, drug testing is a costly and complex issue that needs more study, and more thought.

It is a real fear among student-athletes that the NCAA, with its dismal record in other matters concerning student-athletes, may cause more harm than good with any drug testing program.

Why should athletes be singled out and tested for drugs when other students are not? The idea of drug-testing is discriminatory, unless it is used confidentially, to identify athletes in need of special, educational classes and counseling.

What IS the reason for drug testing among athletes?

Eric Zender, the research coordinator with the NCAA's drug education committee made it clear in an article which appeared in the Washington Post, 8-23-83:

"The basic reason for testing (in athletics) is to see that the kid doesn't have an unfair advantage over others."

The coaches need to make it clear that they are not concerned with slight advantages. What they SHOULD be concerned with is the health and well-being of the athletes.

When it becomes clear that the purpose of the NCAA drug testing program is to help student-athletes, it will deserve widespread support. But not until then.

"You got kids in there who can't hardly quote good English."
—Talk Show Caller
(talking about "Dumb jocks!")

"DUMB JOCKS"

Dumb jocks is a well known, image-tarnishing phrase which the universities and the NCAA do little to combat. They do not permit athletes to get remedial help or a headstart before starting school in the fall of the athletes' Freshman year, they require the athletes to take full course loads (though normal students are not required to do that), and they keep quiet the fact that athletes are doing about as well academically as the rest of the students.

How often have you heard stories about ATHLETES being admitted with low college board scores and poor grades?

They are, at times. No one is disputing that. But is this problem limited just to athletes?

Three University of Texas researchers, according to a report in The NCAA News, 4-17-85, found athletes hardly deserve to be singled out:

"We found that the most selective, the most elite universities in the nation today are up to their eyebrows and elbows with freshmen who can't read, who can't write and who can't figure well enough to be in freshman work."

The researcher quoted, John Roueche, went on, "I don't think colleges will be out of the remedial business in this century."

According to The NCAA News, "the study found that it is not uncommon to find 30 percent to 40 percent of entering freshmen reading below a seventh-grade level."

Don't you wonder why the NCAA wouldn't choose to trumpet this kind of news across the nation in support of athletes? Instead, the report was well hidden on page 5 under a heading, "Skills lagging."

If the media are going to let the world know about the SAT scores of a well-known athlete, shouldn't the National Collegiate ATHLETIC Association be spending public relations dollars to make the public aware that this is a nationwide STUDENT problem, not merely an exception made for a few highly publicized athletes?

Many universities are in an economic crunch. They need students. To get those students, MANY of them are letting in almost anyone who can pay the fees.

———

"I was told it [the procedural process with the NCAA infractions committee] was non-adversarial. All my experience was adversarial and all of my contact with the NCAA was adversarial."

—Lyle Rivera
former Nevada Attorney General
testifying in the Tarkanian case

ENFORCEMENT

One of the chief complaints of NCAA officials over the past several years has been their inability to enforce the association's rules because of an undermanned, inadequate staff.

Yet the salaries in the Enforcement Department amount to approximately $500,000 per year with a total budget of about $1,500,000. Where does all that money go? And, a better question, what good does it do any of the players?

There are not too many major college revenue producing athletes who would care if the NCAA enforcement department were dropped entirely.

How bad is it if some player plays an extra year that he should not have? How bad is it if some player plays who has received some extra plane tickets or some extra meals or some extra cash here or there?

The NCAA enforcement department spends some $350,000 per year on travel. Who is doing all that traveling and for what?

Couldn't that money be better spent on post-graduate scholarships? Three hundred fifty thousand dollars is a lot of scholarships.

WHO APPOINTS
THE ENFORCEMENT DEPARTMENT STAFF?

During the Tarkanian trial, Judge Paul Goldman was very explicit in his criticism of the methods of NCAA Enforcement Director David Berst. Yet, did Berst ever come before a review of the membership? Was he ever asked to account personally for the behavior that a judge found reprehensible?

Certainly Berst never appeared before a group of player representatives to explain his actions.

Is the conduct of the NCAA enforcement department really good for collegiate sports?

What benefits have collegiate sports enjoyed as a result of the recent probations of schools like Florida, Georgia, Illinois and Clemson?

Perhaps it is time to re-evaluate the entire enforcement mechanism.

What "contract services" did the enforcement department utilize that were worth the quarter of a million dollars the department spent in each of the past three years?

Players are never supplied with information of this sort, and they have to be wondering if it wouldn't be better just to let the top schools compete with each other without any NCAA enforcement department at all. Just let them compete. Let them go at it. The university presidents have sufficient power to quell any major violations of the rules of fair play.

What if the top 100 schools got together for a convention each year and talked about their problems, the excesses, and how to control them? If the college presidents are indeed serious about their involvement and their interest in integrity in intercollegiate sports, then what need is there for an enforcement department? What is it that the presidents can not do? Each president has the power, as has been shown at San Francisco and at Tulane, to wipe out a whole program. So why is there a need to spend 1.5 million dollars each year to staff the NCAA's enforcement department? Couldn't one investigator easily snoop around one conference for a year and make recommendations to the presidents of that conference? Wouldn't a warning of that nature be more than adequate to curtail any awful activities that might prove to be an embarrassment to a university?

The NCAA's Select Committee on Athletic Problems and Concerns in Higher Education admitted that most of the problems occur in the 104 football programs classified in Division 1-A (along with about 70 other schools with basketball programs but not Division 1-A football). Does it really take 1.5 million dollars to police so few schools where the presidents hold absolute power and have demonstrated the willingness to cut whole programs in order to establish their commitment to integrity?

Isn't the NCAA enforcement department wasting an enormous amount of money in return for providing benefits of dubious value — all of which could be better accomplished by the presidents themselves? It is difficult to imagine the Division I basketball players voting any money at all for the NCAA enforcement department, yet the NCAA enforcement department is in existence because of the money generated by Division I basketball players — and the department is growing, not being cut back.

"I'm the first to concede that the NCAA's organizational structure is partly to blame.

"I'm gradually coming to the conclusion that there has to be a major rearrangement on the part of the institutions of higher learning as to what they want to do with their athletic programs . . . I think there's an inherent conflict that has to be resolved."

—Walter Byers
NCAA Executive Director

EQUITABLE DISTRIBUTION

During the Oklahoma-Georgia TV case, which the NCAA lost on grounds that it had violated the Sherman Antitrust Act, the NCAA attorneys made a repeated effort to convince the court that the purpose of regulating the TV output was to insure an equitable distribution of revenues from the games, thus supposedly maintaining competitive balance and keeping schools from pursuing a course motivated single-mindedly by the desire to profit.

The Supreme Court ruled this effort in violation of the intent of the Sherman Act, and pointed out (in footnote number 33, p. 2964 of the "Supreme Court Reporter") the following example:

"In this case the rule is violated by a price restraint that tends to provide the same economic rewards to all practicioners regardless of their skill, their experience, their training, or their willingness to employ innovative and difficult procedures."

Didn't the Supreme Court know that this is precisely the NCAA philosophy in dealing with ALL matters concerning student-athletes?

In any case, the ruling went on:

"The District Court provided a vivid example of this system in practice:

"A clear example of the failure of the rights fees paid to respond to market forces occurred in the fall of 1981. On one weekend of that year, Oklahoma was scheduled to play a football game with the University of Southern California. Both Oklahoma and USC have long had outstanding football programs, and indeed, both teams were ranked among the top five teams in the country by the wire service polls. ABC chose to televise the game along with several others on a regional basis. A game between two schools which are not well known for their football programs, Citadel and Appalachian State, was carried on four of ABC's local affiliated stations. The USC-Oklahoma contest was carried on over 200 stations. Yet, incredibly, all four of these teams received exactly the same amount of money for the right to televise their games."

The NCAA was not guilty of a mere oversight here. This kind of injustice is carefully planned and buttressed by arguments in behalf of amateurism and competition and any other feasible-sounding excuse to permit the NCAA's Robin Hoods to get money from the revenue producing programs.

Is it really crucial to the NCAA that distribution of revenues be equal in order to insure the preservation of amateurism or parity or whatever else it may use to justify its actions?

If so, how can it explain the distribution of funds from the national basketball tournament?

Why does it permit the Big East Conference, for example, to reward even its losing teams at a rate greater than many teams who got into the NCAA tournament? Dayton and DePaul, losers in the first round in 1985, received about $140,000, and the four PAC-10 teams who got into the NCAA tournament reportedly received about $50,000. Whereas Seton Hall, who went 10-18 on the season, received $171,000 for its share of Big East revenue.

The excuse can be used that the NCAA has no control over how a conference chooses to distribute its funds, or that it could not have foreseen that three Big East teams would make the Final Four in 1985.

While there may be some validity to both of these points, it still shows a very tiny actual regard for fair distribution of funds, and it shows just how impoverished is the NCAA's whole concept of how to use the players' championship money.

"Legislatively we are too large an organization. And eventually, the victim of the NCAA's lethargy in terms of reform is the student-athlete."
—Dean Smith
Head Basketball Coach
University of North Carolina

REASONABLE EXPENSES

The NCAA Manual is particularly contradictory on the matter of expenses — as they relate to NCAA personnel and to student-athletes.

Student-athletes are permitted reimbursement of expenses in very few cases. For example, even art supplies for an art major are not expenses that can be reimbursed, nor are outside reading materials for an ambitious student reimbursible under NCAA rules.

In the very few cases when athletes are permitted to be reimbursed for expenses — for travel to off-campus practice sites, for travel to official banquets, to award ceremonies, and to post season or holiday tournament games — the language of the NCAA Manual is clear. Only "actual and necessary expenses" may be reimbursed.

The phrase "actual and necessary" is repeated several times. Even on a foreign trip, a student-athlete may receive a maximum, per day expense of $10.

Yet, when reimbursing NCAA personnel, the NCAA rules are much more generous. See for yourself, directly from the 1985-1986 NCAA Manual . . .

"If a committee member travels via commercial airline, the member may travel first class."

What possible justification is there for NCAA committee members to travel first class?

Do they congratulate the thrifty members who save money by not traveling first class? The Manual goes on . . .

". . . or the member may travel coach (or "Super-Saver"), in which case the member would also receive $100 'flat rate' amount to defray expenses not covered by the per diem."

The NCAA per diem is $80.

Why don't the players — who earn the money — get an $80 per day expense payment, while the NCAA committee members be restricted to "actual and necessary expenses?"

Players would certainly love to have a $100 flat rate payment every-time their teams do not fly first class.

If NCAA officials can fly first class or get an extra $100, why not student-athletes?

Don't you wonder how much money the NCAA wastes each year on first class travel, on unnecessary travel, on unnecessary meetings, and on unjustifiable entertainment?

Now that the college presidents have taken such an active role in the policing of collegiate athletics, is it not perhaps possible that the NCAA's role could be diminished, as a money-saving measure?

If the NCAA were to make recommendations to the Presidents' Commission, the peer pressure should be sufficient to assure that the appropriate actions, suspensions, and prohibitions would take place, thus relieving the NCAA of many of its current expenses.

The bills the NCAA chalks up each year in legal fees are staggering enough to make this method worth a try.

If the NCAA lost its power to take players and schools to court, there would be extra millions saved on legal expenses, and fewer meetings and less travel expense incurred as well.

It is not obvious, however, that the NCAA is on any sort of austerity program. Why should it be? Annually, players get less and less, while revenues continue to grow.

First class travel and $80 per day. Doesn't sound amateur at all, does it?

"The NCAA takes considerable amounts of revenue generated from basketball, then uses it for travel, committee meetings, non-revenue sports ... but notice how well those administrators live when they take those trips for meetings; the meetings are always in some fairly exotic place. And then there's the student-athlete, who doesn't have the spare change for a hamburger, trying to scrape living expenses together."

"The sad thing is, we have the money in Division I basketball and football to help these young men, but the college administrations keep getting in the way ..."

"If this sad set of priorities stays intact, then the exploitation of student-athletes will be as difficult as ever to curtail ... "

—Dean Smith
Head Basketball Coach
University of North Carolina

"The trouble, of course, comes after the eligibility is up, when these athletes are light-years from any specific degree. This is a classic example of the exploitation of athletes and is a grave injustice."

—John D. Swofford
Director of Athletics
University of North Carolina

EXPLOITATION

Exploitation is typically used in an athletic context to mean that universities are making money on their basketball and football programs by using athletes who are borderline students, admitting them despite their lack of preparation for college, allowing them to get by for four years while taking courses like basket-weaving and the theory of sports, and then abandoning them after their four years of eligibility are completed. This is certainly exploitation.

But the exploitation does not end here, and it is not missing at those universities which point with pride to their high graduation rates. The universities are exploiting their graduating athletes as well — trading diplomas for millions of dollars in revenue, with the justification that an education is a wonderful and valuable thing.

Exploitation is pervasive in the present system. The coaches use the kids to gain prestige and more earning power. The universities trade the kids a diploma (at best) for amounts of money far beyond that which a regular student must pay. And the NCAA uses basically basketball players' money to pay itself approximately $3,000,000 a year IN SALARIES alone, and another million for "travel and entertainment."

Whether or not a player ends up getting a diploma, he is exploited famously by all of those who claim so staunchly that they want to help him and they have his best interests in mind.

"If a basketball superstar isn't allowed to take $10,000 for wearing a certain brand of shoes, should his coach be allowed to pocket $20,000 for putting the whole squad in that brand?"

—Maury White
The Des Moines Register

ACCENT ON FAIRNESS

Bruce Smith, selected as the outstanding lineman in the nation in 1985, was forced by the NCAA to return his sweater, watch, carry-on bag, and hat to the Independence Bowl, after he requested a "voluntary nonsuit" and dismissed his litigation against Virginia Tech. Smith had gotten a court injunction which enabled him to play in the Independence Bowl, then he dropped the lawsuit after the game.

The NCAA, in its perennial zeal to attain absolute fairness, had no problem justifying the action to get back that sweater and hat. Said NCAA President, John R. Davis:

"The restitution provisions were adopted by the membership in the interest of fairness to institutions forced by court order to compete against teams including an ineligible student-athlete . . ."

"The provisions are designed to eliminate any competitive advantage gained by an institution while permitting an ineligible student-athlete to participate under a court order that eventually is vacated voluntarily or reversed."

The violations which occurred involving Smith and Virginia Tech all happened in the recruiting of Smith as a high school player. He was given three, free campus visits, instead of the one which NCAA rules permit. And, evil of evils, his family received a load of firewood.

These "flagrant" violations, discovered after Smith's Sophomore season, were not deemed by the NCAA to give Virginia Tech a competitive advantage over opponents during two years of regular season games, only against the Air Force Academy in the bowl game.

Suffering under such hardship and unfairness, the Air Force Academy nevertheless managed to win the game — WITH Smith playing — by a score of 23-7.

In consideration of the NCAA's careful distinctions concerning fairness and the fine points of competitive advantage, shouldn't the NCAA make a move to see to it that the Air Force Academy players get to share, at least, in Smith's sweater? Three or four of them could probably get some warmth out of all the yarn it takes to wrap up big Bruce Smith. And that watch he had to give back could save some airmen some demerits some day. Seems a shame not to reward those who overcame such odds, having to play against a guy who had two extra campus visits and some firewood back in '81.

FIDUCIARY OBLIGATION

Fiduciary obligation refers to the legal concept of what might be called 'inherent duties' which arise in a relationship between a professional of some kind and a client. For example, a stock broker or a lawyer, when representing a client, is not permitted by law to act in a way that is not — as far as he knows — in the best interests of his client.

The Law, recognizing the vulnerability of a client who entrusts his welfare to another in some sort of formal relationship, protects the client at least insofar as it requires the fiduciary to try to act in the client's best interests.

When laymen make attempts to explain legal principles, the wording often gets cumbersome. However, John Weistart, Professor of Law at Duke University, is particularly adept at expressing complex principles simply, so I quote here a few of his own words which appeared in the JOURNAL OF COLLEGE AND UNIVERSITY LAW (Vol. 10, No. 2) in an article entitled "Legal Accountability and the NCAA."

". . . principles in modern law reveal a precept that individuals and entities that enjoy significant control owe accountability to those who are regulated." (p. 172)

"There are features of the athlete's dependency that make the case for judicial review of their complaints particularly compelling." (p. 174)

"The lack of volition in the athlete's relationship with the NCAA can be seen as having two important aspects: not only are the rules made without the assured representation of the athlete's interest, but also the rules are unavoidable if the athlete is a football or basketball player who desires further training." (p. 175)

Fans wishing a more complete explanation would do well to read Professor Weistart's books and articles directly. Certainly he has an understanding of the athlete's unique and often unhappy relationship with the NCAA which is as commanding as his expertise in the precepts and expression of the law.

No doubt his views on accountability and fiduciary obligation will be heard in detail at some future time when a court case can be structured in such a way as to end the NCAA's "monolithic" and unjust control over student-athletes.

"I know I've changed my opinion on this rule completely, but times have changed. Kids today need some spending money in their pockets."

—Grant Teaff
Head Football Coach
Baylor University

SUMMER SCHOOL FINANCIAL AID

NCAA rules prohibit a student from getting any financial aid prior to the fall of his Freshman year. That means, if a kid signs with a school and would like to attend summer school to get a headstart in doing college academic work, he is not permitted unless he can afford to pay all of the bills himself.

The colleges are permitted to pay for summer school after a student has gone through his Freshman year, but not the summer before.

This rule is especially ironic in view of the fact that most people recognize the Freshman year as the most difficult, and many critics argue that no kid should be permitted to play a college football game before he has learned where the library is.

Year after year, there are athletes who could benefit greatly from taking some college courses and getting their feet academically wet in the summer before their first full semester. But the NCAA prevents this, to the dismay of many coaches and student-athletes.

A FOOTBALL NATIONAL CHAMPIONSHIP

Currently, football players — especially defensive players and linemen — are generally looked upon as big, dumb jocks stupid enough to run and sweat and pound their bodies on the field so that millions of people can benefit. Football programs pay for all of the minor sports at most major universities, and their holiday bowl attractions are responsible for providing funds for literally hundreds of charities.

There is nothing wrong with charities, but people have to begin realizing that football players are a worthwhile charity in themselves. MOST interior linemen at the collegiate level are unknowns, not glamorous stars; most are borderline students, not Rhodes Scholar candidates; and most do not have a great deal of money nor even a likelihood of graduating from college.

Therefore, letting football-generated funds flow back to football players makes excellent sense, and a national championship playoff would bring football players abundant funds to work with. Let's look at how a national football championship playoff might be structured.

32 TEAM PLAYOFF

A 32 team playoff would give all of the top teams a chance to compete for the championship, yet a champion could be determined in five weeks. That means the teams in the playoffs would play during December (most teams now are idle that entire month) and the college football national championship could take place on New Years Day, keeping to the tradition — and even adding to the excitement of it — with that grand attraction on the first day of the new year.

Using conservative estimates, the 31 games (necessary to reduce 32 teams down to one champion) could expect to draw over two million fans (with just over 60,000 fans per game). At $20 per fan, that's $40,000,000 we're talking about.

The TV contract for a playoff system of this nature would be in the $100 million range. Is that impossible? When you look at what the Super Bowl draws, and the fact that even the present bowl system returns some $40 million to the schools (and that $40 million is just 75% of the total) you begin to see that a $100 million payoff is not dreamworld stuff at all.

One hundred million dollars would provide the kind of guaranteed-for-life scholarship programs, grand remedial programs, and graduation-incentive grant programs already talked about for basketball players in Part I.

HOLD THE HOOPLA

There really isn't any reason for football players to spend a whole week in celebrating, using up piles of expense money that could provide for their futures rather than for holiday hoopla. It would be fine for the players to leave for each Saturday playoff game on Friday afternoon — after classes. Coaches would want to leave earlier, to prepare, to practice once on the playoff field, but such niceties are not essential. Money to fund educations and futures is more important.

A MINOR INCENTIVE

To reward the players on the playoff teams for having to subject themselves to these extra games in December, a very simple "personal expense reimbursement" program could be set up. Give each player, in each round, just $2,000. On a fifty man football team, the total would come to a tiny $100,000 per team — a true drop in the bucket next to the vast amount of money each game would generate.

By this plan, the players who advanced all the way to the final game would receive $10,000 in personal expense reimbursements — not enough to get rich on, but a welcome addition to any player's pocketbook.

BUT WHAT ABOUT FINAL EXAMS?

Assuming that football players would be permitted to take just two courses during football season, they should encounter no great difficulty in studying for two final exams; and since the teams would not leave for each Saturday game until Friday afternoon, on chartered planes, there would be no reason for any player to miss any classes at all.

This puts collegiate football back in the old tradition — when football players were students.

With this plan in effect, the players would be happy to play the extra games, they would have the incentive to stay eligible, and they would reap big rewards for their educations and futures, without getting paid and becoming professionals in the process.

Whatever New Year's Day sick-leaves or strikes are necessary to accomplish this would be well worth it to football players.

Football players are an important charity; but with a national football championship playoff, enough money would be generated to make it all happen. They wouldn't need any gifts or outside help at all.

FREE RIDE

"Free ride" is another perversion of the English language used in association with student-athletes. The term typically means that an athlete is getting his way paid through school in return for playing a sport.

This term had meaning back in the Forties when the average American high school student did not have an opportunity to go to college. Back then, few kids played sports all year around and almost no one practiced with the intensity that is mandatory now. Few players were involved in demanding, weight-lifting programs, few were running stadium steps and miles per day, and few felt the need to put many hours a day into practice in order to improve.

Back then, athletes played, and if they happened to have a knack for a sport, chances are they played it a lot more than others, and they got some wonderful opportunities not available to most of their high school classmates.

An education was something far beyond the reach of the average student back in 1940, so a "free ride" through college by playing ball was indeed a special gift that set athletes apart and made them duly grateful.

But times have changed. Today a "free ride" means getting A BIT MORE grant money than thousands of other students, and it means putting in many more hours per week, many physically demanding hours all year long, and it means trading this time and effort for a diploma that might be obtained more intelligently through federal student grants; guaranteed, low-interest student loans; and college work-study programs.

If young athletes were not so mesmerized by the glitter of applauding fans, by the notoriety conferred upon some by TV, and by the promise or dream of making big bucks in the pros, it would be crystal clear that accepting an athletic "free ride," versus an education via the methods open to other students, would not be worth the effort.

Despite the laudable efforts of outstanding people like Bill Bradley, Tom McMillan, and Pat Haden — all athletic stars and Rhodes Scholars — MOST students who play big-time sports will get lower grades and will be less prepared for the post-graduate job market and for admission to a professional school than classroom competitors who do not spend 30-50 hours a week on sports. They will also be poorer as they go through their four year college experience, since most of them will devote their summers to self-improvement in their sports, while many will need to attend summer school to keep up academically.

What was once realistically named a "free ride" is anything but that today. But it is in the universities' self-interest, and in the NCAA's self-interest, to keep student-athletes believing they are getting something-for-nothing, a gift they should be grateful for.

Why not merely end all of the debating about costs and free rides by giving the revenue producing athletes a fair share of TV and gate receipts and then letting them pay for their educations JUST LIKE EVERY OTHER STUDENT?

Today's revenue producing athletes are clearly NOT getting "free rides." They are being cheated out of many thousands of earned dollars.

FRESHMAN INELIGIBILITY

There is probably only one good reason for barring freshman athletes from competition in varsity sports. If such a rule is coupled with no increase (or better, a reduction) in the total number of scholarships which a school can give, than a freshman ineligibility rule would result in extra, necessary practice players, while decreasing the number of players actually eligible to play.

Any rule which makes the individual athlete more important to the success of the team (and which assures him of more playing time) has to be considered to have merit.

The academic issue, however — the issue most often advanced in support of making freshmen ineligible to play — does not hold up statistically. Supporters of the view that students should have to demonstrate academic proficiency first, before playing sports, must ask themselves if ALL students must then be banned from participation in ALL extra-curricular activities — or is this still one more area where the Division I football and basketball player will be singled out and discriminated against?

What academic rationale can there be for prohibiting a top student from playing during HIS freshman year? Would a freshman student wanting to play basketball be denied that opportunity even after he demonstrated a high gradepoint average in his first semester? By what rationale could he then be kept out of the games in January, February, and March?

Supporters of freshman ineligibility for academic reasons must also rebut a reputable study of data collected by the American College Testing Program, the College Board, and the Educational Testing Service. The study, which was made from data gathered over an eighteen month period at 57 Division I institutions (and reported on in The NCAA News, 11-19-84) showed that scholarship athletes actually did better academically than non-athletes during their freshman year. Said Robert T. Cameron of the College Board:

"The athletes completed more (credit) hours, had the same grades and returned in their sophomore year in greater numbers than the non-athletes."

The study went on:

"In general it seems clear that if athletic participation has a negative effect on academic performance, its impact is not reflected in lower freshman gradepoint averages or reduced levels of persistence."

The results of any study can, of course, be disputed. But this one, taking into account two thousand scholarship athletes and two thousand non-athletes, was probably more thorough than most.

The point is: there seems to be no legitimate reason for punishing a freshman student who is capable of handling both academic and athletic endeavors by keeping him from playing a varsity sport — unless the purpose of it is to make the athletic environment significantly better for the sophomores, juniors, and seniors.

"It's the motherhood trick. You can't vote against it. But it's not as good legislation as it possibly could be."

—Charles Harris
Director of Athletics
University of Pennsylvania

SIX HUNDRED POUND GORILLAS
or
THE REASON BEHIND SO MANY STUPID RULES

The NCAA is widely known for its excessive and stupid rules. Yet, it remains the general attitude of those in power that still more rules, often hastily enacted, will bring about solutions to the problems of collegiate athletics, or at least they will be good public relations.

Indeed, in referring to the same drug legislation as Charles Harris mentioned in the introductory quotation — the SAME legislation that two University of Michigan physicians opposed vehemently — the (then) president of the NCAA, John Toner said:

"I don't mind having the effective date postponed a year. But I think it's important legislation to pass now to get it on the books."

Get it on the books! Put more rules on the books! With that mentality, how can anyone expect anything but a lot of bad rules?

When the NCAA goes into Convention, its primary concern is public relations, not intelligent rule-making. There is the constant fear that the public will react negatively to postponements and to the tabling (for further study) of important issues.

In the Special Convention in New Orleans in 1985, Charles Scott from Mississippi State got up several times to remind the members that often they had had the habit of passing things that they did not intend — because of their haste to "get them on the books."

Mr. Scott, with a low-keyed delivery, made a point of telling a rather long story to the barely tolerant, august body of presidents. He knew precisely what he was doing and did not hurry his delivery. His story was about a 600 pound gorilla. After some considerable detail which didn't seem to make a lot of sense, a questioner in the story asked something like "But what is that 600 pound gorilla doing?"

The answer was "Anything it wants," which was exactly Mr. Scott's point. Rules pushed hastily onto the NCAA books had too often, he said, become uncontrollable, 600 pound gorillas, having implications the voters had never considered or intended.

Despite the repeated warnings, that Special Convention put half a dozen 600 pound gorillas on the books.

But it was great for public relations.

"A lot of universities build their reputations based on board scores of their entering freshmen. That means they have good students.

"Some universities take a challenge and provide opportunities for everyone. When you take that philosophy, naturally your percentage of graduation is not going to be as high.

"Were it not for basketball, many youngsters would have absolutely no contact with education and would be deprived of that ... the abuses that take place in intercollegiate athletics are far outweighted by the benefits."

—Eldon Miller
Head Basketball Coach
Ohio State University

GRADUATION RATES

Graduation rates have become a much-talked about issue in big-time sports. Supposedly they show which schools are keeping their promises to athletes — by trading diplomas for athletic skills — and which are exploiting the athletes, using their athletic skills without giving anything back.

The figures can, however, be misleading. Often the figures are given in terms of the number of athletes graduating in four years. But who really cares how many athletes graduate in four years? When was the last time anyone said to a lawyer or bank president, "Good idea, but did you graduate in four years?"

How long it takes to graduate is not so important as DO THEY GRADUATE AT ALL? Does the university continue to provide money so that players can graduate? Why do NCAA rules prevent schools from offering scholarships for longer than five years? (Don't they want the athletes eventually to graduate?)

There are all sorts of seemingly logical explanations for the various NCAA rules. A five year scholarship SHOULD be long enough for any student making a sincere effort. Yes, true. But what about those admitted who were not prepared, who were not truly college freshmen when they entered? What about those who indeed had misplaced priorities when they entered and who were permitted to squander their first four years of school on meaningless courses in order to get by and stay eligible?

There is fault to be found amoung athletes who have failed to take advantage of their opportunities. But their personal failures in no way exonerate the universities which have let this situation go on and on and on, doing nothing about it.

In isolated cases, it is the fault of individual students who were led to the water but would not drink. But in repeated cases, it is a simple matter of very predictable percentages. Take a group of academically unprepared athletes from poor socio-economic backgrounds with very low grades and test scores, and put them into a highly competitive, demanding athletic environment, and wait four years.

Presto! It doesn't take a gourmet chef or a David Copperfield to predict what will be the result. The athletes will not have graduated in the vast majority of cases, and even many of those who do will not truly be prepared for getting a meaningful job when they are out in the world.

The United States Secretary of Education, William Bennett, has said himself that many universities are ripping off students by failing to provide them a quality education that prepares them for a productive future. This was NOT in reference to athletes, but to GRADUATING students in general.

Add athletic participation and the competitive, demanding athletic environment on top of this general failure in education, and you have a dismal record even among many universities with athlete graduation rates which they point to with pride.

LINK GRADUATION RATES TO SCHOLARSHIP RATES

If college presidents were serious about their intention to educate their athletes, they could go a long way by simply tying scholarship rates to graduation rates.

IF NO ONE GRADUATES THIS YEAR, THERE WILL BE NO SCHOLARSHIPS TO GIVE.

This is remarkably simple to accomplish and it would, overnight, turn coaches into the educators and counselors they are supposed to be. This linkage would assure the athletes of graduating, at least, if not necessarily getting a meaningful education.

WHAT ARE THE EXCUSES?

Can anyone explain why the universities have failed up to this time to tie scholarship rates to graduation rates? If the intent of the universities is really to educate their athletes, why would they even consider any other method for awarding new scholarships?

What excuse can there possibly be for bringing in new groups of athletes each year, even though no old groups are graduating?

How can any college president who has let this go on truly be believed when he claims a commitment to education and integrity in college sports? Dismal graduation rates cannot be blamed primarily on the coaches. If schools are paying the coaches to win, not to graduate players, then coaches can hardly be expected to place THEIR top priority on graduating players.

The hypocrisy belongs to the college presidents. When they let new athletes be recruited and admitted each year even though the old ones are leaving without diplomas, they BELIEVE in exploiting athletes, regardless of what they SAY.

Their actions speak louder than their words. The college presidents who presided over basketball programs at the following schools, between 1972 and 1982, MUST believe in the most basic form of exploitation of athletes, for that is clearly what they have done.

Here is a list of schools with not low, but DISMAL, graduation rates among their basketball players. The two numbers beside each team show the number of scholarship basketball players enrolled in the ten year period, followed by the number who graduated. (Statistics taken from USA TODAY, 5-6-85.)

	Players	Graduates
Austin Peay	100	41
Bradley	63	25
California	46	20
Cincinnati	41	11
Citadel	95	35
Cleveland State	67	30
Eastern Kentucky	76	27
Evansville	53	23
Florida State	48	18
Idaho	57	16
Kent State	69	13
Long Beach	62	23
LSU	39	11
Memphis State	56	6
Missouri	43	12
UNLV	61	13
Nevada-Reno	61	20
New Orleans	66	17
St. Louis	71	25
South Alabama	71	21
Southern Illinois	51	13
Southwest Louisiana	52	23
Tennessee	42	12
Texas South	77	14
VCU	50	18
West Texas State	51	4
Western Kentucky	39	15
Wisconsin	40	17
Wyoming	83	27

Many other schools are below fifty percent, which is roughly the national average for regular students. If a list of football enrollments and graduates were included, the rates would be even more dismal.

Even a graduation rate of seventy percent is not good — as long as the college presidents are pretending to hold academics as their highest priority.

It is not inherently terrible that small percentages of athletes are graduating. There isn't anything inherently terrible about loving sports and not liking academic work. What IS terrible is the incredible, raging hypocrisy of the presidents and the NCAA, who claim that education is their highest priority, but whose rules and actions demonstrate clearly that they are lying.

———————

"The current setup is simply too loaded against the athlete, who receives a year-to-year commitment but is asked to make a four-year commitment in return."
—SPORTS ILLUSTRATED
9-30-85

GRANTS-IN-AID

Grant-in-aid is the name given to athletic scholarships. Athletic scholarships are given, not for four or five years, the amount of time it takes an athlete to graduate, but for one year at a time, renewable upon "satisfactory progress" as measured by the school and by the coaching staff.

Because the grant-in-aid is on a renewable basis, the athlete is essentially there at the behest of the coach, and it is always hanging over a player's head that the coach need not necessarily renew the scholarship.

This is unacceptable. If a university signs a contract with a high school athlete, expecting to utilize his athletic ability, the university should be willing to promise an education in return.

Rather than "one year renewable," the athlete's grant-in-aid should be "for whatever period of time is necessary for the athlete to obtain a diploma." And the athlete should certainly have that grant whether or not he decides to continue participating in sports.

Both the NCAA rules governing amateurism and the clarifications of the courts in past cases have made it clear that the athlete participates in his sport as an avocation — as a hobby — and that his grant is essentially a gift by the university in support of the education of the student.

Back in the Sixties it was made clear to high school athletes that they had their scholarship for four years and that they could quit playing sports if they wanted to, without jeopardizing their scholarships. Coaches believed, if they recruited the right kind of kids and offered them a meaningful athletic experience, that they would not have to worry about having players quit.

There is no flaw in this way of thinking. Very few athletes actually did quit. Yet the rules were changed. The "one year renewable" scholarship is a fact of life now. A four year education is not guaranteed any longer.

The NCAA claims the reason for the change was that athletes were abusing their privileges and many were opting not to play all four years. (No kidding!)

The reason such high numbers of athletes did continue playing, despite unpleasant circumstances, is that coaches back then were adept at exacting promises out of high school players. During the recruiting process — when everyone was still friends — the coaches would be sure to get in comments like "I know that YOU are not the kind of kid who would give his word to come to school and give his best for four years, and then turn around and quit once he got to school. There are kids like that," the coach might add, giving the unmistakable impression that such types were low-character, unsavory sorts that he would never recruit. In the process of shaking hands and exchanging congratulations, the coaches got the player to feel as though he had indeed committed himself, if not by signature, certainly by a gentleman's agreement.

Under these circumstances, the fact that some athletes did drop their sport is testament to how bad the playing — or bench sitting — conditions have been (and still are) at many schools.

HOPING TO LOSE

When a player gets demoted to the bench (and usually when he starts there and remains there over a period of time) his self-image is shattered and, if he is a competitor who wants to play — as most recruited high schools stars are — he has only one real option. He must keep his mouth shut, continue to work hard in practice, and sit on the bench appearing enthusiastic while hoping his team does poorly enough for the coach to see the error of his ways.

Fans who flock to games in the old spirit of the Gipper don't like to look down on the field or court and think about how many of these fine young men on the bench are hoping their good old alma mater loses. It's not a nice thought, but it goes on at every school, to differing extents of course, but to MUCH, much greater extents than anyone in the business or on TV will ever begin to admit.

"[The players] have seen lying and cheating as the norms from the moment they were recruited. Economic justice wouldn't solve all the problems, but it should remove the premium on hypocrisy."

—Sporting News Editorial

HYPOCRISY

It seems necessary, in a Student-Athletes' Encyclopedia, to have a special entry for hypocrisy. But there is so much pretense within the NCAA system that it is difficult to single out one element of hypocrisy that stands out above all the others. One excellent example, though, certainly is obvious when the rules pertaining to eligibility and scholarships are examined.

Despite the fact that the NCAA is considered, for legal purposes, an educational institution, there is no NCAA rule against giving scholarships year after year, even though no player ever uses one of those scholarships to get a diploma. Teams can go five straight years without any player graduating — and many teams have done just that — with no penalty whatever.

Not only is there no penalty, but there is absolutely no competitive advantage provided among the NCAA's myraid rules to the school which DOES succeed in graduating its athletes. In fact, there is an obvious disadvantage to putting educational values ahead of athletic ones; the schools which actually put academics first often lose out in their recruiting because they will not admit into school certain talented athletes who are below their normal academic standards.

There is no way the NCAA can claim a sincere concern for educational values when their rules, instead of offering incentives, put at a disadvantage the schools with academic priorities.

"We worry about victories and losses and postseason tournaments, but it's more important that the athletes are benefitting and developing and preparing to face the rest of the world.

"If we're not doing that, we're not doing our job. It's the NCAA's responsibility to do that. We are the NCAA. And we're all responsible."

—Jeffry H. Fogelson
Director of Athletics
Xavier University (OH)

ILLEGAL GIFTS

USA TODAY ran an editorial on October 18, 1984 calling for, among other things, the explusion from school of college athletes who accept "illegal gifts."

USA TODAY should have already known that it is against **no** law to accept gifts. It IS against NCAA RULES for athletes to accept anything beyond tuition, room, board and books, but it certainly is no crime.

The word "illegal" is incorrect in every case. To use such a word in dealing with an exploited group like student-athletes is totally wrong, not merely from a semantic standpoint. "Illegal" can be said to bear no relation whatever to the student-athlete who has committed no crime and who realizes that he is entitled to fair compensation and attempts to get what is coming to him.

There were **no cases** investigated by the NCAA in the 1980's where a player received illegal gifts. Not one.

"The parents signed the kid's illegal recruiting inducements over to the local booster club: 'For the kid to go to ESU, we'll need the water tower, the radar gun AND a new pumper for the volunteer fire department.'"

"The Recruiter's Tale"
from Tank McNamera

INDUCEMENTS

The NCAA rule book allows student-athletes to receive room, board, tuition, books and almost nothing else. "Inducements," therefore, are defined as almost anything else a player might get from a school which might influence him to attend.

Prohibited inducements include everything from free T-shirts to co-signing of loans, free movie passes, reduction in clothing prices, use of a car, accepting any sort of cash, and nearly everything else. A kid's parents and relatives are not permitted to receive any employment or similar benefits. Parents may NOT be flown to see their son play under any circumstances.

These prohibitions extend not just to the athletic department and the university but to alumni and friends and anyone else who can be vaguely considered to be a "representative of athletics interests." In other words, if I decide I would like to fly the parents of a player at Duke University to Durham to watch a game, or even if I decide to fly the parents of a player at some other school which I might be a fan of, the athlete's parents may not accept my gift. Such gifts are specifically prohibited under NCAA rules.

Why shouldn't someone be permitted to fly a kid's parents in to watch some games? Many families are too poor to get to games when their sons are in school far away from home.

Originally, the feeling within the NCAA was that such rules would encourage kids to attend a school nearer to home. But that feeling fails to deal with the reality of the times. Many schools recruit nationally, and many kids, athletes and non-athletes, attend school far away from home. They don't base their decisions on how much transportation is going to cost, and recruiters hardly mention at all to young high school stars the disadvantages of attending school away from home. They gloss over those mounting transportation costs, saying they can help them get some money to cover those costs. (They SHOULD be permitted to do just that, since the NCAA is gripped by fear of one school gaining an "unfair advantage" over another, and clearly a school closer to a kid's home has an unfair advantage with regard to costs required to attend.)

The coaches KNOW that those transportation costs will mount up and lead to financial pressure on the kids, but they don't worry about it. Either they find ways to get the kids some extra money, or they simply ignore the problem, hoping the kid can get by (or hoping he can get some extra money in his own way).

Certainly it is true that few kids make their decisions on where to attend school with a full awareness of the implications of travel costs on their spending money.

BOBBY KNIGHT DOESN'T BELIEVE IN INDUCEMENTS

There is often a very thin line between inducements — things offered to a kid in order to get him to sign with a particular school — and benefits which a kid may expect once he is already enrolled.

Indiana basketball coach Bobby Knight, for example, is extremely proud of the fact that he does not cheat. In fact, he claims it would be easy for him to get together millions of dollars from boosters and supporters of Indiana basketball and buy all the best players and then just "beat everyone all of the time."

Bobby Knight is fond of calling others "cheaters," yet when asked to supply names by the Big 10 Conference, he refused, admitting he did not have sufficient proof.

Nevertheless, he himself admits to arranging jobs for relatives of players, but he is quick to explain the difference between what he does and what "the cheaters" are doing.

"If a kid is here, say two years, and his brother needs a job, I don't see any reason not to help him get one."

What if a kid is at Indiana, say two months, and his brother needs a job? What if a kid is there, say two days, and his brother needs a job? What if a kid is close to making a decision, say in two days, and his brother needs a job?

A coach like Knight can get away with saying such things because his views often get national attention. A player therefore who is a sports fan knows already that his brother and, say, his aunt (and uncle?) will be able to get jobs after he is there awhile; whereas a coach from East Brady Tech would have to spell that out to a kid during the recruiting process.

Will that make the East Brady Tech coach an inducer while Knight is a humanitarian?

Personally, I don't understand a coach like Knight calling other people "cheaters" without sufficient proof, and I don't understand his self-righteous attitude in the face of the outrageous theft and exploitation that his own players are enduring just like all the others. Nor do I understand the difference between inducements and merely helping out after, say, two years.

The only explanation seems to be the obvious: Bobby Knight is doing extremely well in college basketball. He is doing what he truly loves doing, and he is being very well paid for it. He has no reason to want things to be different from what they are.

You have to wonder what his attitude would be, however, if he were suddenly told that the money he earns would be, say, given to the starving people in Ethiopia — all except for enough to pay for housing, food, books, and tuition. The point is, inducements have been cut to nothing simply to make their control easier for the NCAA, and to keep the NCAA homogeneous, so the athletes at Bucknell are no different from the athletes at Michigan. The players' interests have not been considered in this matter, otherwise there would be many more inducements permitted, and the athletes at Michigan would indeed be getting inducements that the athletes at Bucknell would not be.

Homogeneity is a desire of the NCAA, and of the universities — especially those without the ability to provide inducements — not at all a desire of Americans in general or of revenue producing students in particular.

Prohibiting inducements to players can be justified in all sorts of theoretical ways, but the facts are simply that prohibiting inducements to players is good for the universities and bad for the players.

"The current situation is not fair to the players, with as many hours as they spend on football. It's like a job — and you deserve to be paid for a job."
—Bill Young
Head Football Coach
Texas-El Paso

A JOB

Student-athletes on full grants-in-aid are not permitted by NCAA rules to get jobs while school is in session. This fact is pointed out often by well-meaning supporters of increased compensation for student-athletes to show that revenue producing student-athletes lack one of the traditional means of getting spending money which is open to other students.

However, revenue producing student-athletes are not lobbying heavily for this particular right. Few conscientious, revenue producing student-athletes have much time to devote to outside jobs, even if NCAA rules would permit them to get jobs.

149

The rule prohibiting certain student-athletes from getting a job is stupid and discriminatory and undoubtedly there are SOME student-athletes who need the money and could handle some part-time positions, especially if the nature of those positions might make it possible to study at the same time — the way a baby sitter, night watchman or language lab attendant often can.

Nevertheless, jobs are not really a point of contention. The little bit of money a revenue producing student-athlete could make at a job is not an issue. The issue is the enormous amount of money he DOES make already — but never sees.

"Sports is a full time avocation for anyone with an athletic grant-in-aid and I don't think it leaves him time to work . . . The Pell Grant increase really should have passed because it was limited to particularly needy youngsters. It was most unconscionable that it didn't pass."

—Tom Hansen
Commissioner
PAC-10 Conference

"Frankly some of these kids don't have simple spending money. They aren't even able to afford to take a date to the movies. There has to be some spending money . . . For a kid to have to go through four years of financial chastity, while waiting to see if he can make it in the pros, is not reasonable."

—Marshall A. Criser
President
University of Florida

"The current system has made us guilty of the height of hypocrisy. I can remember back in 1982 that there were a couple of open days at the end of the semester, before our football team left for the Liberty Bowl, and some of our players were out there digging ditches in the rain in order to earn money to go home between semesters. Meanwhile we (the university) came home from that bowl game with a million bucks in our pocket."

—Neale Stoner
Director of Athletics
University of Illinois

"I had tears in my eyes. Coming from a family of 12 children, I'd never seen that much money ($350) before. I was on cloud 9."

—Kenneth Davis
TCU football star
(Dismissed from the team
for accepting benefits not permitted
by NCAA rule)

"[The NCAA] has the power to destroy careers of men who have been in sports and to frustrate the ambitions of the younger men. And it can do it without the basic fabric of protection that we have been accustomed to regard as our rights . . . I know this, I would be outraged if I was summoned before [an NCAA] tribunal and had a judgment rendered . . . The kind of fabric that has been put over the entire intercollegiate athletic movement by the NCAA is an unhealthy one."
    —John Moss, 6-9-78
    U.S. Congressman and Chairman,
    House Subcommittee on Oversight and Investigations

JUDGES' OPINIONS ON THE NCAA

Is the NCAA just a group of hard working, dedicated men doing the best job they can do for collegiate athletics?

According to the August 14, 1985 issue of The NCAA News, the NCAA's own Public Relations and Promotions Committee, at a meeting in Santa Cruz, California, (July 1985) "reviewed the results of a questionnaire mailed in May to various NCAA committee members, media representatives, athletics administrators and college sports fans," and the poll showed that the NCAA has a "negative image."

It would not have required a poll to determine THAT, nor will "more visibility" combat the negative image, as the poll suggested.

When the NCAA puts the concerns of PEOPLE above its love of rules and restrictions, then the image of the NCAA will become positive.

Is this merely the view of a guy with a vendetta against the NCAA? Perhaps the words of state, federal, and Supreme Court judges will command more respect.

NEVADA DISTRICT JUDGE JAMES BRENNAN in the Tarkanian trial, 1977:

"When one sifts through the evidence presented to this court, the action demanded by the NCAA against the plaintiff can be reduced to one word — incredible."

"The evidence shows that every fundamental principle pertaining to the plaintiff's due process rights were violated. The (NCAA) Committee on Infractions and its staff conducted a star chamber proceeding and a trial by ambush against the plaintiff."

"The evidence presented to the infractions committee was 100 percent hearsay without a scrap of documentation in substantiation."

Brennan called the evidence accepted by the infractions committee "inferior in quality to good gossip." He made it clear that the NCAA was out to "get Tarkanian."

NEVADA JUDGE PAUL GOLDMAN, (appeal of Tarkanian case) 1984:

"Both the full-time investigators and part-time (NCAA) Committee and Council members acted and thought not like Caesar's wife, but rather as arrogant lords of the manor."

"This case presents a classic example of how misperception becomes suspicion, which in turn becomes hostility, which leads inevitably to a deprivation of one's rights."

"What started out as an association whose members met and exceeded lofty goals ended up as the NCAA bureaucracy which looks upon its friends, sycophants, with feigned pleasure and its enemies — those who still recognize the U.S. Constitution — with barely concealed malevolence."

"[The] NCAA practices might be considered efficient, but so was Adoph Eichmann and so is the Ayatollah."

"[Says the NCAA] If you want to compete, you must join us, obey our rules, and surrender any claim you have under the Bill of Rights. This Court disagrees with that attitude, as any fair-minded person must."

U.S. DISTRICT JUDGE JUAN C. BURCIAGA, in Albuquerque, in the Oklahoma-Georgia trial, 1982:

"The Court [is persuaded] that the NCAA was aware of the antitrust implications of the football controls, but also that the NCAA has attempted to conceal the intent of its anti-competitive activities."

"[The NCAA] clearly demonstrated its taste for restrictions, and its willingness and ability to strike a crippling blow to the athletic programs of its members."

"[The NCAA used] a campaign of veiled threats and coercion . . . clearly intended to . . . achieve the ultimate effect of coercing the plaintiffs."

"The court does not know and need not determine whether the NCAA administration, in formulating the controls at issue, was motivated by genuine concern for NCAA members, by a lust for power, or by rank and greed. What is clear is that the NCAA has violated . . . the laws . . . "

JUDGE BURCIAGA, 1984:

"The Court is concerned by the lengths to which the NCAA has apparently gone in its zeal to impress upon its membership that somehow the NCAA prevailed in this action. Indeed, in reviewing [the NCAA's] explanation to the NCAA membership of the effect of the appellate court decisions, this Court wondered whether the membership was being given a report of a case different from the one this court heard."

"The Court expressed its reservations regarding the insistence of the NCAA that it would voluntarily abandon its antitrust activities. The Court also declared that it needed to act because the Court had little faith that the NCAA could be expected to conform its conduct to the law in the absence of an order."

"I cannot recount all the subtle ways that the NCAA may still pursue in attempts to . . . reimpose the very activity this Court, as well as the appellate courts, have found to be illegal. I say this in order to impress upon the parties that the Court found illegal conduct on the part of the NCAA . . ."

"It would serve no purpose to repeat the egregious conduct that the Court found to exist . . ."

"What the court does prohibit is the illegal activity pursued by the NCAA and the illegal manner in which it pursued its own interests."

THE SUPREME COURT, June 1984:

"Today we hold only that the record supports the District Court's conclusion that by curtailing output and blunting the ability of member institutions to respond to consumer preference, the NCAA has restricted rather than enhanced the place of intercollegiate athletics in the Nation's life."

"Despite all the stories, most of today's college players don't receive cars and other extravagant gifts. So why should they pay the price of those who do?"
—Jesse Outlar
Atlanta Constitution

A KHAR

The four-letter word for "car," a khar has traditionally been the symbol of evil in big-time college sports. This phenomenon began in the early 1900's when almost no one had cars, and cars of any type were looked upon as luxury items affordable only by the high social classes. This was even before the time that the nation was both shocked and in awe when the greatest athletic attraction of all time, Babe Ruth, was paid $100,000 a year just for playing baseball!

Times change.

Today, on a college campus, as well as just about everywhere else in America, a car is hardly looked upon as a luxury item. Poor people often have cars. Regular students have cars.

The opportunities to get the use of cars within major college athletic programs are abundant. Coaches often have the offer of more courtesy cars than they and their staffs can possibly use.

There are car dealers associated with nearly every major college in the nation. Nor is it uncommon for a booster club to buy a coach a car after a successful season.

Yet, coaches are paid sufficiently to purchase their own cars and, therefore, there is no reason that the courtesy cars should not go instead to the athletes who need them.

It would not be necessary for colleges to provide each player with a new convertible in order to satisfy the need for transportation on campus. Several courtesy cars could be shared by the players, with Seniors having first priority, the newest cars, etc.

The fact that student-athletes are still deprived of the use of cars, if not the possibility of actually receiving new ones, within the rules, is dramatic testimony to the NCAA's consistent policy of considering the athletes last (if at all).

"The slaves don't need cars," goes the typical feeling expressed by NCAA members, "I didn't have one when I went to college."

So what?

Who cares what THEY had back when the two hand set shot was killing opponents and the single wing was an innovation?

"NCAA President John R. Davis noted that the Association spent slightly more than $2 million in legal fees in 1985."

—The NCAA News, 9-30-85

"I'm certain that the already huge legal bills that the NCAA has had in recent years are going to go up drastically."

—Charles Alan Wright
Law Professor, University of Texas
(Former Chairman of NCAA Infractions Committee)

LEGAL FEES

For the year ending in August, 1983, the NCAA's legal fees were $1,180,073. For 1984, they were $1,258,207.

On February 20, 1985, The NCAA News reported that the NCAA would also have to pay the legal fees of Oklahoma and Georgia in the TV case which lasted three years. These fees came to almost a million dollars ($975,702.34) and the judge made it clear that, had he been able, he would have increased his award to attorneys Andy Coats and Clyde A. Muchmore by more than doubling their original $354,543 fee.

In the insane Tarkanian case, the judge ordered the NCAA to pay 90 per cent of Tarkanian's legal fees (UNLV was ordered to pay the other ten percent), which came to another $195,951.

The NCAA, utilizing its unlimited stolen funds, appealed the Tarkanian decision to the Nevada Supreme Court.

Appeal, appeal, appeal. Spend, spend, spend.

It is easy to go to court when you are using other people's money.

Did you know, and were you aware that the judge made special note of the fact, that the NCAA had "at least four attorneys in the courtroom each day" of the Tarkanian trial which concluded on June 25, 1984.

AT LEAST four attorneys in the courtroom in Las Vegas, every day. Can anyone guess why they needed so many?

Why did the NCAA even SEND attorneys at all, to argue a case in Philadelphia in December of 1984 in order to keep a kid, Albert "Truck" Butts, from playing his Senior year when he had done nothing wrong except turn 24, in unknowing violation of a rule not even included in the NCAA GUIDE TO STUDENT-ATHLETES?

Spend. Spend. Go to court. Go to court. Does it give the NCAA leaders a good feeling to have discretionary millions of other people's money to spend and to be able to use whimsically, without regard for the relative value of their actions?

The NCAA's profligate use of money for legal fees is an unpardonable rip-off. There must be a Committee of Common Sense to oversee the NCAA and to put a stop to their ability to finance their lust for power through unending legal action and an unlimited source of funds.

"The amateur requirements were originally adopted by collegiate organizations for the apparent purpose of preventing the results of contests from being skewed by the use of professionals or "ringers," especially when bookmakers were taking an active interest in the contests. Amateurism was seen as a positive virtue, and professionalism was not. In light of the contemporary use of financial aid in collegiate athletics, one may question whether these purposes have been achieved by existing rules, and wonder whether the purposes could not be achieved much easier by a rule limiting eligibility to students in good standing."

—John Weistart
Professor of Law
Duke University

LEGAL CHALLENGES TO NCAA POLICIES

The NCAA and the universities, despite presiding over fundamentally professioinal basketball and football teams, persist in their staunch commitment to a definition of amateurism that assures rank poverty in a high percentage of their participating athletes.

But players and fans alike should recognize that there is no legal, moral, or philosophical reason why amateurism MUST include the concept of poverty. Similarly, there is no reason why each Division I basketball and football player could not, or should not — and fully within the dictates of the NCAA statutes — be given a seven-year scholarship, the use of a car, several free plane tickets, $200 a month spending money, a wardrobe of new clothes, and a $10,000 grant upon graduation.

The figures could all be higher but let us remain conservative while considering several facts of amateur athletic life:

1. Many amateur athletes, both in America and in nearly every foreign country, get many more benefits than those listed above — and still compete in the Olympics in violation of no Olympic principle.

2. The "clear line of demarcation" between college and professional athletes, which the NCAA Constitution requires, would not in any manner be crossed. For proof, the NCAA need merely offer **any** NBA basketball player or **any** NFL football player the opportunity to exchange HIS package of compensation for that of the college athlete getting spending money, use of a car, plane tickets, a scholarship, and a ten thousand dollar grant.

The demarcation remains clear and is untainted by the addition of across-the-board benefits for revenue producing basketball and football players.

3. There is plenty of money available that is specifically earned by basketball and football players, which is not now being used for any essential purpose, and which certainly does not get spent on basketball and football concerns.

With these three facts in hand, a question has to be asked. Why AREN'T basketball and football players getting these benefits?

The answer is simple and not based on contrary philosophy. It is straightforward EXPLOITATION based on greed, or perhaps ignorance, and it takes the form of cost-controls or price-fixing.

As long as the NCAA and the universities can get away with giving the players no compensation for their services, they will do precisely that, just as surely as plantation owners did it to slaves and fruit growers did it to migrant workers.

Human beings do not naturally reward other human beings to the extent they deserve. They reward other human beings to the extent those human beings stand up for their rights and demand their fair share.

Fortunately, there are specific methods available to the players which may be able to remedy the injustice they are suffering. One of these remedies is legal.

The following passages come from Professor John Weistart's eminent book, THE LAW OF SPORTS, pages 775-776, and concern antitrust principles.

"[The courts consistently find] reason to be suspicious when the form of cost-control chosen from among the various alternatives is one which has its main impact on those who exercise little or no control over its formulation . . . Courts are likely to be somewhat more cautious when confronted with a situation in which those who formulate their association's rules choose to encumber the economic opportunities of unrepresented affiliates rather than bear the direct impact themselves."

Weistart goes on to say:

"[When the courts find that a rule has] such a particularized effect on an identifiable subgroup, the court should give serious attention to the availability of less restrictive alternatives."

"If there are alternate forms of regulation which would clearly achieve the same goal with a more diffused impact, it may be appropriate for the court to compel a reconsideration of the regulatory scheme . . . "

"[The courts] have typically shown little hesitancy in striking down direct controls on prices. Such devices represent the most pernicious type of restraint on the operation of a free market, and they have met with a judicial disapproval which is notable for its consistency. Although the NCAA faces a difficult task in trying to provide an answer to the problem of rising costs in college athletics, it is not likely that the courts will feel the NCAA enjoys any special license to tinker with the prices which coaches or others receive for their employment services. The [NCAA] will likely be told that it must choose other, less intrusive forms of regulation to achieve its goals."

(Citing the above passage is not meant in any way to unrealistically raise the hopes of student-athletes for legal redress of their grievances. The above passage was written specifically in regard to the rights of assistant coaches. Yet, it shows a distinct legal basis for the grievances of the student-athletes, even though there are other legal factors to consider in the student-athletes' case.)

The fact remains, in reference to the quoted passages, that nothing could be more intrusive or restrictive than the NCAA's present policy aimed at keeping revenue producing athletes unrepresented and poor, while the NCAA members themselves enjoy very comfortable salaries and expense accounts, and provide handouts to thousands who have no justifiable right to basketball and football players' earnings.

The NCAA has traditionally avoided the legal rebuff that should result from its controls on athletes by virtue of its position as a non-profit, educational association. As Professor Weistart explains . . .

"Many NCAA controls are similar to those which are summarily condemned in a more traditional business setting."

157

Chris Kupec brought an unsuccessful suit against the Atlantic Coast Conference in 1975, contending that the Conference's (and thereby the NCAA's) limitations on compensation amounted to "per se" violations, or price-fixing to eliminate competition.

While Kupec had a logical argument, rooted in the law, the NCAA, being educational, was not deemed to have violated any "per se" requirements, since the "per se concept was devised to achieve the goal of preserving economic competition between traditional business entities . . ." (p. 767)

A future case to be brought against the NCAA, therefore, can not rest on this concept alone, but will better rest on the test of whether the legal "rule of reason" might apply. Is the NCAA using its authority reasonably?

"A rule could reasonably forbid . . . the receipt of things that would affect the amateur standing of the recipient. [But] if an amateur standing rule forbade the receipt of things that would not affect an athlete's "amateur" status, then it might to that extent be unreasonable." (p. 59)

Another legal question may be, is the NCAA, in collusion with the universities, denying student-athletes the benefits they are entitled to in an arbitrary and capricious manner?

To continue the legalese briefly, the NCAA may be seriously challenged in court with these principles and the contention that the traditional concept of amateurism has long ago vanished, and that therefore, "there are less restrictive mechanisms which could be used to effect the association's goals," a point of extreme importance to the courts. (p. 770)

The NCAA currently provides athletes with fewer real benefits than they received twenty years ago — back when star pro athletes were getting tiny fractions of what pro athletes are getting today. In other words, not only would the "line of demarcation" be fully intact with added benefits, it would still be much wider than it was when the concept of amateurism was orginally clarified.

The present disparity between college and professional athletes has become so great that it is actually a DETRIMENT to the NCAA's goals, not a positive factor. Many athletes, for example, have stopped their education, citing poverty as THE reason for leaving college early, even when a pro career was not guaranteed.

The present NCAA policy clearly does not take into account the changing times, and there is dramatic evidence that the NCAA's current policy encourages rule-breaking, requires of many athletes a constant search for needed money, and makes big-time athletes especially vulnerable to scams, scandals and potentially criminal behavior.

The NCAA can not mount a compelling case for the overall effectiveness of its regulatory schemes; therefore, it may have opened the door for athletes to make a realistic legal challenge.

Professor Weistart says:

"The availability of a less restrictive method is usually strong evidence for the plaintiff where he can show his livelihood is endangered." (p. 770)

How many scandals and probations will be necessary before the courts rule that the lives of student-athletes, if not the "livelihoods," are indeed being endangered by the NCAA's repressive policies?

These essentially antitrust-related issues are of course hardly sure things by which student-athletes can get what they deserve. But they constitute a step that may be taken with some realistic hope of success, before more compelling, direct action is resorted to.

The basic issue and righteous cause of athletes will not change, however, regardless of whether the courts provide a legal solution or not. Revenue producing major college student-athletes are entitled to more than they are getting, and it is clear that certain legal principles point to inevitable changes in the NCAA's ability to continue to exert its unjust control over revenue producing student-athletes.

———————

"We are not equal (to other students). They expect you to go out and be like ambassadors, make speeches at variouis functions for them and promote the university. Yet, they do not ask others to do that. They ask you because you're an athlete. They are taking advantage of your status."
—Spencer Tillman
Football Star
University of Oklahoma

THE THREE BIGGEST LIES

There is a common joke about the three biggest lies in the world. "The check is in the mail" and two others of a similar nature.

Of course, with student-athletes, no check is ever in the mail. The three biggest lies for student-athletes are different.

1. **"For the kids."**
People love to pretend they are doing so much for the players, when actually they are stealing them blind.

2. **"One happy family."**
A college team is supposed to be one happy family. Everyone supposedly sticks together, plays hard, enjoys each other, and respects the situation and the coaches. In reality, most teams are riddled with unhappy, bitter players who feel left out, cheated, and disillusioned. We're not talking about one or two bad apples. We are talking about half a team, often more.

159

In the spring of 1985 at Baylor University, a player taped an incriminating conversation with the head basketball coach. Although the kid's action was fraudulent, and although many reporters condemned his "act of cowardice," even the casual fan had to wonder and hold his opinion when 13 of 14 players stood behind the kid who did it.

It is unwise to take sides in any dispute when many of the relevant facts are hidden. Indeed, there may be some teams with groups of basically satisfied players. Maybe even a whole team somewhere. But there are not many among the major college revenue producing programs. Not many of those have even half a team of contented players.

3. "I'm just happy to contribute."

Famous words of former high school stars sitting the bench, trying not to let on how frustrated and sick inside they feel.

Bonus Lie:

"We're mostly concerned about your grades and your future. We want you to get that degree."

When a team has an ambitious travel schedule that forces kids to miss a lot of class — and the team is comprised of a lot of borderline students — there can be no true concern about grades and degrees.

"We have few problems in Division III athletics . . . but the problems in Division I discredit all of higher education."

—Paul Hardin
President
Drew Univeristy

"My instinct tells me that the fundamental difference between small colleges and Nebraska and Florida could be simply that the little fellows are a shade more inclined to give themselves airs about virtue."

—Benjamin DeMott
Amherst Professor, and
Chairman of Board of Trustees of the
National Humanities Faculty

LITTLE SCHOOLS

There are approximately 780 active, voting members in the NCAA. Only 100 or so have athletic programs which generate money. Not surprisingly, there are many issues which, if voted upon by the entire membership, would end up roughly 680-100.

At NCAA conventions, a tiny school like St. Andrews College in Laurinburg, North Carolina has one vote that carries just as much weight as the vote of the University of Michigan or UCLA.

In theory, this one-school-one-vote setup has some merit. It provides a certain equality or equal opportunity, you might say, for each college to compete for the same students. In practice, however, this setup has been largely responsible for the present tainting of major college programs and for the continued theft and exploitation of revenue producing major college student-athletes.

Naturally, the president of North Central College does not see himself as the source of big-time collegiate sports problems. On the contrary, he has a hard time understanding the problems at all. His programs don't generate money. There is little temptation to "cheat," because there is little money to cheat with. His coaches are not under as much pressure to win, because winning teams, though nice to have, are not going to bring in extra millions to the college.

It is easy for small college presidents and administrators to express outrage over big school abuses. They don't have the OPPORTUNITY to have any.

It is easy for small college presidents and administrators to be self-righteous about their clean athletic programs and their athletes' clear sense of priorities and perspective, because there is no money around to dirty their programs, no pro contracts dangling in the sights of their insufficiently talented players.

It has to be a wonderful ego trip for the small school representatives to attend NCAA conventions. They have their weighty vote, just like the others, but they also have their pride in coming from programs which are not under investigation, not being accused of cheating, not being suspected of corruption. "You guys have to learn to mind your store," they can say to the big guys who draw the reporters and the TV cameras.

But why do the little schools have any vote at all in things that do not concern them?

At a recent NCAA convention, an issue was raised about when bowl bids could be extended. Nearly all of the top one hundred schools were of the opinion that it should be possible for bowl committees to extend bowl bids earlier. But the vote went against them, as it often does, because the little schools, who NEVER get invited to bowls anyway, voted against earlier bowl bids.

At the same convention, there was a proposal before the membership which called for moving the issue of player compensation and benefits from NCAA statutes to bylaws. This is an important technicality because bylaws can be changed, division by division, without a vote of the entire NCAA membership. However, the statutes, in order to be amended, must be voted upon by the entire membership.

In any case, the membership voted against moving the issue of compensation to the bylaws, effectively preventing the large schools from giving more benefits to their athletes.

Why should Fitchburg State College in Massachusetts have anything at all to say about how much money or how many benefits Ohio State University gives to its players? The two schools do not compete with each other. There is no reason that Ohio State should be restricted by the will of a tiny school like Fitchburg.

The continuation of this system assures the continued theft of players' money at Ohio State University. Nevertheless, the system goes on. The little schools voted against allowing movement of the compensation issue to the bylaws, because they don't want it to be more prestigioius for an athlete to go to a big school. It already IS more prestigious for an athlete to go to a big school, but the little schools don't want to acknowledge reality. They themselves do not have the money to give their athletes more benefits, so they decide, **"If WE can't give any more benefits to OUR players, then no one can."**

They vote against allowing the big schools to decide their own fate, because they see their association with the big schools as adding to their own prestige. They do not wish to be separate from the big schools, though the big schools would be happy, elated, to be separate from the little schools.

The little schools prevail. They are members of the NCAA, and they benefit from that membership.

SOMETHING FOR NOTHING

When asked his opinion about having a national basketball championship tournament for smaller (Division I-AA) schools, Coach Tom Green of Farleigh-Dickinson was straightforward:

"Our conference (ECAC Metro) has an automatic birth in the 64-team NCAA tournament. That means $75,000 to the team that goes, and $75,000 more for the rest of the conference to divide evenly. But the prestige means more than the money."

The prestige, Coach Green admits, is important, and the payout is money that the schools in the ECAC Metro clearly would never get without their NCAA affiliation. Who pays to see Farleigh-Dickinson play? Who gathers around the TV to watch the ECAC Metro tournament?

This money is nothing more than an undeserved GIFT to the ECAC Metro, made graciously by the NCAA out of the pockets of revenue producing major college players. Naturally, the representatives of the ECAC Metro will vote for anything likely to continue such gifts, even if it means voting for the continued theft of the money of players who really are generating those dollars.

The small schools value their NCAA affiliation, yet they are so accustomed to the something-for-nothing welfare which they have been getting that they almost take it for granted. Howard University's head basketball coach, when asked his response to a Division I-AA national championship, said . . .

"I'm all for it, if the NCAA will throw in some money ($100,000 to $150,000) to get it televised . . ."

The NCAA. Throw in some money. These are typical feelings. The NCAA is rich, the NCAA can do it. And these feelings are justified. As long as the NCAA is permitted to steal the money produced by the big schools, they might as well "throw in" some big money here and there and line a few more pockets with gold. When you consider what the NCAA does with the money it steals, "the least it could do" — or at least so goes the feeling — "is give US some." There are plenty of people eager to share the spoils.

The small school-run NCAA is communism, pure and simple. Hold down the rich. Drag them down to the level of the poor. Distribute their wealth.

There is no justification whatever, in America, for this homogenization. Especially not when there are many acknowledged problems in the programs which generate the revenues. A player who plays at Florida State gets the same benefits as a player who plays at Rollins College. But in many cases the player at Rollins College is held in higher esteem — for having graduated in four years, for having his priorities in order, for having perhaps higher grades (shorter practices?).

Taking money from the rich (the players at big schools who earn it) and giving it to the poor (the players at small schools who do not earn it) and then letting the poor reach a higher plateau in public esteem or in the job market is patently absurd. It is not merely communism. It is communism in its collectivized worst form — a system that reduces the productivity of everyone.

The large schools have, in so many cases, been outvoted by the little schools, that now the large schools are discouraged from even proposing legislation that would help to solve their problems and meet their needs.

"No use, it would never pass," is a TYPICAL, yet unpardonable comment of representatives of the big schools. It is typical because the big schools have experienced a pattern, a history of frustration over votes like those involving bowl bids and player compensation, where the little schools have had no right to be involved at all but where they have nevertheless controlled the process and forged their will.

This pattern continues today. The little schools control the NCAA, and they will continue to control it. The obvious solution is for the large schools to form their own association, apart from the NCAA. But when are they going to do this? How many student-athletes will be ripped off before a new association is formed?

MAJOR VIOLATIONS

One of the most misleading aspects of big-time college sports as far as the general public is concerned deals with NCAA sanctions and punishments as a result of so-called "major violations" of NCAA rules.

When "major violations" are committed, whole programs can be suspended. Dozens of athletes who did nothing against the rules are nevertheless punished summarily, and the school's name, the school's athletics programs, and the school's student-athletes become associated in the public mind with the words "cheating" and "corruption."

Clearly, NCAA suspensions can be devastating to schools, coaches, and athletes. So let's look at some of the things that are classified as MAJOR violations according to NCAA rules.

Fans will undoubtedly begin reading down the following list and think there is some mistake. These violations are MAJOR?

"Minor" violations are classified as those that are inadvertent and not intentional — in recognition of the fact that anytime there is a rule book filled with page after page of ridiculous, common sense-defying rules, there must inevitably be many unintentional infractions. "Major" violations, then, are ALL of the other infractions, committed knowingly, without regard to their size or importance. For example, here is a list of some *major* violations:

Giving T-shirts to prospects.

Giving a prospect a ride — of any distance — in any place more than thirty miles off-campus.

Giving a free meal to a prospect's friend.

Arranging transportation for a prospect to visit a campus more than once.

Giving a prospect a reduced rate in a hotel during a second visit.

Giving a team member a free meal off-campus.

Providing free movie passes for team members.

Arranging summer jobs for prospects where they will make more than they would as regular students applying for those same jobs.

Lending a team member a car for a date.

Lending a player ten dollars.

Giving a player some new clothes to wear to games.

Paying for books not-required or for extra notebooks and pens.

That should give at least a sense of the atrocities that comprise major violations. Take a look at a specific case of major violations.

THE TERRIBLE DEEDS OF THE UNIVERSITY OF FLORIDA

In the NCAA news release of January 13, 1985, in which the NCAA announced the probation of the University of Florida football program, the NCAA President at the time, John L. Toner, was quoted as saying:

". . . the Committee on Infractions and the Council considered this to be among the most serious infractions cases ever processed by the NCAA."

Here is a summary of those violations which were among the most serious infractions in NCAA history:

1. The head coach had a "slush fund" which amounted to about $4,000. (Not even enough money to take the team from Gainesville to Miami on a bus.)

2. Several assistant football coaches and administrative aids were aware that the university football program was being run in a manner against the NCAA rules.

3. Complimentary tickets were sold by players and sometimes for players in excess of the actual cost of the tickets. The most any of these season tickets went for was $250 — much below the "actual" price when you consider that at most large schools substantial donations to the athletic department are required in order for a fan to have the right to purchase the tickets at face value! (When I was in school, nearly everyone I was aware of did this — at all of the major schools. In fact, knowing of the donation requirements, a player would have to be foolish to sell his season tickets at face value.)

4. Some cash payments were made to student-athletes for signing at the University of Florida, none of which exceeded $400. (Didn't they ever hear of shoe boxes down there?)

5. Free lodging in the athletic dormitory was arranged for a few student-athletes not on scholarship; and some student-athletes and relatives of student-athletes received some free nights of lodging at Gainesville motels. At times they even received a free meal; some student-athletes were lent the occasional use of automobiles as well.

6. On 13 occasions during two seasons, some football staff members were paid "to improperly scout" opponents.

7. During the summers, some staff members conducted organized football activities. (Whereas everyone else is careful to write "SUGGESTED Summer Workout Schedule" on the top of their mandatory hand-outs.)

8. One prospect was given as much as $100 and some were bought some meals at some local restaurants by "academic advisors," thereby breaking not just the excess benefit rule but also the coaching staff limitation rule. (A double-whammy!)

165

9. The head coach arranged for a couple of prospects to get a free night's lodging at a Florida hotel.

10. The university exceeded the proper number of off-campus recruiters.

11. Some personnel not specifically designated as "off campus recruiters" did some off campus recruiting.

12. The football staff attested in statements to the chief executive officer of the university that they were unaware of recruiting violations which they were in fact aware of.

13. Two junior prospects got a free trip by car to Gainesville.

14. One prospect got two paid visits to the university instead of the one allowed by NCAA rule, and one prospect got free lodging for one night for his mother and for his two sisters.

15. A high school coach was given thirteen tickets to a Tangerine Bowl game.

16. A few prospects were observed by coaches in weight-training workouts. (A tryout!)

17. One prospect was reimbursed for gas for two car trips to Gainesville — approximately 300 miles total distance.

18. Some prospects were given T-shirts, workout clothing, and other university souvenirs. (Go Gators!)

19. The head coach took a passenger in a university airplane to visit a recruit.

20. A prospect got $41 in travel expenses although it was not clear that the kid actually had to pay for the travel himself.

21. The university employed a graduate assistant football coach although he was ineligible to be one since he had enrolled more than five years earlier.

22. A "representative" of the university helped two prospects get summer jobs.

23. On two occasions during the five year period of this investigation, a coach exceeded the limit of three personal contacts with a prospect.

24. An assistant coach contacted two prospects IN PERSON, OFF CAMPUS, prior to the beginning of their Senior years.

These are summaries of ALL of the infractions listed by the NCAA against the University of Florida, OVER A FOUR YEAR PERIOD FROM 1979 TO 1983 in what the NCAA president termed one of the "most serious infractions cases ever processed by the NCAA."

The average fan has to be asking himself, where's the beef? Is THAT all they could uncover in four years?

WHERE ARE ALL THE SHOE BOXES?

Haven't we all been led to believe that kids everywhere are receiving shiny new convertibles and shoe boxes filled with $10,000?

How can THIS be one of the most serious cases of all time? Was there anything done by the University of Florida that most casual fans didn't already assume was within the rules? Won't the casual fan be surprised to know that some free meals and small cash payments put the University of Florida on the all time villain's list?

Should ANY of what Florida did be against the rules? Is that really all the NCAA could dig up in five years?

It should be possible to get at least that much on every major school in the nation, if the whole truth were known.

And how bad would that be?

The University of Florida did not do a single thing against the law. Ah . . . if only the corruption in government could be so benign.

Do you know the reaction of many booster club members to these terrible findings, which resulted in the firing or forced resignation of Florida coach Charlie Pell?

They bought him a new $24,000 car in appreciation. Few were, understandably, outraged by the list of "crimes" he committed.

MIGRANT WORKERS

It is almost startling to note how similar is the situation of student-athletes to that of migrant farm workers, even though initally the two seem very different.

Like the migrant farm worker, the student-athlete labors in a business which generates a great deal of money. Yet neither benefit from much of that money.

Both big farm owners and university leaders claim noble reasons for allowing an exploitive system to prevail. And student-athletes, like migrant workers, are generally too spread out, too poor, too transient, and too unorganized to realize their collective power and potential economic clout.

Student-athletes, of course, have many advantages over traditional migrant workers — among them literacy, high public profile, and an ability to alter their fate without recourse to secondary boycotts and such actions that require the aid of outside sources.

All things considered, student-athletes should have a much easier time than migrant workers in forming a union and carrying off effective strikes against their exploiters. At this point, however, only the migrant workers have succeeded in bettering their conditions — via nearly a quarter century of effort by leaders like Cesar Chavez and others.

It is becoming increasingly obvious that unions and strikes will be part of collegiate sports terminology and news, since the oppressive leadership of the present system shows no sign of unilaterally bringing about changes that are necessary by any Amercian standard of fairness and justice.

167

MINOR SPORTS

Minor sports have a right to exist just as major sports do, and minor sports offer valuable educational opportunities just as major sports do. Few people have any qualms with minor sports on campus. In fact, many basketball and football players enjoy playing tennis and golf, and often basketball and football players run track or play baseball in the spring.

What qualms exist have nothing to do with the sports themselves, but with the fact that basketball and football money is expected to pay for them all. In many cases, the profits from basketball and football pay for a university's entire minor sport budget, including the salaries of lacrosse coaches, the equipment used in baseball, the trips made by the golf team, and the uniforms used in soccer.

It isn't clear that anyone ever decided that basketball and football money should pay everyone else's way. It just happened, and it continues. Minor sport teams take better and better trips, they play in better and better uniforms, and generally they have come to expect the best modern equipment.

If the universities feel that the educational contribution of these sports is sufficiently important to warrant funding them — as apparently the Ivy League universities do — then by all means they should be funded.

The problem comes, however, not at the Ivy League schools, where these sports are paid for out of the general fund, but at the major schools where these sports are paid for out of football and basketball profits.

Where the money comes from would not be of crucial importance if everything were wonderful in major college sports. But now that the public and the presidents of universities have become convinced that the major schools are the source of a myriad of unacceptable problems — and now that we are all aware of the dismal graduation rates among major sport athletes — it becomes foolish to deprive the major sports of the money — their own money — which they could use to solve their unique set of problems.

It is ironic, as well as grossly unfair and unjust, that minor sport athletes, who are having their way paid through school by major sport athletes, have come to be seen as the "true" student-athletes, athletes with a proper sense of priorities, athletes who wisely place their sports second to their academics.

It doesn't make sense to praise the wisdom and perspective of the minor sport athlete while letting him feed off the money of the guy who is being snickered at and accused of being a dumb jock.

DO MINOR SPORTS BELONG ON CAMPUS?

Few athletes or coaches in the major sports would be so arrogant as to claim that minor sports have no right to be on campus. But major

168

sport athletes and coaches do have a right to question the existence of minor sports if their existence is dependent on money-making major sport programs.

It is time the universities re-evaluate the place of minor sports on campus and decide if their value is sufficient to operate them out of the general fund. If so, they may even get some gifts from the major sports from time to time. But, at least they would be appropriately grateful in that event.

At the major universities right now, the minor sports are existing on welfare, on the largess of the major sports. This makes no sense as long as golfers have higher graduation rates than basketball players, as long as baseball teams are taking post-season trips while the football team stays home on probation.

The money needs to go where the problems are, not to the minor sports.

When minor sports develop sufficiently and create fan interest similar to that of basketball and football, they will be welcomed as major sports. Until then, there is no reason to treat minor sport athletes exactly like, or as well as, major sport athletes.

There is no reason that minor sport teams should go on equally attractive trips, have equally expensive uniforms, or have equally fine equipment. There is also no reason that minor sports losing money should have national championships. Division I football, the sport that fans would love to see decided by a final game, doesn't even have a national championship. Why must minor sports have them?

Minor sport national championships are a tremendous drain on NCAA (i.e., basketball players') resources. These championships need to be abandoned, or paid for through general university funds by individual, participating schools.

Basketball and football players should be free to enjoy minor sports like everyone else — without being obligated to pay for them.

MISPLACED PRIORITIES

When a player does well in a basketball or football game, there are immediate, perceived benefits. People LIKE good players. People ADMIRE good players. People WANT TO KNOW good players.

For a graphic yet daily example, consider the many important men nationwide, who own companies and have a lot of money and a lot of influence and a lot of power who, in general, can't stand the thought of their daughters going out with a Black guy.

But, if that same Black guy happens to play for a certain school and happens to be able to rebound or tackle or dribble or catch passes, those same powerful, wealthy men can actually accept the idea of THAT kid going out with THEIR daughters.

You can come up with all sorts of generalities about racism and about sports in American society and so forth, but the long and short of it all is that people like good athletes. With the attention and admiration given to athletes, **it becomes ridiculous to talk about "misplaced priorities" when a student-athlete puts an inordinate amount of time into his sport and lets his education get pushed to the side.**

Forget the fact that seventeen- and nineteen-year-olds are making these decisions. The excuse of youth or immaturity is not needed. Let thirty-year-olds make those same decisions. It boils down to this:

A player has four years to do his athletic thing, four years to make it in the sports world. And he has fifty years or so to educate himself. He can educate himself at age forty while walking with a cane. But he can only star in football while he is in college. If he doesn't show it then, he will never get another chance.

In terms of timing, then, and in terms of immediately perceived benefits, it makes sense for a player to put his emphasis on his sport for four years, not on his education — ESPECIALLY if he has a realistic chance of making it as a pro.

When was the last time you heard anyone talking about what a fool Magic Johnson was for leaving Michigan State two years early in order to sign a 25 million dollar contract with the Los Angeles Lakers? People watch him on TV, they buy the shoes he endorses in commercials, and when they stick a card in a national banking relay system, they may repeat, "It must be MAGIC."

He speaks intelligently to reporters. He seems like a great guy.

"Isn't it a shame that he didn't get a college degree?"

Who cares? He can go back and take one course per summer for the next sixteen years, or he can take correspondence courses, or he can take none at all. What difference does it make?

What difference does it make that Moses Malone of the Philadelphia 76'ers didn't attend college at all?

For the successful guys, it doesn't matter — obviously. So it shouldn't be looked at as strange or stupid or even as "misplaced priorities" if a young athlete puts his best efforts into his sport for awhile.

The tragedy is that, fully aware of the benefits and the potential future the young athlete aspires to, the NCAA has nevertheless structured the system in such a way as to make the emphasis put on sport appear stupid if the athlete does not make it to the pros.

FULL COURSE LOADS?

There is no inherent reason why an athlete must take a full course load while competing, but the NCAA has ruled it a requirement for eligibility. There are plenty of people associated with universities who are taking less than full course loads. There are plenty of professors who, because they have special research duties or because they add prestige to the university, do not have full teaching loads. In other words, there is abundant precedent in every university for having people associated with the university who are not full time students or full time professors yet are considered an integral part of the university. Why not athletes?

Why shouldn't a football player be permitted to take a half course load during the fall semester? Why shouldn't a basketball player be permitted to take a half course load during the spring semester? Why shouldn't football and basketball players be permitted six years to graduate?

What is so bad about getting a degree in six years instead of four? A degree is a degree. All sorts of regular students take more than four years now. THEY aren't considered failures. Some even are considered wise — because they are putting time into a job or a special interest which enhances their education process, making it more relevant, more meaningful. Some are praised for working their way through school.

In statistical studies, athletes are considered failures for not graduating in four years. Who put this special emphasis on four years? Many of those who do graduate in four years would be better off to take longer, so they could put more time into their courses and consequently get more out of them.

If athletes were permitted to take half course loads, they could put a lot of time into each course they did take, and they could — even while personally emphasizing their sport — compete very favorably in the classroom, with a much improved chance of keeping a positive self-image in academics.

This is not to make excuses for athletes. There are many athletes who do well both in the classroom and on the field. But why make it so difficult?

What is the rationale for taking a borderline student/fine athlete and putting him into a situation where you know he is going to have to struggle academically? Why not let him take two courses during football season and give him a legitimate chance to succeed? And then why not offer him a scholarship for as long as it takes him to graduate, so he can feel that his priorities are in order? He will do his best on the field, give the classroom his best shot, and still have time to get his degree and concentrate fully on academics when his eligibility is completed.

Some critics may argue that letting players take half course loads will just give them more time to waste, and let more borderline students be able to get by. But getting by is not the issue. The issue is providing a positive environment for student-athletes. The issue is setting up a situation which compensates student-athletes for what they are giving to the universities. **The issue is taking into consideration the unique needs and abilities of a special class of people — and responding to them.**

171

With a few simple rule changes, the self-image of student-athletes would soar. Many more would begin to look upon themselves as successes in the classroom, and they would look toward getting a degree with pride and expectation, not as an impossible dream.

The all-too-common case of a good athlete/good person, not quite talented enough to make pros, completing his four years of playing and finding himself out in the cold, fifteen courses short of a degree, is a national disgrace. These kids have been responsible for producing millions in revenue yet they are cast aside and considered failures. They aren't wanted hanging around the athletic department. This athlete, as Harry Edwards has said, is no longer looked upon as "big gun" but as a "loose cannon on the deck, a potential source of embarrassment to the athletic department . . . a potential source of disenchantment and dissension within the ranks of new recruits and athletes with remaining sports eligibility."

There is no justifiable reason that things should be this way. But they are. And the exasperating thing is, few people in power in the NCAA are doing a thing about it. They sit back and self-righteously make claims against this or that school when the fault is clearly in the system they help to propagate.

There are always going to be some individuals with misplaced priorities, of course. But the present system robs the athletes of their rightful compensation, and makes likely the eventual failure of large numbers of them. Their priorities make sense right up until the time of being cut from a pro tryout camp.

Just because we can all point to a Bill Bradley or a Tom McMillan or a Pat Haden, star athletes and winners of Rhodes Scholarships, or to a few schools and programs where the athletes have been able to play and graduate in four years, there is no justification for letting so many athletes fall by the way, feel like failures and not get degrees.

If the players got a fair share of the money they earn, neither these problems nor the self-righteousness of the administrators who benefit from their money would exist. The players' priorities are only misplaced because the system is set up for distributing massive free rides at their expense. The gladiators, you might reasonably say, are fighting for the enjoyment and aggrandizement of the fat cats in the front row seats.

The true example of misplaced priorities in big-time athletics rests with the universities and the NCAA — who place pomp, platitudes, and public relations ahead of people.

MORAL DILEMMAS

Moral dilemmas are what coaches, players, and to some extent special boosters are faced with constantly as a result of the NCAA's stupid rules. There is a general awareness of need. Players are on campus — in many cases, nice, hard-working kids — who barely have enough money to get by on.

Does the coach give them money? Does he find a way for them to earn some? Does the player accept money? Does he tell the coach he needs some? Does he ask a booster club member or some special fan to help him out?

A fan sees a need and has a desire to help. He has a business of his own. He went to the school. He gets a great deal of enjoyment from his association with the team. And he has money. Can he give some discreetly? Should he let the coach know? Should he keep it from the coach? How can he get the money to the player in a way that will embarrass no one and not have any later negative repercussions?

The NCAA can make all the rules it wants while everyone sits in three piece suits and talks over the situation at plush resort hotels. The annual convention costs more than $100,000 of NCAA (basketball players') money. But what does this have to do with human need? With friendship? With what one man sees and recognizes as need as he makes friends with a young athlete?

The NCAA rules are broken constantly by sincere people not looking for an unfair advantage, not looking to get by with something extra, not looking to put one over on the competition. The NCAA rules are broken constantly by good people because the rules are often petty, often stupid, and because they put people at odds with their own consciences.

The NCAA rules should not put so many sincere people in moral dilemmas over whether to obey their humanitarian instincts or whether to follow strictly the rules.

THE MOREHEAD SCHOLARSHIP

Neither "Morehead Scholars" nor revenue-producing student-athletes are just like other students. In the classroom, EVERYONE is equal. No intelligent person has ever claimed that athletes, or anyone else, should get special privileges in the classroom. Obviously, we all want a good doctor when we get sick, and we don't care whether he (or she) once played a sport or sang in the choir. We want to know that the doctor absorbed the knowledge necessary to help us get healthy.

But sameness in the classroom is not at issue. Uniqueness in terms of value to the university is the crucial consideration to student-athletes. Just as some professors are more valuable to a university — and therefore get paid more — some students are more valuable to a university and deserve different treatment.

Is some principle of fairness violated when one student must pay for his education while another, for example a Morehead Scholar, attends without paying? This is standard practice at most colleges and universities. So, going a step further, what principle of fairness is violated when a student who is responsible for bringing many thousands of dollars into a university, is provided with extra benefits to attend?

UNETHICAL BENEFITS?

The Morehead Scholarship is given annually to outstanding students who wish to attend the University of North Carolina at Chapel Hill. Called the Morehead, after its founder, it provides a high school student with a full, four year scholarship, the opportunity to be paid for summer internships, a certain allotment for spending money and travel allowances, and the opportunity to continue the scholarship into graduate school. Outstanding athletes, such as Mark Maye of Charlotte, after winning Morehead Scholarships, naturally have chosen to accept them, rather than athletic grants-in-aid.

Is the integrity of young scholars on the Morehead Scholarship somehow compromised when they accept these scholarships? Aren't THEY just like all the other students? These are obviously stupid questions when asked about Morehead Scholars. Of course they are NOT like all the other students. They are award winners. They have demonstrated specialness, and to my knowledge, they are seldom, if ever, criticized for their failure to pay and work their way through school, nor are they criticized for the extra benefits they receive.

Can anyone explain why a top athlete (who demonstrates HIS specialness by generating many thousands of dollars for his university) should not get a scholarship at least equal to that provided by the Morehead Foundation?

Are Morehead Scholars to be considered professionals by virtue of their selection?

What ancient commitment to the nebulous, old-fashioned concept of athletic amateurism requires that a producer of big revenue be compensated to a lesser degree than a Morehead Scholar?

"I'm not in favor of a national championship playoff. Our players aren't paid enough ... "

—Don James
Head Football Coach
University of Washington

NATIONAL CHAMPIONSHIPS

There is no Division I national championship in football. It is sufficient to VOTE for the champion. Therefore, it makes good sense to VOTE for the champions in all the other sports as well — most certainly those many that lose money. Here are the sums to be spent on national championships, as shown by the estimated NCAA championship expenses for 1985-86:

Championship Transportation Guarantees	$5,698,500
Championship Game Expenses	$2,582,400
Championship Per Diem Allowances	$1,974,000
Championships Department	$ 978,000
Other Championship Distributions	$ 634,500

The championships that are making money certainly deserve to exist and to go on making money. But it remains a sickening kind of rip-off to see so much basketball championship money going to pay for national championships that simply are not necessary.

Basketball and football players' educations and futures versus minor sport championship playoffs. THAT is the choice. THAT is the hypocrisy. The NCAA has chosen the championships.

Give the money away, lavish it on unnecessary games, WHILE basketball and football players are failing to graduate and looked upon as dumb jocks by the public. It is impossible for intelligent basketball and football players to understand how this Robin Hoodism can be justified.

Incidentally, the estimated revenue for the 1986 Men's Basketall National Championship is **$37,000,000**, fully **75% of the NCAA's TOTAL revenue for 1985-86.** Does it suddenly become clear why basketball players have a right to be outraged over the way they are treated by the NCAA?

"The NCAA is a multi-million dollar business operation which makes tons of money on various business activities which it uses to keep its status as the secret police of college sports. Its powers are excessive and uncontrollable ... Byers and his staff have a great thing going for themselves. They are big time partners in a huge sports business which craves money and power. Their 'Pick the Winner' promotion with Gillette shows how two-faced they are. Picking winning teams is okay if the NCAA has part of the action; otherwise it isn't."
—Roger Stanton
Publisher
Basketball Weekly

NCAA

Though covered in detail in Part I, a succinct definition is appropriate here.

The NCAA is a group of parasites numbering some nearly 600 schools and hundreds of bureaucrats — all sucking the blood of some hundred-plus schools and growing and prospering while their host organism (the hundred-plus money-producers) is suffering degenerating health.

"Following the NCAA Convention in Nashville, I asked an administrator from one of the top conferences how things went and his sarcastic response was: 'Well it was close. There for a while I thought we were going to pass something that would benefit the student-athlete. But we kept our record perfect and didn't.' "

—Larry Donald
Publisher
Basketball Times

NCAA CONVENTIONS

The NCAA annual convention costs over $100,000 per year, which is a significant waste of basketball and football players' money.

A thousand people are too many to run the affairs of collegiate sports. The group in attendance is simply too large — and represents too many diverse interests — for meaningful work to get done, so the Convention itself, according to many members, amounts to little more than a social gathering.

The NCAA, at least, deserves credit for its selection of sights for these social gatherings. They are of uniformly high quality, as the sites and hotels for recent conventions below attest:

Convention	Year	Hotel	City
80th	1986	New Orleans Hilton	New Orleans
79th	1985	Opryland	Nashville
78th	1984	Loews Anatole	Dallas
77th	1983	Town & Country	San Diego
76th	1982	Hyatt Regency	Houston
4th Special	1981	Stouffers Riverfront	St. Louis
75th	1981	Fontainebleau Hilton	Miami Beach
74th	1980	Fairmont	New Orleans
73rd	1979	St. Francis	San Francisco
72nd	1978	Peachtree Plaza	Atlanta
71st	1977	Fontainebleau	Miami Beach

'NEED-BASED' RECRUITING

When you know the inside story of how so-called "cheating" is carried on, you see the events in a much more positive light than the impressions left by typical media headlines.

There are two essential points that govern most recruiting and the potential offer of inducements to top players.

First, middle class kids don't get many inducements. There are several possible explanations for this, the most obvious being that coaches realize middle class kids don't need them. If a kid already has his own car, already has spending money, he isn't going to be particularly enticed by the things a coach could possibly offer him. Furthermore, the

176

coaches do not, philosophically, feel that middle class kids need added perks, so for that reason too they are less likely to offer them. Finally, coaches fear offering inducements of this type to middle class kids because they know the approach that their competitors are taking. Almost universally, it goes something like this:

"We are well aware of your character and your upbringing. We know you aren't the kind of kid who is looking for handouts or trying to break rules that would jeopardize your future. We respect your intelligence and common sense, and we wouldn't even consider offering you anything against the rules even if you asked us, which we know YOU would never do."

Using this psychology, the coaches know they can recruit the kid on equal footing with all of the others, realizing that, if the kid does have an offer of inducements, recruiting him with this honest approach will likely make him doubt and become suspicious about any school which did offer something extra.

The poor, truly needy kid, however, is in a completely different situation. He may hear something like this:

"Listen, what I am going to talk to you about right now is technically against the rules. If you want to pick up the phone right now and make a call, you could get me in big trouble and make me lose my job. But I'm not worried about that. I think we've had a chance to get to know each other well enough now that you know that I am truly concerned about your future. I want what's best for YOU as a person, and as an athlete, and I wouldn't be taking this chance if I didn't. Listen, I know what kind of kid you are, I know what you think of your family, and I know you want to help them. I know your mother can't be sending you money while you're away at college, and I know you would very much like to help HER out if you can. I mean, what do a group of rules-makers in Kansas know about your mother, you know what I mean? Just because they say we're not supposed to give you anything, doesn't mean we can't do it. Personally, I'm willing to break a bad rule to help a kid and his family."

It makes sense. If a recruiter is any good at all at forging a personal relationship with a young athlete, he should be able to solicit a sufficient sense of loyalty in the kid to keep him from squealing regardless of where the kid decides to go to school. (A picture of the coach's wife and family wouldn't hurt, along the way, in impressing on the kid that the coach has a lot at stake, yet is willing to risk all that to help the kid.)

Such tactics can be berated as being manipulative, but since they are almost solely directed to kids who really do need money and extras, what is the real harm? The recruiter, in fact, probably is most often sincere. He DOES feel more of a desire to help the kid and his family than he feels a desire to follow NCAA rules which he does not believe in. Why shouldn't the kid get money? The kid is poor, his family is poor, and the university will make many thousands of dollars from the kid.

From this perspective, "cheating" looks like not much more than giving "according to financial need."

Although the media and the NCAA may name such offers "cheating," a transaction of this type may be morally more correct than when a wealthy coach at the helm of a successful program withholds money from his needy players out of deference to immoral rules which rob players of their fair share of the income they generate.

"If I were a younger man, and had nothing better to do with my life, I wouldn't mind heading a commission to revise those NCAA rules and get them in a little better shape . . . grown men have better things to do than try to investigate whether or not somebody bought somebody a coke."

—John Cribbet
Former Chancellor
University of Illinois

NITPICKING

At the June, 1985, so-called "historic," special NCAA convention in New Orleans, the delegates — mostly university presidents — made a point of making a particular statement over and over again as various issues came up for discussion.

"Let's not nitpick the details. Let's make the statement, establish the rule, and leave the details for later."

This was a very curious, and unhappy, development in view of the fact that nearly every NCAA rule that is applied to players is little more than nitpicking of some kind or other.

The presidents' willingness to leave the details until later can only come soon to harm some student-athletes, as other nitpicking details have done to student-athletes over and over again throughout recent NCAA history.

Players are denied eligibility often due to technicalities they are not even aware of. LaSalle's Albert Butts (whose story is told under "Outrage" in this section), is an excellent example, though excellent examples are legion. Whole teams are put on probation for violations amounting to little more than technicalities. Do you doubt it? Ask the University of Kansas what they did to get a football probation. Ask San Diego State University what they did to get a basketball probation? Check out the University of Illinois football program or the Oregon State basketball program.

What's the use of nitpicking the details here? NCAA rules are little more than nitpicking details from start to finish.

OKLAHOMA-GEORGIA CASE

This court case, which eventually went to the Supreme Court, prevents the NCAA from restricting each school's ability to make its own contracts for televising games. The effect of the victory for the individual schools has been, first, to limit rather than raise the amount of money the schools are making from TV revenue. But much more important is that this case established that the NCAA is subject to antitrust laws, and it swept away the notion that the NCAA has broad powers to regulate all forms of intercollegiate athletic activity.

This intelligent judicial decision gives athletes, finally, a realistic hope of getting the NCAA beast off their backs, in order to benefit from a free market system.

The case made it clear that free market principles are given higher priority by the courts than the "efficient" regulation of college sports.

"I believe that in the near future, there will be a change in the relationship of amateurism as we find it in college athletic programs and professionalism as it is rapidly emerging. I do not know what the change will be; people who deal with the Olympics have suggested some approaches that have not yet found their way into collegiate athletics. These kinds of changes hold great promise.

"Consider the fact that the student-athlete is the only one who doesn't in some way share the revenues he helps to generate. As the revenue pool gets larger, I think the willingness to accept this kind of arrangement will get smaller and smaller. Consider for example the quarterback who is central to the success of a football team. He may have a coach who is receiving a quarter of a million dollars a year, while he, the quarterback, is getting tuition, room and board, books, and fees. I can't help but think that legitimate economic forces considered by the student-athlete and his family will cause them to question this kind of allocation, and whether this interpretation of amateurism is rational."

—Cecil Mackey
President
Michigan State University

THE OLYMPIC GAMES

The Olympic Games have little influence on the lives or aspirations of major college football players, since football is not an Olympic sport.

From the standpoint of the basketball player, it is important to say just one thing.

There are athletes in America and around the world making hundreds of thousands of dollars and still competing as amateurs under international Olympic rules. These are not isolated cases either, but rather a consistent occurrence throughout the world.

For this reason, the NCAA's claims that the severe limitation on players' benefits is necessary in order to preserve the ideal of amateurism is hogwash.

There are hundreds of different concepts of amateurism around the world and even many within the United States. But few, if any, are as repressive as that espoused by the NCAA.

What purports to be a noble ideal amounts to nothing more than a smoke screen.

Until the NCAA has exhausted all means of providing deserved benefits to basketball and football players through legitimate scholarship funds, remedial programs, and other endowments, it will be clear that the ideals of amateurism are merely disguising blatant theft and exploitation.

"A different view of these scandals is that they are unavoidable, if not pardonable, as long as the opportunity for further physical training carry the inextricable linkage to academic pursuits. Given the lack of alternatives, we should not be surprised that the programs attract some participants who are more interested in one part of the dual (scholar-athlete) arrangement than the other."
—John Weistart
Professor of Law
Duke University

THE ONLY GAME IN TOWN

WHAT SHOULD A COACH DO . . . if a kid approaches him and says, Coach, I am not a good student. I hate reading. I know education is important, but I just can't stand learning from books. I like carpentry and the outdoors. THAT's what I want to do when I get older. But right now, I want to play basketball. I am 6'8" and I can run and leap and shoot. I never lifted weights. I got these bulging muscles from lifting two-by-fours. I think I have an excellent chance to become a pro, but of course I am not ready yet. Can I come and play for you? Is there any way you can get me in some courses in carpentry? And maybe in physical education? Just long enough for me to stay eligible for a couple of years so that I have a legitimate chance to make pros? You know, Coach, there really isn't any other way to prepare for a career in the pros. I can't make it playing street ball or at the YMCA. I have to be playing against Georgetown and North Carolina and Kentucky. Please Coach, I'll do anything you ask. Isn't there some way you can get me in and keep me eligible?

"If there was even a less than one percent chance we had done something wrong, then the NCAA is right. But we did nothing wrong. So [the NCAA's] decision is 100% wrong."

—Lefty Ervin (12-84)
Head Basketball Coach
LaSalle University

AN OUTRAGE TO JUSTICE

Federal District Judge John P. Fullam was sympathetic. He admitted that the rule preventing Albert 'Truck' Butts from playing his Senior year for LaSalle University was a bad one. The judge himself suggested that Butts might try to appeal on the grounds of racial discrimination.

Other than that, the judge explained that he was powerless to help Butts:

"There is little doubt that plaintiff LaSalle, and at least to some extent Big 5 basketball in Philadelphia, will suffer irreparable harm from enforcement of the NCAA bylaw."

There was even less doubt in his mind or in anyone else's mind that the enforcement of the bylaw would do irreparable harm to Albert Butts.
Said Butts' coach:

"What about the irreparable harm done to his life? He'd be robbed in ways we don't even know about."

Said Marty Blake, a pro scout, in discussing the effect of the decision on Butts' chances of making the NBA:

"We're not talking about a can't-miss guy. We're talking about a guy who needs his Senior season."

But Albert Butts did not get his Senior season. The NCAA went to court against him to uphold the bylaw that says that each year over the age of 20 counts as a year of competition.

The rule wasn't even made for basketball players. It was made in 1980 (while Butts was in prep school) in response to some schools which were recruiting older foreign track stars and winning championships with them.

Mike Stanton explained it best, in an article for "Eastern Basketball" in the January 16, 1985 issue:

"Concerned about all those foreign soccer players and track stars washing up on American shores (Give us your tired, your poor, your huddled masses . . . but keep your jocks), the NCAA banned an athlete from participating in a fifth year of competition after his 20th birthday" (if he starts school after he is 20.)

The value of this exclusionary, discriminatory rule was questionable from the beginning. From Butts' standpoint, it made no sense at all. Butts had not been told of the rule throughout his career. He had not been told of it while at Frederick Military Academy where he went for two years in order to prepare himself to be able to do college work.

Had Butts known of the rule, it would have been possible for him to gain entrance to an American university — based on his size and basketball ability alone — as has been often documented. But Albert Butts chose to go two years to prep school, so he would not have to rely on GETTING BY on meaningless courses, but instead, so he could actually GET EDUCATED while attending LaSalle and hoping to become a pro.

Butts' purpose and his effort should have been an inspiration and an example. The NCAA should have pointed him out to the kids — and the admissions directors — of the nation who would have a player enter college before he is capable of doing college work.

The NCAA rules should ENCOURAGE prep school attendance. But instead, the NCAA went to court.

The NCAA will argue that they were only upholding the will of the member institutions. But, if put to a vote, few if any member institutions would have voted against the eligibility of Albert Butts.

No good athletes nor any good coaches want to beat other teams on rules technicalities. The NCAA ought to know that.

But, were the NCAA's hands tied by the rule? Did they have no choice but to enforce it?

What stopped them from getting in touch with LaSalle's competitors and presenting the basic facts of the case as follows?

"The kid had not been informed of the rule. He came under this rule because of his sincere desire to educate himself and to prepare himself for college. His Senior year is very important to his future as a potential pro player. Do you object to us not appearing in court to pursue the case?"

Ask the coaches at Villanova, at St. Josephs, Penn, and Temple. Ask the coaches at Fordham, the team which stood to benefit most from Butts not playing. If THESE schools were against the eligibility, then go to court. But were they?

So often, when the NCAA justifies its rigid, inflexible posture, it does so with the contention that "we are only enforcing the will of the member institutions." What it fails to admit is that the will of 800 schools is unimportant in many of the NCAA's nitpicking actions. Eight hundred schools didn't need the NCAA's protection. What was needed was an injection of common sense that was understandable to any reasonable person.

The NCAA does not comprehend the freshness and joy that we all experience when someone sees clearly a situation and deals with it — on its individual merits — rather than by falling back on the prescription that "A rule is a rule."

The NCAA may argue, with 800 schools to preside over, that dealing individually with each circumstance would be an impossible task. And perhaps they are right. Maybe that is why President Edward Foote of the University of Miami (FL) said:

"The NCAA is just too big for sensible operation, too unwieldy, too slow to respond . . . Possibly, the NCAA can be restructured, but I'm not optimistic. I would welcome it, but I see little reason to expect it."

The Butts case, among so many others, makes it clear that student-athletes' interests cannot be fairly served under the present NCAA.

"We are putting more and more restrictions on athletes . . . We have over-legislated."

—Donald B. Canham
Director of Athletics
University of Michigan

"The problems are not a result of bad people but of too many rules."
—Al McGuire
TV Commentator
Former National Champion
Basketball Coach
Marquette University

"The structure for governing athletics today is incredibly complex. It overburdens the entire system of intercollegiate athletics. Much of it makes no sense now; much of it cannot be enforced. The system is so unwieldy that it cannot work. Something has got to change."

—Cecil Mackey
President
Michigan State University

"The NCAA rule book is more complicated than the U.S. Constitution."
—Joe B. Wyatt
Chancellor
Vanderbilt University

"College sports might not be facing a torrent of rules violations if the rules were realistic."

—Hugh Cunningham
Professor
University of Florida

"Many problems get back to the NCAA structure and size. It has grown and become cumbersome."

—John Swofford
Director of Athletics
University of North Carolina

OVER-LEGISLATING

Many of the top people in the sports world have said the same thing for years: There are too many restrictions on athletes, too many rules.

But no one is calling for a moratorium on rules.

At each new convention, student-athletes lose more rights, get new restrictions, find their benefits reduced. They are not just losing, they are getting thrashed. But student-athletes do not even have a say in their affairs. They are not invited to the NCAA conventions. They are not represented. They have no vote.

Student-athletes are controlled by a so-called voluntary association which they have no desire to belong to, but which just keeps on ruling and restricting them.

There is simply no end in sight to this rule-making frenzy. The NCAA does not have a long range plan of any kind with which to alter the present intolerable situation. It is their sincere hope, for all anyone can see, to make rules more and more stringent, to increase the size and effectiveness of their enforcement activities, and finally to strongarm their subjects into an unwilling compliance.

There is no foreseeable future under NCAA auspices of a national collegiate sports program where participants are grateful for their opportunities and at sufficient ease to open their operations to the public for an inside look at day-to-day operations.

A pervasive paranoia and secrecy exists in big-time college sports, and few people even want to talk about it.

It is easier, of course, to make new rules than to find creative solutions which will inspire compliance.

The tragedy of major college sports is that more than a few general rules have to be made at all.

Is it really impossible to get a hundred people together, with common interests, to iron out what they really want, how they want to compete, and what general standards they wish to live by?

Is it really necessary to have hundreds of nitpicking rules about phone calls and quiet periods and visits and contacts? Wouldn't it be a hundred percent better to give a hundred coaches seniority, and job security, and let them attend a week-long convention to make the general principles by which they would compete?

Couldn't they correct their own mistakes at their annual meetings, reprimand their own members, vote the "bad guys" out of their ranks?

There seems little doubt, even acknowledging that this is a much oversimplified view, that almost any organization, starting over (and yes, with the benefit of hindsight) could do a much better job than is being done.

Why not throw away the rule book and start from scratch? Rule number 1: Let's keep the group small and let's try to make college sports an enjoyable endeavor again — like it was back when the Four Horsemen were trampling people and winnin' 'em for the Gipper!

"Give me six weeks, and I can get any college in the nation on probation."
—'Credo' of NCAA investigators,
According to Brent Clark
Former NCAA investigator

PARANOIA

Paranoia is defined as a mental disorder characterized by delusions that are ascribed to the supposed hostility of others.

But are big-time sports programs victims of paranoia? When a former NCAA investigator tells a House Subcommittee on Oversights and Investigations that the NCAA feels it can get anyone, and when a judge finds that the NCAA was 'out to get' a well known national basketball coach, is it a delusion? The proper term is FEAR.

College football and basketball coaches around the nation run closed-shop types of programs, in constant fear that someone is going to contaminate, or perhaps merely find out something about their programs.

Naturally, with so many foolish NCAA rules in effect, there is indeed always an opportunity to find a school in violation of something.

It is a tragedy that student-athletes must be subjected to a daily diet of secrecy and suppression, being cut off from interested fans, alumni, and press, because of the pervasive fear that something might go wrong.

There is no paranoia any longer in major college sports programs. The word is fear. There are no disorders, no delusions. The hostility of others is real. The rules themselves are hostile to the interests of athletes.

PELL GRANTS

Pell Grants are federal funds available to students in need of financial aid for college. A regular student, through this program, can receive as much as $1800 per year. But student-athletes, in recent years, could receive only $900 by NCAA decree, even though studies have shown that a student needs at least $1400 above the cost of room, board, books, and tuition in order to pay typical expenses of living and going to college. A new ruling for 1986 may permit student-athletes to receive more than $900 in Pell Grant funds, but the amount will remain LESS than regular students are permitted to receive.

Interestingly, the NCAA has been more inclined to point out the few times when Pell Grant money has been abused rather than the many cases in which more money is truly needed.

Tom Yeager, the director of legislative services of the NCAA, was quoted in several publications calling Pell Grant money "play money" used for buying stereos and making car payments.

Supposedly, the reason the NCAA does not allow a poor student-athlete to keep the full $1800 — like regular students — is that there is fear that universities will use all their Pell Grant funds on athletes, leaving none for regular students.

Would universities be giving all this money to athletes just because they like them? Obviously, there are good financial reasons behind such actions. Not many universities consider themselves as being in the charity business. You can be sure, at any time they are giving money out, it is with the realization, or at least with the expectation, that they will be getting a handsome return on their investment.

———————

"There is a kind of collective action of a myriad tiny elements on low levels that tips the balance — exactly as in a country that decides' to go to war or not. It will flip or not, depending on the polarization of its citizens. And they seem to align in larger and larger groups, aided by communication channels and rumors and so on. All of a sudden, a country that seemed undecided will just 'swing' in a way that suprises everyone."

—Douglas R. Hofstadter
Author

PHASE TRANSITIONS

This term has no usual tie-in to athletes, except perhaps as it explains the phenomenon of momentum and team spirit — the way a whole group of down players can suddenly, simultaneously, catch fire and produce a far greater collective effort than they could muster just moments before.

Douglas R. Hofstadter, in a very provocative book called "METAMA-GICAL THEMAS: Questing for the Essence of Mind and Pattern," explains the mystery and some of the workings of a phase transition. This is the process by which cells in a brain or fish in a school or people in an audience interact in such a way as to make dramatic shifts of direction or movement or opinion. The people of the nation, just like cells or fish, form collective units that "create self-reinforcing loops of interaction."

As a result, dramatic change often takes place imperceptibly. A seemingly inactive hill of snow suddenly becomes an avalanche, as billions of snow crystals sweep over houses and trees and bury everything in their path.

What has happened? How did all that snow start moving? Hofstadter explains these phenomena with regard to public opinion shifts, as well as with natural events, and the implications for the student-athlete are profound.

A nation, Hofstadter explains, can shift dramatically much like a person may suddenly decide to take a new action.

"It will happen when enough citizens band together, seeing some common interest, sensing some common goal. There is a sort of 'critical point' when that number reaches a threshold and suddenly, there is a turnaround at a national level." (p. 794.)

The nation is reaching that critical point. What were a few voices in behalf of student-athletes just a couple of years ago have suddenly become a torrent of opinion. What seemed to bother almost no one has suddenly come to be seen as an outrage, as theft, as unconscionable exploitation. The collective opinion of the nation is undergoing a dramatic shift. It is turning rapidly, and the NCAA is out of step.

The elements, the features of a classic phase transition have been set in motion. It is only necessary to let 'the self-reinforcing loops of interaction' continue. A whole new era of collegiate athletics is about to begin. The threshold is at hand.

"I have not heard any mention of the players, nor have I felt any real concern for the players themselves in all of the years I have attended NCAA conventions."
—A Respected Director of Athletics
Who asked that his name be withheld

AN ANNUAL PLAYERS' CONVENTION

Will the NCAA encourage the creation of, and then provide funding for, an annual convention of major college revenue producing players?

The answer to this question will determine without doubt whether the NCAA is "for us or against us."

The NCAA funds public relations campaigns on drugs and sports; it funds studies on lacrosse injuries and the effects of effort "upon the foot during high jumping;" the NCAA makes grants to associations of basketball, football, volleyball, tennis, baseball and swimming COACHES; it makes grants to associations of sports information directors and to directors of athletics; it grants money to two national youth sports programs; and it spends money on posters, on film production, and on the production of public service radio and TV announcements.

It is not the contention of student-athletes that any of these expenditures are necessarily bad. It is merely obvious that the immediate concerns and the fair treatment of student-athletes should be the FIRST PRIORITY for NCAA funding.

Accordingly, it makes sense that the NCAA provide funds for an annual convention of revenue producing major college student-athletes. The convention should include an elected representative of each major college basketball and football team. In the first year, this list might be limited to the 100-plus football teams in the CFA, Big Ten and PAC-10, and to basketball players at these schools, along with basketball players from any of the 64 schools which participated in the most recent NCAA basketball tournament and are not already included. (Most of the 64 schools are also big-time football schools, with notable exceptions like St. John's and Georgetown.)

The Players' Convention should be similar to the NCAA annual convention. Players should be flown to a resort hotel where they would have the opportunity to conduct meetings and establish a program of activity, with the purpose of presenting an agenda of concerns and desires to the NCAA membership at the NCAA annual convention.

Certainly, the players should be empowered to propose legislation to the NCAA membership; and national player representatives, elected at the Annual Players' Convention, should be integral parts of each annual NCAA convention.

Naturally, the athletes' complete expenses — for rooms, food, travel, and incidental entertainment — should be a cost born by the NCAA.

It not only makes perfect sense that there should be an annual players' convention tied directly into the NCAA structure, it is astonishing that there is not, nor is there currently any procedure by which athletes can realistically present their concerns and desires to the NCAA for consideration.

Currently, revenue producing student athletes are NOT members of the NCAA, nor are they represented at NCAA conventions. An Annual Players' Convention will be one positive step which the NCAA can take to demonstrate its desire to include players in the legislative process.

A failure by the NCAA Council to recommend an Annual Players' Convention to the NCAA membership, or a failure to provide funding for this players' convention, will announce to the players, loud and clear, that more active efforts will be necessary.

[A suggestion for an Annual Players' Convention has already been sent to the NCAA Council members, to the NCAA administrative staff, and to a large number of Division I presidents and faculty representatives. Their failure — or willingness — to act will show where they stand.]

"If you run up the score, it will come back to haunt you. I don't believe in running up the score."

—Frank Broyles
TV Commentator
Former Football Coach
University of Arkansas

POINT-SHAVING

No one who loves sports can possibly be in favor of point-shaving. Shaving points, or in any way tampering with the result of a contest, defeats the whole purpose of the effort.

Student-athletes who shave points can not be tolerated. This is simple. It is understood.

Nevertheless, most people would have different feelings about a kid who shaved some points in order to get some money for his needy family than about a kid who shaved points to support a drug habit.

Even in the sordid business of point-shaving, there are differing degrees of reprehensibility.

Poor kids, stolen from and cheated by those who purport to be their educators, are especially prime candidates for point-shaving. This is not to say that point-shaving would never happen again if players were given a fair share of the revenue they produce. But certainly it is true that having some money and being grateful for it and for personal good fortune would eliminate a great deal of potential temptation. Grateful, basically satisfied people are decidedly less vulnerable than desperate, penniless ones.

As far as point-shaving itself goes, a player really doesn't care much whether his team wins by twenty or only by ten. A win is a win, as the saying goes; therefore, in the NCAA-ruled world of college basketball, where hypocrisy and deception are commonplace, a poor kid can be expected to be a prime candidate to give in to the temptation to make some extra dollars.

It is wrong. It cannot be tolerated — not in any form. Without integrity, sports become meaningless.

Yet, where on the spectrum of point-shaving reprehensibility does "coaches' etiquette" fit in? How many times have you heard a coach accused of "running up the score?"

"Accused" was the word. Because so many people seem to believe that it is wrong to run up the score. **IS it wrong to run up the score? Or is it wrong not to?**

Why do coaches get away with comments like, "If you do it to him, he'll do it to you someday?"

Why would any coach EVER want to lose by less than the other team was capable of winning by?

Why does anyone tolerate this attitude of going easy on the losers? Why does anyone expect a basketball coach to call off his full court press when he gets a twenty point lead? or a football coach to keep the ball on the ground late in the fourth quarter with a 28 point lead? Why not try to win by 35?

It doesn't make sense. When a team beats another team by twenty points — when it was capable of winning by forty — THAT is point-shaving.

It is hard to imagine a player spending years in prison for doing something very similar to what our top coaches do often — and get praised for.

Of course there are arguments. The coach isn't doing it for money (but then, he already has money in most cases) and the coach is doing it in a controlled, acceptable way.

But how acceptable is that? How abominably different is the kid from the coach? The kid refuses to lose but will see to it that his team wins by only nine — for some money. The coach will see to it that his team doesn't win by more than nineteen — so he doesn't embarrass a colleague. Don't laws against point-shaving protect only illegal gamblers?

The "etiquette" doesn't seem much better than the nine point win that could have been thirteen.

Money seems to be the only real difference between the two. The coach usually has some, and the players usually don't. That IS a factor.

So is the matter of control. The coaches' point-shaving is often equally bad, but presumably not in danger of getting out of control. A player's point-shaving, it is feared, could get completely out of control — to where big-time gamblers would be deciding the scores of games, not the players.

Certainly it would be terrible if that happened. But wouldn't it be better, too, if EVERYONE, at ALL times just did his best?

Even coaches.

———————

"I am too old not to be thankful for the greatest catalyst desegregation in the South has had — college football.

"I asked Bo Jackson about the bad old days, how much he knew about them, what he thought about them.

"He gathered his brow, sincerely searching back through his mind.

" 'That's something,' he said earnestly, 'I've never thought about.'.

"Things are far from utopian now, but in one 22-year-old lifetime, things have changed that much. And college football has been the finest example along the way."

—Ed Hinton
Atlanta Constitution

PRIMARY PURPOSE OF UNIVERSITIES

One of the favorite tactics of critics of big-time sports or of those temporarily mesmerized by an abuse of some sort within a big-time sports program is to make the apparently safe claim that our institutions of higher learning are not there primarily to support professional sports.

Those people may be politely thanked for such totally uninformative, superfluous comments, and then they should have it pointed out that the mission of universities in America is diverse. Naturally, universities are educational in nature — which sports are, according to the NCAA's relationship with the IRS — but "education" obviously has a very broad definition.

Are universities only for nuclear research? Should they be for nuclear research at all? Should university medical centers be doing abortions? There are those who claim that universities should not conduct research on social diseases or offer courses that are military in nature.

Critics forget that the universities are "the people." And the people love basketball and football. They love basketball and football being a part of the universities. The connection has been a very positive one over the years, and one that need not be severed because the media or a few presidents overreact to public pressure at certain times.

Our universities do not exist primarily for sports, anymore than they exist primarily for nuclear research. Universities are an instrument of democracy, a civilizing, educating force. They exist for any purpose deemed important by the American people. Therefore, universities promote pure research, they produce teachers, and they offer opportunities to students in business, religion, medicine, music, militarism, and art.

There is no clash between sports and education — only a desire on the part of weak-thinking alarmists to make some personal impressions (which they apparently can't express satisfactorily) sound more awesome.

The next time someone comes forward with the grand proclamation that the-universities-aren't-there-primarily-for-sports, ask to see the charters of the particular universities they are talking about. THEY may be surprised.

"[The players] are giving you four of the best years of their lives, so why not give them something they can live on? . . . They're working very hard to bring the school money, give them a salary . . . It would be like a professional league, but there's nothing wrong with the word professional."
—Lou Carnesecca
Head Basketball Coach
St. John's University

PROFESSIONALISM

General Motors, AT&T, and IBM executives strive for it. But the NCAA sees it as the most evil of words.

Executives define professionalism as dignity, competence, organization, and reliability. Included in the concept is the expectation that a professional person will act responsibly, yet with awareness of his own self-interest, with intent to maximize his abilities and his profits in a fair, straightforward manner. "Professionals" are expected to dress well and project an image which exemplifies the success they aspire to.

The NCAA defines professionalism as any amount of money over "necessary and actual expenses." In THAT concept is included the idea that accepting a new suit or a few ties is corrupt. Self-interest is not seen as extending to any awareness whatever of maximizing abilities and benefitting from self-worth.

The NCAA would do well to alter its definition in recognition of the reality of big-time collegiate sports. It would dirty no one to have a group of student-athletes rewarded with post-graduate scholarships, spending money, new clothes, and transportation allowances.

Only the NCAA's greed and narrow-mindedness prevent student-athletes from attaining the standards of professionalism that are the pride and aspiration of the rest of American society.

"Why should we impose different standards on an athlete than we do on a student who wants to participate in the band or as a pom pom girl?"
—Joseph Johnson
President
Grambling State University

PROPOSITION 48

Voted on by the NCAA a few years ago and scheduled to take effect in 1986, Proposition 48 requires athletes hoping to play Division I sports to have a 2.0 average in a core curriculum of eleven basic, high school courses, along with an SAT score of 700.

The proposition has been criticised as being racist, because a high percentage of Black athletes do not meet those qualifications. As a result of this and other reservations, there have been some modifications. Many people are uncomfortable with establishing a rigid minimum score of any kind, and especially on the Scholastic Aptitude Test, which is often cited for being culturally biased.

The upholders of universal good are crying out against any attempt at modifying Proposition 48. They call it "giving in to the pressure of athletic interests," and they are quick to bring up the greedy, win-at-all-costs attitude as the only justification for modification.

Nevertheless, despite the zealousness of a vocal group of administrators (and sometimes reporters), there are reasons for caution. Nearly everyone, in principle, is for higher academic standards for colleges, and for better education in primary and secondary schools. But being for an unmodified Proposition 48 does not mean one person is pro-education anymore than it means someone for modification is anti-education.

What has been disconcerting throughout the Proposition 48 debate of the last couple of years is the almost typical view that ATHLETES ALONE are always getting away with something, that they are universally being admitted to college with below-standard grades and below-par scores on the entrance tests.

At times, of course, they are. But what the widespread critics fail to point out is how often other students are admitted in the same way.

Is the big, non-athletic donor's son not admitted with below standard grades? below-par test scores? (The athletes, remember, ARE big donors.)

Researchers at the University of Texas claim that 30-40 percent of ALL freshmen entering college have reading levels below the seventh grade level. Therefore, critics have to realize that the problems go much beyond athletics. Most universities HAVE lowered their standards. They have had to — for the same economic reasons that have tempted them to admit unprepared athletes.

Four times as many students go to college now as did in 1950. The schools grew with the influx of baby-boomers in the Sixties and Seventies, and now most schools are competing hard to fill their dormitories. They need the money from more students — even if those students aren't the best prepared.

Big-time athletes get singled out because they get so much publicity. But the unprepared Freshman whose grandfather built the administration building doesn't end up with HIS name in the New York Times. Neither do the other fifty students admitted solely to collect their tuition money and fill the dorms.

This is no attempt to get athletes off the hook, or to praise their degree of preparedness for college. But as long as they are taking the flack, the whole situation has to be looked at. Why subject athletes to a standard above that of any other student?

If the son of the million dollar contributor can get in school with 600 on his SAT, then athletes should too.

If, on the other hand, the universities are prepared to set admissions standards from which they will not deviate for anyone, then of course athletes would rightfully be included.

If the university presidents are so unanimously in favor of integrity in athletics, they should certainly be in unanimous favor of integrity — and equality — in admissions policies.

What is most important is not so much at what minimum level students are admitted, but whether or not a real effort is made to see that they end up educated once they are there.

The National Institute of Education has said that too many students are "ill served by too many of our institutions." The Wall Street Journal, in several reports cited by The NCAA News (11-19-84), has indicated "a common theme" that "while many students pile up course credits AND [even] EARN DEGREES, they don't learn much of value."

Certainly that news casts doubts on the very value of getting a degree and on the importance of the graduation rate itself — which has become synonymous with academic success to the NCAA.

If colleges make a sincere attempt to educate their athletes, and to compensate them fairly for their economic value, it won't be so crucial that they graduate — with a diploma of sometimes questionable value.

A fair amount of money, and a solid "four year advance in knowledge and thought" (regardless of how close that takes an athlete toward graduation) would likely be preferable to what many athletes now leave college with, even the many who do graduate.

So, Proposition 48? Yes, of course — as long as it applies to every other student.

Right now, it doesn't.

"Colleges fall over themselves playing this (amateur) charade. If, for example, a large corporation offered to fund a new lab on campus, the school would genuflect in gratitude. But if, say, the Philadelphia 76ers offered to underwrite the scholarships of three basketball players, that same college would recoil in horror and moral outrage.

—Bill Lyon
Columnist
Knight-Ridder Newspapers

PRO TRAINING GROUNDS

When discussions come up about compensating or paying student-athletes, someone usually brings up the point that the colleges provide great training grounds — valuable apprenticeships, you might call them — for pro sports. "Isn't that worth a lot?" ask those who feel the athletes are already getting a lot by getting an education.

Obviously, one answer is that not many athletes can take advantage of that training and make it to the pros. But a second answer is, yes, it is a great training ground. For the 4% of the major college athletes who can use college as a training ground for pros, it is indeed worth a great deal.

"Then why not make them pay back the costs of their scholarships?" the questioners usually ask.

"Because they did not get nearly what they were entitled to in the first place."

"But shouldn't THE PRO TEAMS have to pay it back? The pros are getting something for nothing. Why shouldn't THEY have to pay? For them, it's like having a paid-for minor league."

WHY DON'T THE PROS PAY
FOR THEIR COLLEGE "MINOR LEAGUES?"

Most fans will be surprised to learn that the pro teams cannot, even if they want to, reimburse a college for the training it has given to a student-athlete. The first answer in the 1985-86 NCAA Case Book makes this clear.

"Receipt of [funds from a professional organization] would be contrary to a fundamental policy of the Association to maintain a clear line of demarcation between college athletes and professional sports. Further, receipt of such funds by an institution would make available additional monies that could be realized in some form by student-athletes and result in student-athletes receiving indirectly funds from a professional sports organization."

The stupidity of that answer speaks for itself.

The reason that such monies are turned down is that the NCAA is already accustomed to stealing so much money and wasting so much money there is really no need to seek out viable sources of additional revenue.

When players start getting their rightful share of revenues, the NCAA will find it within its power to justify immediately accepting grants from professional teams that could be used for specific, worthwhile purposes. These would not infringe on the "line of demarcation" — especially if the salaries of NCAA officials are in danger of getting cut without such funds.

"Somebody cheats, nail the team. That's the way they've been doing it for a long time."

—RON GREEN
Sports Editor
Charlotte (NC) Observer

"If the NCAA wants to impose sanctions for what it believes are violations of its rules, then impose them on the school, not the fans.

"But when the NCAA says that the people of the state of Illinois — those people whose tax dollars fund the operations of the state universities — cannot watch their team on television, then it becomes a matter to be considered by the general assembly."

—George Sangmeister
State Senator
Illinois

PUNISHMENTS

Somewhere, back in something like 10,000 B. C. or earlier, some Cro-Magnon man must have wanted to punish some Neanderthal-looking creature but he didn't know who was at fault, so he just smacked his club against the ground and tried to wipe out the whole other tribe. In a world where everyone looked alike in the distant caves — without cameras, finger printing, eyewitness testimony, and Xerox machines — that might have been the best way to accomplish the task.

Indeed, blanket punishments of this nature are common throughout history, but they are also un-American. Our system of justice says, "Better a hundred guilty men go free, than one innocent man be hanged."

The NCAA, however, in meting out punishments, apparently has never felt bound by the dictates of the American form of justice. Their punishments, down through the years, can be characterized as thoughtless, uncreative, or just plain stupid.

Unfortunately, nothing has changed. It is still the habit of the NCAA to punish all sorts of innocent victims in order to be sure of getting the people who are guilty of violating NCAA rules.

It is not necessary to search diligently for examples of the NCAA's wholly unjustifiable punishments. EVERY probation puts dozens of athletes, who have done nothing wrong of any kind, off TV, out of the spotlight, and makes them ineligible for post-season play.

Elements within the NCAA are even aware of this injustice, but they do NOTHING about it, which is even worse. Below is a report from the NCAA Select Committee on Athletic Problems and Concerns in Higher Education. Their report was published in October of 1983, but the NCAA's mindless probations not only are still going on, they are becoming more far-reaching, more stringent, and more damaging than ever. The Select Committee said:

"There is much support for the notion that penalties should apply to the individuals who have been party to a violation and that innocent persons should not suffer because of what others have done. One institution is presently under a penalty that will bar it from a bowl game after the 1983 season and will prevent its games from being televised live in the 1984 and 1985 seasons. The most recent violation found against it was in 1980. The coaching staff and athletes who will feel the brunt of the penalty had nothing whatever to do with any of the violations." (p. 19)

The report goes on to explain to the reader that "the solution for seeming inequities of this kind is not easy to find."

But the NCAA seems to have no difficulty at all in finding a solution. They do it the easy way. They punish everyone.

You have to wonder if this kind of punishing can hold up in court under the rules requiring "reasonable exercise of authority." In a case in Iowa in 1972 (Bunger vs. Iowa High School Athletic Association) the court ruled in favor of an athlete and against the association, concluding:

"[We] realize that the rule has been made broad in an effort to avoid problems . . . but rules can not be so extended as to sweep in the innocent in order to achieve invariable conviction of the guilty." (THE LAW OF SPORTS, p. 49)

The NCAA's consistently unjust punishments certainly seem to be in direct contradiction to such a ruling, yet the beat goes on.

It may be true that no one has yet taken the NCAA to court to test this particular application of their authority; and it can only be hoped, since the NCAA shows no signs of changing its Neanderthal policy, that someone will soon challenge the NCAA legally and put an end to these injustices.

"INELIGIBLE FOR LIFE"

In a court case involving two Canadian players who were ruled ineligible by the NCAA in 1973, (Buckton vs. NCAA) the court made the following comment:

"[It is] naive to assume that because the source of aid happens to be a school, the motivation behind that aid is not, at least sometimes, an effort to induce a good athlete to attend a particular school in order to be of assistance to the athletic program. Even the most casual reader of sports pages is aware that such inducements are an everyday fact of life in American amateur athletics. This fact of life underscores the frivolity, if not more, of holding student athletes responsible for the motives of their benefactors, whether they be American athletic directors or . . . team managers." (p. 61, Weistart, THE LAW OF SPORTS)

Professor Weistart is careful to point out, however, that "it is certainly not uncommon to impose sanctions on athletes for the derelictions of their coaches."

The NCAA Special Convention in New Orleans in 1985 made it quite clear that athletes found guilty of violating NCAA rules are in jeopardy of losing their eligibility permanently.

This is hardly surprising. With the NCAA record being what it is with regard to unjust punishments, it is actually astonishing that this has not been done all along.

It is to be hoped, though, that the courts will not permit a player (whose earned money is being stolen hand over fist by the NCAA) to be denied eligibility — permanently — for the crime of trying to receive a small fraction of what he is entitled to.

The present rules now call for permanent loss of eligibility if a player is found, for example, to have accepted twenty dollars from a coach.

197

Does permanent loss of eligibility — especially for a kid who has a realistic chance of becoming a pro prospect during four years of college competition — sound like a reasonable punishment for a poor seventeen-year-old who might accept that money from a coach or alumnus after being convinced by that adult that it would be okay to accept it? Would the fact that the kid or his family truly needed the money influence YOUR feelings? Would the fact that the kid might be worth perhaps millions to the university influence YOUR feelings?

Facts such as these do not influence the NCAA rule-makers or enforcement department at all.

"The players are bigger and stronger, and when there is a collision, something has to give. The scholarships have to be upped. The players have surpassed their protective equipment. Nowadays, you not only have to be a good coach, you have to be the luckiest guy in the world."

> —Hayden Fry
> Head Football Coach
> University of Iowa

"Nobody listens to the coaches. I'd like to have ten more scholarships, but it won't happen. You no longer have five tackles at one position. You have two or three, and if one gets injured, that's when it really hurts."

> —Earle Bruce
> Head Football Coach
> Ohio State University

"We'll pull our belts tighter and lead the team . . . The freshman class has been brought closer together by this. We're gonna get to play early, and we're ready for that challenge."

> —John Stollenwerck (1985)
> Quarterback, SMU
> (Indicating the positive feature
> of SMU's loss of scholarships
> due to NCAA sanctions)

SCHOLARSHIP QUOTAS

Reducing scholarship quotas is one wonderful way to make nearly everyone happy but coaches; and the coaches would get over it soon.

The NCAA rules permit 30 new grants per year in football and a total of 95 players on scholarship at any one time, while in basketball they permit fifteen players on scholarship at a time. Numbers like these simply aren't necessary. Pro football teams have only 45 players on their rosters — and they have bigger players and longer seasons. Sure, they have access to players on taxi squads, but statistics show that six or seven players per year must be replaced — not fifty.

In basketball there is no excuse for having fifteen players on the squad. Two hundred minutes of playing time in basketball is simply not sufficient to disburse happiness to fifteen people.

By reducing scholarship quotas in football to 68 total — 17 per year — and in basketball to 12 total — 3 per year — the athletic atmosphere would be a hundred percent better for the players. Additionally, the money not spent on travel, equipment, unnecessary coaches, and of course on the scholarships themselves would be a welcome cash savings that could be distributed back to the players, thus NOT forcing the university or overall sports program to find any new money with which to compensate the revenue producing athletes.

Coaches might protest and give all sorts of reasons why they couldn't possibly function with so few players, but very few of them would resign due to this hardship and thousands of qualified, capable people would be happy to take the place of any who would resign.

The result of having so few players on a team (especially if coupled with a freshmen ineligibility rule and a scholarship rate linked to the graduation rate) would be that coaches would have to be the counselors and educators, in fact, that they have always claimed to be; the benefit to the health, education, and general welfare of the players would be dramatic.

Players would have a chance to be part of what might truly be a happy family atmosphere. Each player's personal and athletic development would be important to the success of the entire program. Coaches' would have to recruit PEOPLE, not bodies, and they would have to do it very meticulously, careful to select not just good athletes but kids very likely to maintain their enthusiasm, kids that are fun to be around, and kids who are very likely to go to class and graduate.

You could do ALL THAT just by reducing the scholarship quotas and making freshmen ineligible. Tying the scholarship rate directly to the graduation rate, additionally, would take the wonderful, resulting atmosphere for players even one more giant step beyond.

"There could be deductions in recruiting expenses. That's the biggest single expense in any football department."

—Prentice Gautt
Commissioner
Big 8 Conference

RECRUITING

Mediocre coaches have demonstrated consistently that a successful athletic program depends primarily on effective recruiting; and the increasing attention given by the media to this issue bears further witness to the degree of interest which fans have in this process which coaches call their "second seasons." From the student-athletes' point of view, there are three major issues, (1) the conspiracy and collusion of the universities and the NCAA which deprives student-athletes of many privileges as well as the opportunity to make a sound selection, (2) the deception which most of the schools are guilty of, and (3) the unnecessary, or faulty notion of, pressure associated with the recruiting process.

CONSPIRACY AND COLLUSION

The NCAA's own Select Committee on Athletic Problems and Concerns in Higher Education supports without question the conclusion that the NCAA, in collusion with some universities, conspires against prospective student-athletes. In its October 1983 report, the Select Committee (p. 15) said:

"Many of the existing rules in recruiting are intended to protect institutional treasuries and personnel from wasteful and unproductive activity that institutions otherwise would feel obliged to engage in to keep pace with the competition."

No kidding. Isn't that "wasteful and unproductive activity" what competition is all about? Does the NCAA suppose that Coke and Pepsi deem all of their advertising expenditures useful and productive? Listen to the Select Committee's reasoning.

"It is a truism among those knowledgeable about recruiting that it is never possible to be sure in advance what little thing will turn out to be decisive in whether a talented young person chooses State or Tech.".

Does it require a person "knowledgeable in recruiting" to know THAT? Do you know why YOU choose Coke over Pepsi, or Chevy over Ford?

Go on, Select Committee, keep talking . . .

"If a coach from State is in the stands every Friday night to watch a recruit perform, Tech will feel that it must have one of its coaches there also."

Yes, that is absolutely correct. If unlimited visits and contacts are permitted, THAT is a sure sign — especially when the head coach comes himself — that the school is sincerely interested. If the head coach comes twice or three times or six times, a player knows he is truly wanted.

Knowing you are wanted — TRULY WANTED — if you are a player, is THE crucial issue. The Select Committee may not have known (it should have, although only 2 of the 16 members were coaches) that many players are recruited who are not really wanted, and who are likely to be unhappy at the school which eventually signs them.

200

Perhaps the point is not clear enough. THE crucial issue for a player, in wading through the incredible deception of smooth talking, highly competitive, motivated salesmen, is to find out if he is truly wanted. Does the coach EXPECT him to start?

"Oh c'mon, no one can be promised he will start." But a kid has to know where he fits in the plans. Is he the first choice, or is he a necessary body who MIGHT develop? Is it expected that they will be able to get someone else next year who is better?

No Select Committee, no group of coaches, and no NCAA Convention can dispute the central importance of this issue to the player's welfare in college, yet the recruiting rules, as the Select Committee admits, are made to reduce competition and to take away the crucial barometers which measure REAL interest.

Prospects are in real danger of making uninformed choices precisely because the rules which protect the institutions' treasuries deny them the opportunity to have sufficient contact with the head coach in order to get to know him personally.

The contacts (strictly limited in number and in time) now permitted do not give a coach or a prospect adequate time to make truly informed judgments. It is easy for trained salesmen to come off looking like wonderful people in such restricted circumstances, and the process works again and again to the players' detriment.

It remains, as far as I know, an open legal question as to whether the NCAA has the right to make such unnecessarily restrictive rules which limit a player's ability to choose.

Currently, a player can not even receive two paid visits to a particular college, even if there is sincere interest in both quarters and the kid, who perhaps may have visited in the fall of his Senior year, would like to return in the spring to evaluate the school in light of all he has learned about schools in the interim.

The concern here is clearly not for the kids. It is, as the Select Committee admits, for the schools.

RECRUITING DECEPTION

"Hey Coach, how do you like your new job?"

"Actually I don't know yet, I haven't been there long enough."

"But you've already written dozens of letters to prospects. I guess you know the situation well enough to know that THEY would be crazy not to go there."

"Oh yeah, hey, no problem."

The conversation above actually took place between two friends. They laughed. They understood. Assistant coaches are changing jobs all of the time. They do the best they can at the place where they happen to be. That's how they get promoted. Of course.

Below is the kind of letter they write to prospects:

BEAUTIFUL, TWO-COLORED

LETTERHEAD UNIVERSITY

May 14, 1982

Dear [name omitted]:

Congratulations! We have been corresponding with several coaches and teachers in your area, as well as with some of our alumni, and they have all recommended you as an outstanding student and athlete who has exhibited just the qualities we are looking for in a young man who will represent our basketball program. Your community speaks of quality, dignity, and character when referring to you, and we applaud this.

Our basketball program has a very rich and cherished tradition. Our prestigious reputation speaks for itself, but we want you to take time to investigate us and see for yourself why Letterhead University ranks among the elite in the country. Briefly,

— The academics are unique. We have degree programs in **every** imaginable field of study!

— The environment is unique. There's not another like it in the entire nation!

— The basketball program is unique. The opportunity to play is unparalleled. We are expanding our national schedule and we are playing some of the top teams in the nation.

Finally, our entire basketball staff and administration are committed to championships and quality people. We believe that college should be fun, rewarding, and stimulating. Letterhead University offers this and more. Please find time to return our questionnaire so that we can get to know you better. All of us here at Letterhead University are looking forward to meeting you in the near future. Together, we can soar to great heights.

Sincerely,

Signature

[Coach's Name]
Coach of Basketball

"Two-colored letterhead" is a good name for one of these letters. Nearly all these letters look terrific. The letter above is an *actual* letter from a head coach at a major university to a prospect. The name of the college has been changed (and specific information identifying the college has been omitted) to protect the guilty school from being singled out for its guilt, which would be unfair since hundreds of schools use this identical recruiting method.

Although the letter looks very personal, it is a computer-generated form letter which most likely was sent out to hundreds of kids who went to all-star camps or whose names happened to get on various recruiting lists.

This coach, despite having signed his name, had no knowledge whatever of the qualifications of the prospect he was writing to. The coach had no knowledge whatever that the kid had not yet passed any Junior year courses, nor that the kid had been thrown out of school on an alledged drug violation, even though the letter explains clearly that several people had recommended the kid highly as a fine student and as an outstanding citizen in his community.

COMPUTERIZED RECRUITING

Allowing these computerized form letters to go out EACH WEEK is one of the most deceptive practices utilized by college coaches. Every year hundreds of kids, and especially their unsuspecting parents, go through the year believing they are being highly recruited, when in fact they are not even being considered. Their names, if indeed on any real list at all, are far down the way, the fifty-eighth or fifty-ninth choice, just in case everything goes wrong or the kid shows some real, actual promise later on. They figure, they can't know everyone right away, so it's better to recruit everyone as though he's a top prospect. Then, when they finally identify who it is they really want, they will already have been recruiting him heavily and they won't be behind anyone else in the battle for his services.

SORTING THROUGH OFFERS

How many times have you read that so-and-so, some fine little high school athlete, is "sorting through the offers" still trying to decide where he is going to go to school? What he is trying to decide in many many cases — though he often doesn't know it until it hits him like a boulder late in his Senior year — is if he has any offers at all, in all that mail.

Some schools go as far as to offer definite scholarships by mail in one of their voluminous weekly mail-outs. Then, when the kid calls and asks them for that scholarship later in the spring, they say, "Oh, since we didn't hear from you, we thought you didn't want it. We went and offered it to someone else." (They were of course careful to word the offer originally in such a way that the kid would have no sense that he needed to give an immediate yes or no.)

Oh well, it's a tough business, right?

SOME OF THE TOP SECRETARIES IN THE NATION!

We warn our kids at the Prep Stars Invitational All-Star Basketball Camp that they are likely to be recruited by some of the top companies — IBM, Wang, Texas Instruments — and some of the top secretaries in the nation! They DO have to be warned not to mistake the mail for sincere interest, and they have to take time to explain to their parents not to carry those letters to work, beaming with pride. Better to wrap the cat's droppings in them and wait for a personal visit.

BRING IN THE SURGEON-GENERAL

If the NCAA wants to stop this deception perpetrated on students and their families, it can quit wasting time visiting the top one hundred prospects — which may be done more for ego-gratification than to help the kid — and begin stamping a warning from the Surgeon-General on the top of EVERY recruiting letter that any college sends to a prospect.

"WARNING: This letter may be hazardous to your health. Please recognize that this letter in no way indicates sincere interest in you or your future, nor does it imply any knowledge whatever of your ability as a student or athlete."

BOOKLETS ON BEING RECRUITED

If the NCAA sincerely wants to help the athlete in the recruiting process, besides enlisting the help of the Surgeon-General, the NCAA should put a great deal of effort into producing booklets that would explain the recruiting process thoroughly, as well as how to deal with it. For example, the Select Committee reports:

"Students report telephone calls around the clock, volumes of mail that are incomprehensible, and a total loss of privacy."

Then why not a booklet on "Handling Calls and Mail, and Maintaining Your Privacy During the Recruiting Process?" The NCAA falls short of actually helping anyone. Their specialty is regulation, which brings us to the final phase of recruiting, the so-called pressure.

RECRUITING "PRESSURE"

Most of the people who term the recruiting of high school prospects as "pressure" have never gone through the process themselves. When a prospect does use that word in relation to his own experience, it is usually because he has learned the terminology from newspapers. Actually, it isn't really so tough being heavily recruited.

The NCAA has hundreds of rules to restrict recruiting. High school coaches, often with ambition and egos in the way, may isolate their stars still further, while they try to orchestrate a player's contacts and narrow his choices according to their own preferences. In many cases, a high school coach merely wants attention himself. It's his brief time to get the ear of the big-timers, to be invited to work at college summer camps, and to get to rub shoulders with, and be recognized by, the big names in the sports world.

Coaches claim they do these things "for the kids," to keep them away from high rollers and shady characters and would-be exploiters. But in the process, more often, they merely do the kids a disservice.

I personally feel that the college recruiting process was one of the highlights of my life both socially and educationally.

Through contacts with hundreds of people and through the bombardment of questions — what do you plan to major in? what factors will influence your decision? do you prefer a small school environment? what do you want to be? — a prospect has to learn about himself, and he has to learn how to express his ideas.

Every super salesman has a story. They all claim to be THE BEST. If they come from schools with less than the best academic reputation in the nation, then perhaps they have the best athletic program in the southwest corner of a particular state. The variety of claims and angles force a player to learn to separate fact from fiction.

It CAN be a great education. But most athletes don't get it anymore. The chance to make lifelong associations through constant contact with alumni is impossible. Rules strictly limit the associations possible, even with the man who may become the prospect's coach. The restrictive rules no longer permit real friendships to form. Nor do they permit enough contact to make good decision-making likely. It was better for prospects — more personal, more human, more enjoyable, and more informative — when coaches could take prospects and their families out to dinner as often as both groups wished to go.

In the guise of protecting prospects, the NCAA has stripped them of a once-in-a-lifetime experience, and in its place are early signings based often on scanty information. The limited contact allowed gives the superficial, insincere coach a real opportunity to compete — with little time for his true personality to be revealed.

High school kids who have been taught to say they "just wanted to get the decision over with" so they can "enjoy their Senior year in high school" don't know what they are missing. But the NCAA should.

It really isn't so much pressure being wanted, and being pursued. Mostly it's fun. And it's controllable. Coaches don't purposefully try to irritate a kid. They will take no for an answer once they are made to realize the guidelines a kid or a family has set up. In fact, they are anxious to follow those guidelines in order to make a good impression.

Recruiting "pressure" is largely an NCAA-inspired concept, to justify recruiting restrictions which keep schools from having to spend a lot of money to compete for players. It's price-fixing. It's unconstitutional. It's typical NCAA. Limit the kids' benefits so there is more money to spend and scatter among friends.

"When we made it possible to red-shirt freshmen, we created a new problem. We can sign 30 recruits a year and have only 95 on scholarship . . . Now we have five years and a potential of 150 athletes who must be reduced to the 95 limit."

—Jim Whacker
Head Football Coach
Texas Christian University

RED-SHIRTING

Red-shirting is the practice of keeping a student-athlete out of action for a year, usually while he gets stronger or matures. A student-athlete, under normal circumstances, has five years in which to complete four years of playing eligibility, so a coach is free to keep any player off the playing roster whenever it appears that such an action would be beneficial to the team.

Originally, the rule seemed like a good one for players. It gave a few late maturing or physically weak kids more time to reach their potential, and it gave an injured kid an opportunity to make up a lost year. However, in recent times, the rule has often been used to keep the whole Freshman class out of the lineup so the whole group could mature and get better. As a result, the practice of red-shirting probably hurts more athletes than it helps. It makes all athletes have to compete against an extra class and leaves the possibility of a 'bench career' (and the accompanying unhappiness) greater than it was before wholesale red-shirting was a common practice.

Schools like Duke University, which do not red-shirt except under extraordinary circumstances and which graduate nearly all of their athletes in four years, are accordingly penalized athletically.

The NCAA rules arising out of the "unfair advantage" concept take no notice of disadvantages suffered due to putting priorities on people and on academic excellence.

"The most discriminated-against single group of people I know is the student-athlete. If you made a list of all of the things where he's restricted and the average student is not, you wouldn't believe it . . . we're putting more and more restrictions on athletes . . .

—Donald B. Canham
Director of Athletics
University of Michigan

"I used to have the opinion they (football players) had an easy way to go. But they put in far more hours. I think during the season they should not be asked to take a full (course) load."

> —Sharon Keitel
> Tutor
> University of Missouri

"Athletes are treated like gold mines to be mined for the enrichment of others, yet they are the only category of students who generate rather than consume revenues."

> —Ernest Chambers
> Nebraska State Senator

"From our perspective, we would think that (drug testing programs) are not the way to clean up athletics. Every athlete is presumed guilty until he's cleared by the results of urinalysis.

"If they (the Big Eight schools) think it's such a great thing, then why are they just doing it for athletics? Why aren't they doing it for faculty and students? It's really a discriminatory program."

> —Joyce Armstrong
> Executive Director
> American Civil Liberties Union
> Eastern Missouri

REGULAR STUDENTS

Perhaps THE crucial consideration affecting the lives of student-athletes is the NCAA's commitment to maintaining the idea that a revenue producing student-athlete is a "regular" student. The implications of this contradictory position become obvious quickly, upon examination of two of the NCAA's own fundamental philosophies and policies.

First, the NCAA Constitution clearly states that athletics are to be pursued, as far as the athletes are concerned, as an "avocation" — as a hobby or "recreational pursuit," though it is clear to everyone that big-time collegiate sports are much more than that.

Second, as far as the NCAA is concerned, great care is taken to assure the public that NCAA sports are fully "educational" in nature. This fully educational nature is especially crucial when it becomes necessary for the NCAA to establish its non-profit status with the IRS, and when, in court cases (like that versus Oklahoma and Georgia regarding television rights), it becomes necessary to explain that various NCAA restrictions on players and regulations on universities should not be subject to typical commercially-intended provisions of the Sherman Antitrust Act (since, of course, the NCAA's mission is an educational one.)

The NCAA has difficulty, however, even with its own identity and definitions of its functions. It is odd, for example, that the schools which make a great deal of money from sports are often cast by certain elements of the NCAA in the role of greedy commercialists — tending too far in the direction of professionalism — in spite of the fact that these greedy commercialist schools in fact put ALL of their profits back into their minor sport programs, which are supposedly educational.

Are sports indeed educational? If they are, then it should be eminently possible to change one fundamental fact of student-athlete life which would be a major step forward for the welfare of student-athletes.

ARE FULL COURSE LOADS REALLY NECESSARY?

Why is so great an effort made to see that athletes must take a full academic course load like every other student? If sports are indeed educational, then the student-athlete should get academic credit for his participation or, at the very least, he should be able to take a reduced course load, especially during his season. Doing this would NOT make him any less an integral part (as required by the NCAA Constitution) of the student body.

There is a perverse insistense on the part of the NCAA that each student-athlete be a full-time student, taking the same course load as other regular students (who are not participating on athletic teams) even while the athletic season is in full swing. In this regard, no consideration whatever seems to be given to the educational nature of the athletic endeavor. If participation in a sport is indeed educational, then a full course load PLUS a sport might arguably be viewed as overload.

There is no apparent recognition by the NCAA that an athlete may often be absent from class, through no fault of his own, and therefore must compete academically at a distinct disadvantage with regular students not forced to miss class.

Why this insistence on regular student status? For all the theorizing and moralizing over this insignificant issue (to the universities), the fact remains (and graduation rates show) that only a small percentage of big-time athletes graduate in four years anyway. So why force athletes to take more courses than they can handle? Why not let them have a chance to compete favorably in fewer courses, rather than poorly in many?

What difference does it make if an athlete takes six years to graduate? Is a normal citizen looked down upon for working and taking just two courses per semester in night school?

Universities are filled with part-time students, "associated" students, part-time professors, and visiting artists. The university serves a wide variety of needs in a community and is generally proud of its diverse forms and associations. Why shouldn't the revenue producing student-athlete be one of these diverse forms? Why does he have to be exactly like everyone else in an environment where no one is exactly alike? Why is the NCAA trying desperately to force the athlete into a traditional pattern while the universities are simultaneously making sweeping changes in order to accommodate and respond to a wide variety of community needs and life styles?

A PHOBIA FOR PROFESSIONALISM

Clearly, the NCAA is so beset by fear of the extreme situation — that of pro teams attached to the universities by the thinnest thread or by name only — that it is afraid to propose even the most obvious, intelligent changes. Any change is apparently looked upon as a chink in the armor, a crack in the pristine mantle of education.

Nevertheless, in consideration of the diversity of forms and associations within a university community, it is illogical to insist on full, regular-student (academic) status for athletes who are participating in the physically demanding, time-consuming, psychologically pressurized environment of major college sports. This is especially true in view of the fact that the revenue producing student-athlete makes a unique and very significant contribution to the university — literally paying the way of (often) the entire minor sport program — which the other students do not make.

STUDENT-ATHLETES ARE INDEED SPECIAL

Student-athletes PRODUCE revenue. They contribute MORE to the universities than they take away. Why is this fact of university life so seldom acknowledged?

The athlete, instead of being recognized for his specialness, is put in an academically disadvantaged situation and denigrated for his failure as a regular student.

The NCAA's foolish insistence on regular student status for athletes is akin to requiring regular citizens associated with the universities to take full course loads, even though they may perhaps be holding full-time jobs in addition to attending night school.

What justification is there for forcing the student-athlete to succeed in as many courses as a regular student not participating in athletics?

Why not reward the student-athlete for his special (financial) contribution to the university? Why not reward him with different status? He IS indeed different.

It is time the NCAA openly acknowledges that big-time athletics are not pursued by athletes as a mere "avocation" and that this is NOT bad. It is time that the NCAA lets the athlete raise his self-image and lets him compete favorably academically by allowing him to take a reduced course load at least during the time his season is in full swing.

This is easily enough accomplished. Football players could take reduced course loads, perhaps just two courses, in the fall semester, when all of their games are played; while basketball players could take reduced course loads in the spring semester. Further, schools could see to it that only non-conference, close-to-home basketball games would be scheduled for December, so that games would not interfere with final exams and study schedules in the first semester.

There is a variety of ways to minimize the student-athlete's burdens while enhancing his image and chances for success both on and off the field, but the NCAA seems either unable or unwilling to do anything bold and positive, apparently because of narrow-mindedness related to this out-dated and unrealistic (but nevertheless cherished) concept of 'regularity.'

The NCAA's philosophies with respect to major college football and basketball players are old-fashioned, inadequate, and unacceptable. They are replete with contradictions. See for yourself. Here are the words of the NCAA's Select Committee on Athletic Problems and Concerns in Higher Education, on the "regular" student issue.

"Academic standards for Division I student-athletes should be more demanding . . . consistent with the fact that other students who receive performance scholarships are expected to exceed the academic performance of the student body in general."

Are those 'other students' in turn expected to exceed the ATHLETIC performance of the student body in general? How can such a statement be made by a "select" committee?

The NCAA is excessively concerned that the athlete be a regular student in many ways (academic and financial) which are detrimental to him, yet it is quick to single out the athlete in other areas and discriminate against him.

The same Select Committee that concluded that Division I student-athletes should be required to attain higher academic performance levels, also said:

"This set of recommendations [basically consisting of singling out Division I football and basketball players for varsity ineligibility as freshmen] has been structured to constitute a "package" that recognizes the greater pressures on Division I football and basketball players . . ."

How did the Select Committee arrive at such conclusions? How can any committee recognize greater pressures, yet require higher than normal academic levels? How can they expect athletes in general to compete equally with students who generally have better academic backgrounds, higher SAT scores, and more time to devote to their studies — to say nothing of a less distracting "avocation?" Don't they realize that requiring equal course loads dooms most athletes to inferior performances in the classroom?

An NCAA in tune with the times, which recognized that special students need special student status, could do much to raise the self-image of student-athletes while raising their public image and graduation rates as well.

The out-of-touch leadership of the NCAA may be the only people who look upon big-time student-athletes as "regular" students. They aren't. They haven't been for at least twenty years.

A GRAND REMEDIAL PROGRAM

A special remedial program would solve the problem of good athletes being admitted to college before they are ready to do college work.

A grand remedial program, funded with basketball and football championship money could allow each major school, each year, to designate several athletes to enter the program.

The program would be run by academicians with no connections to the athletic teams. As soon as the students were prepared to do college work — based on standards that the academicians would develop (perhaps the standards set up by Proposition 48?) — the students would be eligible to move into college.

The entire program could be run within one specially created school. Certainly, such a school would feature great basketball and football games — all within the school itself — yet the focus of the school would be on academic preparation.

A program of this nature would provide a place where athletes unprepared for college academic work could go to remedy their problem areas — without paying a cent, without losing any eligibility. It would be collegiate basketball and football players, through their championship funds, helping up-and-coming basketball and football players.

Imagine a school of 250 basketball players and 250 football players, doing no traveling for games, having only short periods for athletic practice each day but plenty of time for the best instruction available in order to educate themselves.

What a tremendous use of championship money — to send athletes to college prepared to get the most of their educational experience.

"This is something that goes on all over the country. It has happened because the NCAA Constitution has changed over the last ten years and has allowed the universities the right to refuse or discontinue the scholarship. Oh, there has to be 'justifiable cause' found to prevent this, but in reality, these are one year scholarships.

"They (a major university) said he (a player) had a bad attitude and was a bad influence to the team. They gave no substantiation to that . . .

"I have heard of other cases where kids were kicked off or run off the team, and they had nothing to do. They couldn't afford an attorney. So they just went home."

—Scott Britan
Attorney for an athlete who appealed
a non-renewal of his scholarship.

SCHOLARSHIP RENEWAL

In the August 14, 1985 issue of The NCAA News, the first line of a story reads:

"ONLY four percent of 16,000 student-athletes representing a majority of NCAA member institutions, were denied renewal of their athletics grant-in-aid in 1983-84, according to a study conducted for the Association's Administrative Committee."

ONLY four percent? That is FOUR players off EVERY major college football team in the nation. Does that sound like a small number — when you consider how avidly each kid is recruited?

Does it sound like a small number when you think of the likelihood that, here and there, there are three schools together that renewed ALL of their athletic scholarships? That would mean, somewhere, SIXTEEN football players off one team did not have their scholarships renewed. Seen in this way, four percent suddenly becomes an enormous number.

The reasons cited for the non-renewals were "poor academic performance by the athlete" (29 percent), and "discontinued participation in athletics" (26 percent).

What does "discontinued participation" mean? Did these kids — one per team on every team in the nation — just lose interest in their sport after being so avidly recruited just a year or so before?

And why do the percentages stop at 29 and 26? That only adds up to 55 percent. What happened to the other 45 percent?

The article cites "poor athletics performance, disciplinary problems, injuries, and transfers to other institutions."

Is POOR ATHLETICS PERFORMANCE a reason not to renew what is claimed to be an educational "gift?" (They ARE called "gifts," you know, for legal purposes, in order to make sure that athletes are not eligible for workmen's compensation and other benefits when these scholarships are terminated.) Why would an educational grant be terminated for INJURIES?

"Only four percent" — four guys off your favorite football team — seems like a very high number in terms of human lives; numerically, though, it's only four of a hundred. No big thing for an educational association with TV contracts and big economic issues to fight for.

REPRESENTATION

Representation is what athletes lack. Athletes do not have any form of representation whatever within the NCAA. They do not have any voting power, nor do they even attend the conventions.

The NCAA bureaucrats claim that student-athletes have representation because they can take their problems and concerns to their 'faculty reps' (who athletes seldom can even identify) or to their coaches, although the views of both of these groups are often in direct conflict with those of the players.

More than two hundred years ago, at the Boston Tea Party, the New

England colonists acknowledged, to the lasting benefit of all Americans, the intolerability of "taxation without representation."

Today, the revenue producing student-athlete is even more egregiously taxed than was the colonist in Boston, yet he hears, in the same paternalistic tones, that everything is being done with his best interests in mind.

"We have abundant money available in Division I basketball — so much so that many schools endeavor to become Division I teams, and clumps of teams form new conferences, just to partake of the NCAA tournament and regular season revenues.

"Division I basketball needs the same kind of grouping (as Division I-A football) with the schools that are paying the freight of all the others being able to regulate their own affairs . . . I find it unfair for a group of schools within the 276-member Division I, wanting to pare their athletic budgets down to the bone, to be able to trim down the staffs of the bigger schools as well."

—Dean Smith
Head Basketball Coach
University of North Carolina

RPMCAA

An RPMCAA — a Revenue Producing Major College Athletic Association — is precisely what is needed, in place of the NCAA, to run big-time collegiate sports.

The NCAA has more than 800 member schools, yet admits readily that nearly all the problems are centered in the hundred or so schools that have sports programs which make money.

There is no intelligent reason for continuing to let the NCAA rule the hundred-plus revenue makers, whose needs and concerns are vastly different from the rest of the NCAA's constituency.

It makes perfect sense for the revenue makers to split from the NCAA, but as government agencies have so capably and consistently shown, special groups of people are not inclined to relinquish their power willfully, merely because logic and intelligence may warrant it.

George Washington, though famous for his presidency and his victories as a general, is REVERED for his rare willingness to step down from a position of power. Few organizations or individuals do that from any other sense but obligation or ill health.

When basketball players find a method by which to withhold their earnings from the NCAA, then the association may graciously decide to step aside. Until then, it is very unlikely that the NCAA will call for an overhaul as a matter of practicality and intelligence.

213

RUN-OFF

Run-off is what coaches often do to players when they recruit more players than they can use in order to get a few players that they need.

The process is simple. Bring in a lot of players, run-off those who fail to produce, and do the same thing next year. A player who doesn't quickly contribute to the team needs to be pushed out of the program. There is a limited number of scholarships permitted, so a coach has to make sure he gets the most from each one.

If a mediocre player sticks around for five years, he is a drag on the program. He decreases the odds, each year that he is in school, that all the team's voids will be successfully filled.

Recruiting is not an exacting business. No one knows for sure what high school players will be stars in college. Some high school players develop tremendously in college, while others never seem to improve at all. Players especially fail to get better once they realize they have been shoved to the side and labeled a disappointment.

Players sense quickly when they are being ignored in practice, and many know in advance that they have almost no chance of being put in a game. At this point, the sport itself usually quits being enjoyable.

This cycle happens to many players each year, at every school, but nevertheless, the present system continues to allow coaches to make up for their recruiting mistakes at the cost of very unhappy experiences for the people involved. Put another way, it BENEFITS a coach to treat his reserves poorly — in particular the ones far down the bench — because there is a better chance they will decide to transfer, thus opening up a scholarship that can be given to some new hopeful, young player who believes HE can make it big.

This system goes merrily on, though seemingly in direct contradiction to the NCAA's stated purpose of providing an enriching experience for the participants in each NCAA sport.

The worse a coach treats his players who did not pan out, the better chance there is that they will leave and permit him to bring in more players with the potential to help the team. This is one of many NCAA rules that reward behavior that is directly in opposition to players' interests and humane principles. The willingness of a coach to run a player off his team actually gives him a competitive advantage over those coaches who treat all of their players with respect and who attempt to work with and develop each of the kids they recruit.

"You see, coaches' jobs compared to 15 years ago, are incredibly lucrative. Salaries are escalating unbelievably ... "

—Bobby Knight
Head Basketball Coach
Indiana University

SALARIES

In a New York Times article of 6-21-85, entitled "Coaching Salaries Zooming," columnist Sam Goldpaper reported that Joe B. Hall's earnings at the University of Kentucky, before he left, were $600,000 while Eddie Sutton, Hall's replacement, earned $400,000 at Arkansas. Said Goldpaper, "(Dean) Smith, (Digger) Phelps, (Bobby) Knight, and (John) Thompson are thought to be earning more than $300,000 a year" — along with Villanova coach Rollie Massimino now that he has a national title under his belt.

Pro coaches are known to average about $300,000 a year, so the figures above for the college coaches are presumably accurate, otherwise Dean Smith would not be likely to claim, as he did in that article, that "in recent years, the earning gap between the college and pro coach has been closing."

Perhaps the figures are inflated somewhat. But a few tens of thousands notwithstanding, these are nice earnings. So are the $3500 per TV show known to be paid to Ohio State football coach Earle Bruce, or the shoe company contracts of several coaches, reportedly in the neighborhood of $100,000 in some cases.

How much does North Carolina State basketball coach Jim Valvano make for his many promotions? Raleigh (NC) newspapers put it at well over $100,000 — with some reports of his total earnings getting near the half million mark.

So the top coaches make a lot. So what? These coaches have risen to the top of a very competitive profession. They deserve what they are making — maybe more.

Yet it seems unbalanced that they are able to benefit so handsomely from the public interest in their sports while the athletes themselves may not benefit at all.

Even more unbalanced, though, are the salaries of the NCAA bureaucrats, whose actions are often contrary to the public interest — at least if you believe the Supreme Court — and who, in any case, certainly can claim no widespread public support.

Here are the salaries paid in 1984 to NCAA employees as a group, in each of the various major departments:

Administration	$891,233
Championships	$414,609
Communications	$482,886
Enforcement	$453,891
Publishing	$343,773

Over $2,500,000 just to pay NCAA bureaucrats' salaries.
    Hmmm. Amateur sports. Amateur sports.

"There's something less than logical about the NCAA giving 45 post-graduate scholarships to students who are from wealthy families. True, these NCAA Scholars have had excellent grades, but why not give them an honor — and give the money to the student-athlete who needs it?"

—Dean Smith
Head Basketball Coach
University of North Carolina

THE NCAA POST-GRADUATE SCHOLARSHIP PROGRAM

Based on the reports in The NCAA News, and based on various NCAA public service announcements, you get the impression that the NCAA is very proud of its post-graduate scholarship program. The NCAA News of June 19, 1985 reported that, since 1964, the NCAA awarded scholarships worth $2,304,000 to 1624 student-athletes.

Do these sound like impressive numbers for a non-profit, educational association whose national basketball tournament was sold to CBS for 1985, 1986, and 1987 for $96,000,000?

In 1985, when the Division I national basketball tournament made a net profit of more than $30,000,000, Division I basketball players received a paltry, abysmal, outrageous $10,000 in NCAA scholarships. Five Division I basketball players received grants. (They are not even assured that many. One Division I player pulled in an 'at-large' scholarship!)

The current NCAA program calls for the awarding of ninety, $2,000 scholarships annually — 25 to football players, 20 to basketball players (10 to men and 10 to women in all three divisions), and the remaining 45 to players in other sports.

It is difficult to understand how the NCAA can publish facts and figures like these with a straight face, as though they have such a wonderful record on education.

Providing only 180 thousand dollars per year, and less than 2.5 million over twenty years, is less than most forms of acknowledged tokenism. Giving $10,000 back to the players who generate more than $30,000,000 is an outrageous insult that can only inspire cynicism and disdain.

This policy would be egregiously wrong even in a climate where one hundred percent of the Division I basketball players were graduating and were the object of consistent public adulation. In the present climate, it is pure theft.

What would make sense would be a $10,000,000 or $20,000,000 annual scholarship fund guaranteeing that any basketball player who wished to further his education — whether to graduate or to go on to become a surgeon — would have a full scholarship, spending money, and other expense allowances to enable him to get as much education as he wished throughout his life.

Basketball players generate sufficient revenues to fund a program of this far-reaching nature. But this year, the NCAA granted them five, $2,000 scholarships.

Hooray, hooray.

"I haven't talked about bowls after five football games during 27 years at Penn State. Not even to the (13 representatives of) bowls did I talk about bowls. I just visited with them socially."

—Jim Tarman 10-12-85
Director of Athletics
Penn State University

BOWL SELECTION COMMITTEES

Bowl selection committees are among the biggest farces, the biggest wastes of money, the biggest testaments to the crony system that steals money annually from revenue producing major college athletes.

Selection committees representing each of sixteen bowl games spend the weekends throughout the football season wining and dining colleagues on expense account money that will be deducted from the profits that the players generate during the holiday bowl season.

Assuming that each bowl has at least, like the Sun Bowl, eleven selection committee members, that makes 176 "scouts" criss-crossing the country watching football games — all just to select some 27 teams to play in the sixteen bowls without two previously-committed teams.

The Orange Bowl, though needing only one team (having already a commitment each year from the Big Eight champion) annually spends over $50,000 on "Team Selection" even though Selection Committee Chairman Nick Crane admitted in the Pittsburgh Press (10-16-85):

"There are no negatives with Penn State as far as a bowl prospect is concerned . . . It's strictly a question of their won-loss record and their rating in the polls."

So why was HE there watching the game in person? What a waste that thirteen bowl representatives appear at a Penn State-Alabama game in October — and they don't even talk to anyone about football! Thirteen bowl representatives here, a dozen there, ends up costing more than a million dollars by the season's end.

I have said repeatedly, with all due deference to the bowl selection committees, that my brother Dave, an avid sports fan with a Masters Degree in Physical Education, could — if armed with just a subscription to USA TODAY and a good TV set — undertake the selection process, arrive at approximately the same group of 27 teams, and do it for not more than half a million, if asked politely.

A savings, for football players, of a whopping $500,000!

SEVEN YEAR SCHOLARSHIPS

In 1967, while being recruited as a first team Parade Magazine All-American, I was personally offered a seven year scholarship by representatives of a university. I had indicated a desire to attend law school after graduation from college, and the representatives of this particular university felt my value to their program would warrant providing me with a seven year scholarship to fulfill my personal goals.

It was necessary to turn down the offer, because it was — and still is — against NCAA rules for a player to accept an offer which includes provision for graduate studies.

You read that correctly. The NCAA, a non-profit, EDUCATIONAL association, prohibits a student from accepting even a scholarship which would further only pure, educational objectives.

There is only one reason for this seemingly absurd prohibition. The six hundred-plus small schools within the NCAA — the schools with sports programs which do not produce revenue — cannot afford to offer seven year scholarships.

Therefore, to protect themselves, they vote consistently to prohibit the schools which are capable of providing such scholarships from doing so.

The result is crystal clear. The NCAA consistently subjugates the rights of individual student-athletes to the arbitrary desires of the small schools which want to compete at levels which their means do not warrant.

This "one room schoolhouse" syndrome — making the gifted students learn at the pace of the dull — is THE central fact of collegiate sports life which assures that student-athletes cannot get what they are entitled to. (The dictates of so-called amateurism in denying players their fair share pale in comparison to this one room schoolhouse effect.)

There is no logical or legal reason why the large, financially able schools should not be able to compete against each other and reward student-athletes in proportion to the value that all of the major schools recognize they have.

This is blatant COLLUSION on the part of the NCAA and the six hundred-plus schools with non-revenue producing football and basketball programs AGAINST student-athletes, denying them the opportunity to realize their economic value in a free market system. It defies any sense of American justice, especially because the NCAA, even within the legal scope of the broad authority of voluntary associations, can show no essential goal being furthered by this excessively restrictive policy.

The NCAA, by already recognizing the need for divisions within its membership, has given up any case it may have wished to make in behalf of homogeneity and conformity.

The present system furthers no end but the NCAA's perverted brand of Robin Hoodism, stealing from the rich and the potentially rich in order to consolidate their own personal power.

SLUSH FUNDS

This is one more of those castrations of the English language, perpetrated by the NCAA and the media, which mislead the public into thinking that big-time sports are rife with corruption and abuses intolerable to society and to institutions of higher learning.

A slush fund as existing in college athletics today, is some money — and not very much in most cases — which a coach may use to help out players who need some financial assistance. If NCAA rules had any relationship at all to economic realities, each school would be permitted by the rules to have such a fund, though of course they would name it a "contingency" fund, not a slush fund.

A contingency fund would require no dramatic change in the rules or focus of collegiate athletics, and it would go absolutely unnoticed by the public as the schools ran their day-by-day operations. A rule might merely state that schools may collect $20,000 from alumni or friends of the university for the purpose of the contingency fund. The NCAA could even require an annual accounting, making each school submit a report noting the amount, purpose, and recipient of each expenditure.

Most casual fans would suppose that there already IS such a vehicle or mechanism for providing, within the NCAA rules, for emergencies and special situations which may arise.

As for the terrible slush funds themselves, there are no cases reported of $100,000 slush funds, where each football player, for example, could get a whole thousand dollars during a year with which to do up the town. The University of Florida's "extremely serious" slush fund of 1983 and 84, notably, was just $4,000 — enough for each football player, over the course of the year, to receive a menacing 14 cents per day!

There's no telling what kind of corrupting effects THAT kind of money might have on a young man.

"It's the unfairness that I don't like . . . we sacrificed for the symbolic character of what's going on here."

—Dr. Charles Young
Chancellor, UCLA

"I think it was a chicken vote. You can not separate harsh penalties from due process. That's a large omission.

"The presidents are not as yet knowledgeable about what the NCAA does in terms of enforcement procedures . . . "

—Donna Lopiano
Director of Women's Athletics
University of Texas

"If they do know the full consequences of their actions, then they have demonstrated a cold-blooded determination to protect the images of their schools at heavy cost to the innocent."

—Ron Green
Sports Editor
Charlotte (NC) Observer

THE NCAA SPECIAL CONVENTION

The NCAA Executive Director, the NCAA President, and reporters throughout the nation hailed it as a great step forward for athletics and for higher education. The university presidents themselves, it was said, grabbed the reigns of power and took unprecedented initiative to bring intercollegiate athletics under control.

The Convention, supposedly, was organized around two basic issues, integrity and economics. Oddly, however, there was no discussion of the integrity of stealing the money of a certain group of athletes, nor was there any discussion about fairly compensating those athletes. As the presidents view integrity and economics, these matters concern only the public perception of the integrity of the universities, and the economic impact of athletics on the universities' treasuries.

Essentially what the presidents did in this "historic" special convention in New Orleans was make a grand statement for the benefit of the public that they were cleaning up college athletics. There was little discussion, little opposition on any of the twelve items on the program. Everyone went to New Orleans with the purpose of making a statement to the public. They reiterated that central concern throughout the convention — at any time someone brought up anything of a dissenting nature.

So, the presidents spoke. They established greater "institutional control" of athletics programs — something any good president certainly should have had all along. They provided for outrageous penalties that

220

could suspend whole programs for two years — probably illegally. (But they weren't at all concerned about legality. They wanted to make a STATEMENT TO THE PUBLIC.) They added new restrictions and punishments for the players — ALL NCAA conventions do that. They added some strict punishments for coaches, and they added some paper work for their members.

There wasn't really anything particularly special about the 5th Special Convention, except that it showed that even college presidents, when subject to public pressure, can act hastily and put rules on the books with little thought regarding the consequences of their actions.

The presidents went to New Orleans to make a statement to the public, and they succeeded famously. Student-athletes, in typical fashion, were totally unrepresented, and their interests were trampled once again. The Convention further implanted the propagation of pettiness and the climate of fear and paranoia surrounding college sports.

With a full measure of piety and self-righteousness, the presidents voted for each proposition in landslide, nearly unanimous fashion. No one present felt guilty or responsible for any abuses that have become rampant throughout collegiate sports. Of course the 600-plus little schools don't have such problems, and the presidents of big schools which did have current probations (or investigations going on) felt sufficiently removed from the unscrupulous coaches whose win-at-all-costs attitudes brought on the whole mess. There was no recognition, no discussion, of their own hypocrisy, their own willingness to steal from one group, to provide for a national sports welfare program at the expense of the big producers, no discussion of unfairness, no concern whatever expressed for the welfare of student-athletes.

The 5th Special Convention was a grandstanding gesture, a public relations ploy that assuaged public concern for the moment and kept the crucial issues neatly under the rug.

Blame it on others, look what THEY did. Without a trace of culpability noticeable anywhere, the proceedings were reminiscent of Orwell's "Animal Farm."

But the neighing and bleating and baa-ing won't truly be heard by the public until the innocent victims are slaughtered.

"I said years ago that some athletes will have the guts — and I'd like to be coaching that night — somebody will tell them (officials): 'Gentlemen, we will not go out until we get paid.' And, someone will come up with a check."
—Dale Brown
Head Basketball Coach
LSU

PLAYERS' STRIKES

No one likes the idea of a players' strike; and players will likely use strikes only if there appears, after repeated efforts, that there is no other way of bringing about a distribution of benefits that in some way attempts to recognize the real economic value of revenue producing athletes to the NCAA and universities.

Before anyone makes an issue over how repugnant the thought of a strike is, careful consideration should be given to the even more repugnant theft and waste and exploitation occurring now, coupled with the incredible educational benefits that would accrue to players — and to society — in a post-strike era of permanent full scholarships, remedial programs, and the other benefits which could be realized by basketball and football players benefitting from their own multi-million dollar championship playoff events.

Any rational citizen can see immediately the value and the far-reaching benefits of the proposed scholarship funds. For causes like these, strikes are not excessively radical measures.

Striking players suffering the brunt of undue criticism, especially, will merely need to focus their attention on their very worthy goals, not on their methods of achieving them.

Weighing the benefits to be gained against the current waste — and keeping that mismatch firmly in mind — should enable even the faint of heart to stay the course.

To hold up some big games due to 'team sicknesses' wouldn't be the end of the world. It would simply put things in proper perspective, cause some changes, and help the players make speedy recoveries from their illnesses.

222

STUDENT-ATHLETES

When you hear the term "student-athlete" used by the media in these times, it usually is accompanied with rolling eyes, snickering, and comments like "yeah, but can he READ?" The NCAA, on the other hand, has a nice, long, official-sounding definition for student-athletes which involves words like "solicited" and "matriculation" and "jurisdiction." Nevertheless, most student-athletes are simply kids who are trying to get an education and play some ball, and they are doing their best at both, generally bewildered by all the fuss over them, both positive and negative.

"$TUDENT-ATHLETE$"

"$TUDENT-ATHLETE$" is a newsletter published periodically for the purpose of keeping student-athletes, the media, and collegiate sports fans abreast of the latest developments of importance in matters related to the welfare of revenue producing major college student-athletes.

The address of "$TUDENT-ATHLETE$" Newsletter is Box 25824, Charlotte, NC 28212.

STUDENT FIRST

One of the rallying points of administrators — and of do-gooders who suddenly become interested in functioning democracies — is the "student first" concept.

Most of the people who refer to this concept and the need to keep educational priorities in proper perspective (that is, ahead of athletic priorities), usually bring it up with a rise in their voice as though they have made a sudden discovery or have been struck by a wondrous revelation.

"THEY SHOULD BE STUDENTS FIRST!" trumpet the suddenly inspired.

It is best for everyone, at a time like this, be they coaches, students, administrators, or good citizens, to begin nodding approvingly until the inspiration dies.

No reasonable person has any real argument with the relative importance of education on the college campus. And few student-athletes even understand the point. They are students when they are in class or in the library, they are athletes on the field or on the court, and they are eaters in the cafeteria, sleepers (and perhaps lovers) in the bedroom.

What's the big deal about first and second? Student-athletes do not fly to games that are not scheduled, they do not set practice times; and most of them would rather read Mark Twain than a playbook or scouting report, and hear Bruce Springsteen instead of another rousing pep talk at halftime.

For the most part, student-athletes don't give much thought to what they are first and second. They try to do as well as they can at whatever they do, putting in the time necessary to enjoy some degree of success at everything they are involved in.

Some students, of course, drop all classes once they believe they are headed for the pros; and some students fail to improve their athletic skills while spending hours trying to turn a B+ into an A-.

By some perspectives, it might be wise for a student who has but four years to attract the pros — and fifty to become a lawyer — to concentrate more heavily on athletics, especially during his junior and senior years. What difference does it really make if a student takes a bit longer to graduate? The nation is filled with people taking just one course per semester — while working full time jobs. Are these people deluding themselves and victimized by a faulty sense of priorities?

The point is, the whole issue is not as clear cut as the self-righteous proclaimers would have the public believe, and in any case, fortunately, most student-athletes don't pay much attention to these kinds of concepts anyway. They leave that to people with more time to waste.

———————

"[The Division I athletic fund-raising] programs probably raise over $100 million dollars annually."

—John L. Toner
former NCAA President
to the IRS, 1-7-85

STUDENTS ENTIRELY

With all the debate over whether kids are primarily students, or primarily athletes, or athletes first or students first, it might be worthwhile to adopt a totally new concept.

Make athletes "students entirely." Make them EXACTLY like all other students.

That would satisfy typical criticisms like the following one of Rick Taylor, Director of Athletics at Boston University:

"It seems fairly evident that we are doing a poor job of making the scholarship athlete think and do for himself. [We are] creating an environment that has someone else do virtually everything for an athlete."

Certainly someone SHOULD be doing SOMETHING for athletes in

return for all the money they keep athletes from getting.

But why do anything at all? Why not compensate the athletes fairly and let them sink or swim on their own? The answer, of course, is obvious. The coach, making a fat salary off the players, is willing to do whatever he has to do in order to keep the kids in school. It is not the athletes who are demanding that everyone do things for them.

Neither were slaves. Yet plantation owners were more than happy to provide them with housing and food and all the "actual and necessary expenses" they needed. It was a sweet arrangement, all that free labor in return for what could be made to sound like benefits.

If the colleges want to change their relationship with student-athletes, the athletes stand ready.

The athletes could be called "students entirely," meaning they would not be identified as student-athletes, but merely as students. They would not have special dorms, no tutoring programs, no special food, no scholarships.

The universities would be free to put their hand solely to education. If an athlete flunked out, so be it.

How would the athletes survive? On incentive. The alumni could be permitted to give athletes whatever they felt like giving them. Recruiting could take whatever form it wished — the way IBM may offer more inducements than Westinghouse — and athletes could struggle to stay in, and hire their own tutors when necessary, in order to remain a student in good standing.

The alumni could hire coaches and directors of athletics. Why not? One hundred million dollars annually ought to be able to support some good solid football and basketball programs.

With the alumni running the show entirely, the teams could have the same POSITIVE associations with the universities that they have now, but the universities could not be tainted by any abuses that might occur, and there would be no public perception of lack of integrity in the institutions.

What is wrong with this? The sports program would go on — at least the ones the public supported, the athletes would be free to realize their fair market value, and the universities would be free to turn their full attention to the task of educating.

The universities, to make their association with a team real in the minds of the public, could simply stipulate that wearing a State uniform would require being a student in good standing at State. Period.

(Personally, I don't feel this degree of detachment is necessary, but it would certainly solve both the integrity and the compensation problem.)

If universities are sincere about their desire to turn their full attention to education, they should be more than happy to turn over sports to alumni and booster clubs — entirely — and let their students be students — entirely.

225

"They get money and material things in return for their athletic performances. But they alone among career-bound college students are expected to hide that fact from public view, as though there was something shameful or reprehensive about it . . .

"We admire a business student who starts his own business or the drama student who gets a foothold on the stage while still enrolled in school. We should admire the student-athlete in the same way and for the same reason."

—Jeff Riggenbach
Columnist
USA TODAY

SUMMER SCHOOL FINANCIAL AID

NCAA rules prohibit a student from getting any financial aid prior to the fall of his Freshman year. That means, if a kid signs with a school and would like to attend summer school to get a headstart in doing college academic work, he is not permitted unless he can afford to pay all of the bills himself.

The colleges are permitted to pay for summer school after a student has gone through his Freshman year, but not the summer before.

This rule is especially ironic in view of the fact that most people recognize the Freshman year as the most difficult, and many critics argue that no kid should be permitted to play a college football game before he has learned where the library is.

Year after year, there are athletes who could benefit greatly from taking some college courses and getting their feet academically wet in the summer before their first full semester. But the NCAA prevents this, to the dismay of many coaches and student-athletes.

THE TARKANIAN CASE

This court case showed the NCAA to be the power-hungry bureaucrats that they are. The judge in the case, Paul Goldman, admonished (several times) NCAA investigator (now Director of Enforcement) David Berst for his failure to cooperate with the Court, and for his failure to give straight answers to the questions he was asked. The judge made it clear in this case that the NCAA was out to get Jerry Tarkanian, the University of Nevada-Las Vegas coach.

Fortunately, the NCAA lost this case, and fortunately the transcripts of the case are a matter of public record, which makes it impossible for the NCAA to persist with credibility in their contention that they are merely carrying out "the will of the member institutions."

"They build 20,000 seat basketball palaces such as the one at the University of Kentucky and they manufacture so much post-season football that you can imagine watching Arkansas and Southern Cal in the Toilet Bowl one day, but they never tell you why. It is for victory and the glory that accompanies it, of course, but most of all, it is for money."

—John Schulian
Playboy Magazine, 1982

TOILET BOWLS

Each year, under the auspices of the NCAA, a tradition carries on and supports the habits of a useless crony system that lets a group of athletics administrators travel the country, in style, in the guise of setting up a group of important football games that are often referred to by fans as "toilet bowls." These bowls may often feature mighty clashes between seventeenth and nineteenth ranked teams, not exactly the kinds of spectacles that bring family and friends away from the dinner table to gather around the TV set.

The players on many of the teams headed for Citrus and Bluebonnet Bowls are often reluctant to go. Some change their minds, once assured by their coaches that December practices will not be too tough. Many never want to go at all, but they will try, when the time comes, to make the most of the party atmosphere and hoopla surrounding these non-events.

It is not a bad time for the players, since the schools usually feel compelled to spend somewhat lavishly and to treat the players especially well for those several days away, since they can reward them in no other tangible way throughout the year.

Nevertheless, even the players themselves realize what a foolish waste of money it all is. These annual holiday blowouts where everyone throws money around and enjoys the festivities bring to mind old Hollywood portrayals of the fall of ancient Rome — fat people eating big meals, and celebrations carried on vacuously for no particular reason. It is not a pleasant picture. But it is seldom pretty to watch a group of people waste money that belongs to others.

When you consider the money that could be made, AND THE USE THAT MONEY COULD BE PUT TO, from first round championship playoff games, the farce of the present bowl system comes more into focus.

It is a shame to hear the Independence Bowl or the Holiday Bowl be labeled "Toilet Bowls," knowing that many fine people give a lot of their time and effort to make them happen. Yet, it is a shame that Sun Bowl and Liberty Bowl committee members have to put in all that time and effort just to promote games that no one really cares about, between teams which often don't really want to be there at all.

These also-ran bowls pay out to each of their teams a meager half million for all those efforts, tribute to a system that generates little fan interest, has no need of money, and no place to spend it except on floats, parades, and strained hoopla over games that should never be staged.

THE TOXIC WASTE SYNDROME

Almost any time an industry or enterprise is generating a valuable product or service there are residual side effects that are negative. This is true whether you are talking about cotton fields losing nutrients, steel mills spewing smoke, or nuclear power plants producing toxic waste.

What is crucial to any of these endeavors is that money generated from profits be put back into the enterprise in order to deal with the negative side effects. Farmers traditionally planted alfalfa to restore their cotton fields. Industries have had to comply with increasingly strict environmental protection laws, requiring filters and special, often expensive, systems to nullify the side effects of their production.

The Federal government, for example, has a 1.7 billion dollar 'Superfund' in order to deal with hazardous waste, and Congress has present plans — and little disagreement — to expand the present program to at least $7.5 billion.

These statistics are important in that they demonstrate a basic recognition that side effects must be dealt with, not shoved under the rug.

The NCAA has been fond of shoving the problems of major college sports under the rug, while freely and wildly wasting the profits of big-time college sports on totally unrelated matters.

When vast amounts of money start flowing back to the football and basketball programs which generate them, the negative side effects so often talked about will be quickly brought under control.

There are few problems in big-time sports that $100 million could not solve. The problem is, the money generated is quickly stolen by the NCAA or, as they would claim, put to other purposes.

It is time that the universities and the NCAA acknowledge that the problems they point to are a result of their own failures to put football and basketball money back into football and basketball — to solve football and basketball problems.

If, nationwide, the profits from productive enterprises were kept from flowing back to those enterprises, the United States would have no cotton, no blue skies, and nothing but radioactive fallout in the air.

The NCAA has to be blind not to realize this. But the theft goes on.

228

THE "TRUE" STUDENT-ATHLETES

Today's "true" student-athletes in the public eye, and to some extent in their own eyes, are the students who play a sport at a small school with no associated financial aid, or the students who play a minor sport at a big school.

These athletes, supposedly, have THEIR values and priorities in the proper perspective. They don't have some 'whack-o' impression that everything is supposed to be handed to them, that they aren't supposed to have to do anything for themselves, that they don't have to spend most of their time in the library.

This is not meant to assail the minor sport or lower division athlete. He is, usually, as unresponsible for these sentiments as the revenue producing athlete is. Both are victims, or lucky recipients, of the environments they happen to find themselves in.

It is merely ironic, and undeniably a source of irritation at times, that the players now recognized as the "true" student-athletes are often having their ways paid through school, and their equipment and uniforms and travel expenses paid too, by the very athletes who are so often looked down upon.

It isn't often that revenue producing players hear expressions of gratitude coming from the recipients of this welfare. Maybe that's because they know the producers are finally tiring of passively giving.

"There's only one reason for the transfer rule — to keep the stud in the barn."
—Ernest Chambers

THE TRANSFER RULE

The transfer rule requires that any athlete who wishes to switch from one school to another must sit out a full year before he is eligible to compete again.

This rule was never made with the players in mind, but instead to keep coaches off each others' backs.

So, what happens if a kid goes to a school and decides he does not like it? He has to sit out an entire year before he can play at another school. If he is a Senior, perhaps deciding he does not like a new coach, he has to find a school that will offer him a two year scholarship just to get one year of play out of him (and even that could not happen if the kid had already red-shirted or sat out a year with an injury). Of course, there aren't many coaches interested in giving a two year scholarship for a year of play. But it gets more complicated than just that.

A school has to ask and get permission from another school just to talk to a kid who has already indicated a desire to transfer — and the school where the kid is may deny one school that opportunity yet give its approval to another.

Of course a coach would moan and groan over a rule that permitted other schools to recruit kids in his program, but that would be what is "best for the kids" — precisely what people are so often claiming to be doing.

Coaches, athletic directors and college administrators know well that there are many unhappy kids in their athletic programs, but they appear to have no intention whatever of changing the rules in any way that will alter that, especially if a rule change would in any way make their lives more difficult.

This "do what is best for me" method would be more acceptable if players had any representation of their own and any opportunity to push their own interests. But they don't.

An ironic aspect of this rule is that, provided that the violations of a school are bad enough, for instance in the case of Tulane, the players may transfer without having to sit out a year. However, in a case, like that of Mike Giomi at Indiana — where neither the kid nor the school violated any NCAA rule at all — the one year sit-out period is in effect. Giomi could not play at NC State or at any other school until after sitting out one full year.

The difficulty in transferring enables bad coaches to get by — all they have to do is keep a smiling face during three recruiting visits — and it ensures that each school will have unhappy players who feel as if they have no attractive alternative so they stay where they are.

The transfer rule, like so many NCAA rules, was made solely with coaches' benefits in mind. It never did and still does not help the players at all. It does much to hurt them though.

Rarely do any rules get passed that benefit the players. Why should the schools bother? They have slave labor — gladiators, if you like — AND a guise of educating and character-building at the same time. It's a tremendous racket.

There is no moratorium when coaches transfer to another school yet this is usually more disruptive to a sport program than the departure of a player. There shouldn't be one for players either if their happiness is worth consideration.

UNDER THE TABLE

When does anyone ever get MORE than he is worth? What athlete has EVER received inducements that were more than his perceived value?

Student-athletes would be elated to receive, on top of the table, in full view of everyone, whatever inducements, perks, and benefits they are perceived to merit as a result of their abilities.

There is no reason, in America, that the tables should not be turned over so that there is no underside.

"It's incredible no one else has thought of it! We can order a batch of 18-karat gold paper clips and send out attachments with every letter. Gawd, we'll funnel millions to the kids and the NCAA will never know it!"

—Very Innovative
Director of Athletics
State University

UNFAIR ADVANTAGE

If the actual use of solid gold paper clips strains the limits of your imagination, they don't come close to expressing the far-reaching, consequential absurdity of the NCAA's interpretation of the concept of "unfair advantage."

The NCAA's notion of this concept, perhaps more than anything else, is responsible for turning the atmosphere and aura of big-time sports inside-out and making a mockery of it. The natural character of the' enterprise called big-time sports is competitive, high-minded, noble, and proud. With few exceptions, the people involved in big-time college sports have the ability to demonstrate these qualities consistently. To rise to these positions, to have a chance to be successful, these people have had to develop at least a mental toughness, an abhorrence for excuses, and a disdain for frailty. Given any kind of inspired leadership at all, big-time college sports would be a model for the nation and the world.

To a very real extent, Dean Smith, the former U.S. Olympic coach and head basketball coach at the University of North Carolina has exemplified this kind of model. At a school where the football team has a typically inadequate graduation rate, Smith nevertheless graduates nearly 100% of his basketball players year after year. And he has gone far beyond that. He has influenced the state of mind of an entire state of people, not as a result of his notable success but moreso because North Carolinians (even those from rival schools who claim to dislike him) sense (or fear) that he has fully grasped the elements necessary for success in any endeavor — things in combination like pride, unwavering commitment, acknowledgment of others, and meticulous organization.

But it took more than twenty years and something of a legend to build this model in Chapel Hill. And sadly, the rest of the nation has few parallel examples to look to. Within the climate and atmosphere created in big-time sports by the NCAA, a coach has to be a Houdini to balance the rules with common sense, breaking a few ridiculous rules here and there — without developing a general sense of disdain for the aggregate — and yet maintaining not merely a consistent sense of integrity himself but the ability to project and extend that commitment to those around him. It takes, as I have said, a balancing act, especially for colleagues and associates not to be put off by the gray areas of hypocrisy that must inevitably surface periodically.

The NCAA rules, if it is not already clear, FOSTER AND ENCOURAGE PETTINESS and a mean spirit; most of the rules and pettiness can be traced directly to the NCAA's gold-paper-clip rendition of "unfair advantage."

There is an abiding fear, a consistent, outrageous, laughable, mind-boggling, unexplainable concern that someone is going to get some slight advantage over someone else in some trifling way, and not even all the king's horses and all the king's men will be able to patch up the damage after that happens.

My literary abilities are insufficient to adequately explain the totally unnecessary, fundamentally-absurd concern which the NCAA has with this concept. Their interpretation of "unfair advantage" is wholly out of touch with the goals, character, and values of the coaches and programs they preside over.

The big-time coach teaches, on a day by day basis, and imbues — if he does anything character-building at all — those around him with a real disdain for pettiness and excuses and looking over the shoulder at the other guy. The examples of John Wooden and other great coaches have not been lost on those striving to achieve success in sports professions. "Don't worry about what THEY are doing, let's make sure WE can execute perfectly what WE are doing."

In perhaps more typical coaching slang it might go more like, "Hell, let 'em have better equipment, let 'em have their Astro Turf, let 'em fly each kid in here on a Lear jet if they want to, cause when they walk in here on Saturday afternoon, we're gonna kick their ass."

The high-minded spirit, or at least the don't-bother-me-with-pettiness attitude is a sine qua non of the big-time sports experience. If big-time sports has a character-building contribution to make, it is with the development of mental toughness and a consistent requirement to rise above the mundane and get the thing done.

In stark, common sense-defying contrast to this is the NCAA's posture that one team can get an unfair advantage over another by giving one kid a ride home, or one kid's sister an extra meal, or somebody's grandmother a T-shirt she may never wear.

This isn't a writer's carefully constructed hyperbole, to make a point. This is a daily, minute by minute, DEHUMANIZING FACT OF NCAA LIFE. A proof of this viewpoint could read like a Ripley's "Believe It or Not" on pettiness.

CAN CEDRIC HENDERSON PLAY?

Former University of Georgia center, Cedric Henderson, was declared ineligible to play in May of 1985 at the same time as the school was placed on a one year probation for recruiting violations. USA TODAY reported . . .

"The school has appealed Henderson's penalty to the NCAA eligibility committee, arguing his single violation — accepting a 26-mile car ride from a Georgia coach — was neither serious nor intentional.

"Tom Yeager, the NCAA's director of legislative services said the five-member committee will probably conduct a teleconference hearing 'within a couple of weeks.' In a majority of such cases, the player's eligibility is restored, he said.

" 'But I don't think anything's a formality,' Yeager said. 'WHAT'S AT ISSUE IS WHETHER THE VIOLATION GAVE THE SCHOOL A RECRUITING ADVANTAGE.' "

How does anyone read that without amazement? Better yet, how does the NCAA find people willing to sit on a committee and spend part of their lives deciding the whys and wherefores of 26-mile drives?

When are the major universities going to stand up and say **Hey! you are welcome to a recruiting advantage, you can have it, go ahead, it's okay?**

(I assume it is understood that the reason that "unfair advantage" is such an issue is that the NCAA must protect all the tiny schools which have little to offer and therefore fear greatly the possibility that someone may give something they don't have to give.)

AN INSULT TO THE PLAYERS' INTELLIGENCE?
or
AN INNOVATIVE ADMISSIONS PROCEDURE?

Apparently no one has a greater disregard for the intelligence of student-athletes than the NCAA. If the kids are so stupid as to be making their decisions based on T-shirts and 26-mile drives, then clearly they do not belong in college. Is it time that a new form be used to replace the one currently used when a student-athlete signs a "national letter of intent?" The new form might ask why the kid chose the school he is signing with. If the kid explains that "it was an extra 26-mile drive that did it," or "it was the day my sister got the one night's free lodging in an off-campus motel," then the kid can be informed on the spot that he has not passed the entrance qualifications!

Facetiousness is warranted by the character of this subject. However, if the NCAA seriously wants to alter the environment of pettiness which it has created, and if it wants to free people like Dean Smith from having to worry about insignificant matters like the number of contacts he can make and when the quiet period starts and where you can drive a kid or what you can send him in the mail, there is a simple solution.

A COMMON SENSE, EDUCATIONAL APPROACH

In the May 29 issue of The NCAA News is an essay written by University of North Carolina Director of Athletics, John D. Swofford. In the essay, Swofford lists six criteria that might be used to evaluate the success of an athletics program. They are:

1. Consistently competes to the best of its abilities.
2. Graduates a high percentage of its athletes.
3. Adheres to the principles of integrity.
4. Represents its university in a positive fashion.
5. Enhances the college experience of its participants.
6. Produces contributors to our society.

The criteria may not be particularly new or creative, and they may be considered subjective or nebulous. Nevertheless, rather than sitting around Mission, Kansas talking about the relative recruiting advantage a school might gain by giving 26-mile rides, wouldn't the NCAA spend its time more productively by developing a formula for determining an athletic program's success and then **using that formula to determine how much financial aid each school could offer?**

SOME SCHOOLS SHOULD BE GIVEN AN UNFAIR ADVANTAGE

Wouldn't it be great if the NCAA scrapped the pettiness and decided to group the member schools according to their success rating, allowing the more successful schools to offer a kid more financial aid than less successful schools? Wouldn't THIS help educate the kids on which were the better schools to attend? Why not USE the kids' so-called greed to make a buck in order to get them into the best schools?

Would a nationwide draft make sense — with the top selections going not to the losers but to the schools judged most successful?

Easier said than done? Of course. But it would be better than the present system. Wouldn't there be squawking when the NCAA rated one school higher than another? Of course. But there is squawking now, and nearly all of it is over issues that do not truly deserve the attention of intelligent human beings.

A REALISTIC, IMPLIMENTABLE PLAN

Whenever rules get ridiculously petty, the system has broken down. It is time to start over. Clearly, what is needed now in big-time sports is not more rules, but less rules and more education.

In place of the handbook to prospects which explains the uninspiring, lengthy list of NCAA rules, it is time to send booklets on "Making a Wise Choice of a College" and "How to Handle the Recruiting Process."

When students are educated properly, they will make choices based on substantive issues, not on things like T-shirts, car rides, dinners, and plane trips. Then the NCAA and, more importantly, the coaches will not have to concern themselves or give deference to matters below their dignity.

The sweeping, fire-breathed, dragon of the NCAA's interpretation of the "unfair advantage" concept has dragged big-time college athletics down, far below anything that a few isolated (real) cheaters could accomplish. If the NCAA would attack the education-of-athletes concept with the same religious zeal and fanaticism that they use on interpreting 'unfair advantage,' you would have to turn over stones to find an athlete who made a foolish choice.

A SOLUTION EMERGES

Perhaps the answer, after all, is for sports fans everywhere to send some T-shirts to Mission, Kansas; take some NCAA members out to dinner; contact them, personally, more than three times (off-campus!); and send their mothers a small gift. Then, presumably, we could get them to do anything we want!

"John Wheeler has become the scapegoat of (Coach) Jim Haller's resignation... John has been made out to be a disgruntled player seeking revenge, but in reality he represents a disgruntled team seeking justice.

"We would like to emphasize that this statement and the entire investigation was initiated by the team ... "
—Baylor Basketball Team
(Statement signed by 13 of the 14 members—after one of their players taped a conversation with his coach, which led to the coach's resignation.)

"I've always admired (long time AFL-CIO union leader) George Meany ... "
—Walter Byers
NCAA Executive Director

PLAYERS' UNION

Despite the fact that some coaches, administrators, and even many fans will say that they are dead set against the forming of a players' union, it is probably going to be necessary for revenue producing basketball and football players to form one.

When you consider how unjustly these players have been treated up to this time, and the magnitude of the theft and exploitation they have endured, it is unrealistic to think they will get more than nickels and dimes, if anything at all, through the efforts of others.

The attitudes and opinions of those ruling the universities and the

NCAA were formed in earlier times, and they have — many of them — become set and hardened. Few people can be expected (especially not those who have had a hand in the forming of the present policies) to alter their course dramatically, even if the case against them appears obvious to others.

The players will need to act in their own behalf to form a union, but they should be able to accomplish that, and some sweeping reforms, rather easily once they realize fully how much they are worth to their schools and what their union could accomplish.

[See also Part I, chapter 8, "Making the Dream Come True: A Union, a Strike, Whatever it Takes."]

"Hugh Cunningham, highly respected professor of journalism at the University of Florida, has made a long and thorough study of the problems of colleges, athletes, and big-time sports. He points out that a regular student at Florida, eligible for full support because his family can't provide monetary help, can receive $5,020 for two semesters from financial aid sources. Under existing NCAA rules, a scholarship athlete at Florida gets compensation totaling only $4,877."
—Jesse Outlar (11-84)
Atlanta Constitution

"Most colleges promise to make you better culturally and morally, but it is not evident that they do. If my own son came to me and said 'You promised to pay for my tuition at Harvard; how about giving me $50,000 instead to start a little business?' I might think that was a good idea."
—William J. Bennett
U. S. Secretary of Education

"All I can say is 'Wake up everybody.' You can't just offer athletes an opportunity for an education. That is no longer important enough."
—Ernest Chambers
Nebraska State Senator

THE VALUE OF AN EDUCATION

When people start justifying the theft and exploitation of athletes, they are fond of citing the value of an education in terms of earning power over a lifetime. Via this method, they arrive at figures in the hundreds of thousands of dollars, and they try to advance the claim that players are getting literally hundreds of thousands of dollars in return for their athletic ability.

To put this in perspective, I want to give a typical example of the costs of an education, using students from the city I live in, Charlotte, North Carolina.

A student can attend Central Piedmont Community College for a total of $204 per year.

After two years at CPCC, a student can transfer to the University of North Carolina at Charlotte, where the yearly tuition charge is $670.

Two years at Central Piedmont, then, costs $408 (maximum cost) and two years at the University of North Carolina costs $1340. Added together the cost of an education for ANY student in Charlotte, North Carolina is $1748.

Seventeen hundred forty-eight dollars is the value of an education. You need less than two thousand dollars — and NO ATHLETIC ABILITY AT ALL — to get an education.

In many states, the cost is even less.

If you are determined to add in the cost of room and board, let's just take the estimate from the University of North Carolina (at Charlotte) bulletin.

The estimate of total costs for an in-state student at UNCC is $2,720. Multiply that by four and you get LESS than $11,000.

Of course, any student can apply for grants and have much of that $11,000 paid.

Nevertheless, even accepting the $11,000 price tag, it becomes clear that the purveyors of the education-is-valuable justification for robbery are using pure sophistry.

The NCAA and its supporters continually try to make student-athletes grateful for what they are getting BY VIRTUE OF BEING AMERICANS, by virtue of being citizens in a nation that values and provides for the education of its citizens.

But the NCAA deserves no credit for the educational opportunities available to Americans.

What the NCAA offers, in return for athletic ability that fills a 100,000 seat football stadium in Ann Arbor and a 33,000 seat basketball dome in Syracuse, is a scholarship worth somewhere between $1748 and $11,000. This is robbery.

"I know the value of athletics to the student experience and, frankly, we and other public institutions need the revenue and support that athletics can generate."

—Bill Atchley (in the NY Times, 12-12-82)
former President
Clemson University

THE VALUE OF SPORTS

Big-time football programs often pay for a school's entire athletic program. (See "Athletic Budgets") But, as BUSINESS WEEK showed, in a March 25, 1985 article, basketball programs can have an enormous financial impact as well. There is no better example than Georgetown University, a small, 196-year-old Jesuit school "with towering academic credentials" which, in 1973 had a 3-and-23 record and no thoughts of defraying the cost of running a sports program via basketball victories. (Georgetown does not have a football team.)

But along came Coach John Thompson and then superstar Patrick Ewing, and the rest is history — and economics.

The Big East Conference (of which Georgetown is a member) has the most lucrative TV package in basketball. The Conference currently has contracts with CBS, at about $2,000,000 per year; with NBC, at over $1,000,000 per year; and with ESPN for similar sums and even more weekly games.

Take Georgetown's share of that TV revenue and add the Final Four appearance worth $750,000, a dozen or so home games per year averaging at least 13,000 fans, and (don't forget) "booster items" such as hats, T-shirts, mugs, and banners which, according to BUSINESS WEEK, brought in another $200,000.

Those are only the direct sources of income. Patrick J. McArdle, director of the alumni association's annual fund-raising efforts, told the magazine that the basketball team was responsible for "geometric" increases in contributions. Gordon D. Chavis, a regional director of admissions, claims the team deserves "a great deal of credit" for a 33% increase in student applications since 1983.

BUSINESS WEEK added that "the Hoyas, as the team is called, have become a kind of profitable venture that impresses even Georgetown's well-heeled alums."

The revenues for the season ending in 1984 were estimated to be in excess of three million dollars, while the revenues for the season ending in 1985 were likely even more.

There is just one more question to ask. Was there any money left over, after funding fifteen other sports programs, to get the players a couple of pizzas?

VOLUNTARY ASSOCIATIONS

Athletes down through the years have generally fared poorly when trying to take grievances to court against the NCAA and other voluntary associations. This has often been confusing to players and fans who have failed, in many cases, to understand the courts' reluctance to overrule the authority of voluntary associations, even when the injustices involved in some of the cases seemed clear.

The courts, however, have generally reasoned that, since membership is voluntary and since withdrawing, presumably, is possible at any time, there is no LEGAL cause to interfere. In many cases, the courts may even have agreed (morally or logically) with players and others in some particular contest, yet they still ruled in favor of the association on the principle already cited.

According to Professor John Weistart in "The Law of Sports:"

"It is important to reiterate that the court's review will be limited to insuring only that the rule in question is a proper exercise of the rule-maker's authority. It will not evaluate the wisdom or desirability of the rule as drafted, and will not substitute its judgment for that of the rule-maker, even if it would have adopted a different rule had the initial decision been its to make." (p. 48)

This seems inherently wrong, but let me go on, first, to clarify (or at least raise) some other legal issues involved. For example, the courts have "clearly indicated that the right to participate in amateur athletics is not fundamental," (p. 51) and therefore not a right guaranteed by the Constitution. On the other hand, the courts have begun to look harder into the facts of particular cases before them on grounds that the athlete's interest in participating is, in a legal sense, "substantial," not merely extra-curricular. In other words, some courts have recognized that athletes may have significant economic interest in participating, especially if they are talented enough to be pro prospects. Indeed, in Behagan v. Intercollegiate Conference of Faculty Representatives, "The court took judicial notice of the fact that 'to many athletes, the chance to display their athletic prowess . . . is worth more in economic terms than the chance to get a college education.' " (p. 23)

Additionally,

". . . several courts have reached the conclusion that athletic participation is indeed an integral part of the student's 'education,' and is, as such, entitled to the same protection as are other aspects of the educational experience." (p. 22)

These comments are at least more hopeful and they bring us back to THE major issue involving voluntary associations and athletes, because this could be the basis on which athletes eventually get redress against the NCAA when going to court.

Professor Weistart explains that the rules applying to voluntary associations developed from questions primarily involving fraternal, social, and religious organizations, whose problems were considerably different from those which have arisen in the field of sports. (p. 38)

Nevertheless, the courts are convinced that the nature of the relationships within social, fraternal, and religious organizations is parallel to that involving voluntary associations and schools. However, the rules of law which have resulted never did seem — and still don't seem — as though they should apply to the relationship between associations and individual athletes.

"Such reasoning might justify the application of the rules to the schools, which are members of the association, but it would provide a rather slender basis for application to the athletes themselves." (p. 43)

Curiously, Professor Weistart admits:

"Although the courts have commonly applied the private association law to actions brought by amateur athletes, they have never made it clear why these rules should be applicable to the relationship between athletes and those who regulate their efforts." (p. 42)

Certainly it seems entirely obvious to student-athletes, who are not members of the NCAA and whose substantial interests can not be pursued by withdrawing, that the courts' custom of applying association laws to them is itself unjust. The NCAA, for all intents and purposes, is the only game in town. Were it not for that monopoly, the NCAA may not have survived at all. Players have no realistic alternative to the NCAA, and they are brought within its auspices involuntarily.

The obvious injustice here and the gaps in the Law's attempt to deal with student-athlete problems in the past, portend positive changes in judicial findings in the future and offer realistic hope for legal opinions that will significantly limit the NCAA's power.

The NCAA is NOT a voluntary association as far as athletes are concerned, and the courts are just beginning to demonstrate that they recognize that fact.

WELFARE

The NCAA and the universities have created an enormous, wasteful welfare program by exploiting revenue producing basketball and football players.

What other name can be given to the NCAA's massive, money-losing, national championship program or to the funding for the total sports programs at the large universities? Money is taken from revenue producing basketball and football programs and given to all of the other sports.

What justification is there for this? What steps has the NCAA taken toward assuring that minor sport championships will be able to sustain themselves financially?

It is interesting to note that, in principle, this socialist concept is contrary to most of the stated goals that educators have put forth for a considerable period of time. In 1970, when I was in college, Lloyd H. Elliot, the president of George Washington University, said in the Congressional Record (August 12, 1970):

"[Education] would be spurred along if our society could bring greater competition into the educational mainstream by encouraging profit-making educational ventures . . . the profit motive should be put to work to effect economies in education."

Although President Elliott's comments were not aimed specifically at the NCAA at that time, the NCAA has clearly failed to establish that principle with regard to the running of minor sport programs and championships. This is not to over-state the case and imply that educators have not believed in the value of supporting sports programs financially, but it does underline the NCAA's failure to promote the concept of profit-making, adequately, where minor sports are concerned.

Is the NCAA bent on pouring basketball and football money permanently into minor sport national championships? If not, why has the NCAA given travel guarantees and expenses in recent years to participants in minor sport championships even though this was not the case for fifty years in the past?

In view of all of the acknowledged problems associated with the major sports, it is truly astonishing that this Robin Hood welfare system is permitted to go on.

"When a big contributor's son gets into college with sub-par grades and test scores, it's called 'business' or a recognition of economic realities, but when an athlete gets in, it's called winning-at-any-cost."
—Dave DeVenzio

WIN-AT-ANY-COST

This is a phrase that media and NCAA members frequently throw around. Not coincidentally, however, they NEVER name names when they use it.

I challenge anyone to name any coach in America about whom it can be said, 'he wants to win at any cost.'

The point is, there aren't any coaches like that. Some are more exploitive, less sensitive, than others. Each coach has different priorities that become more obvious at one time than another. But, with so much talk of the winning-at-any-cost attitude, it should be possible to name dozens of proponents of that philosophy.

No one can name ANY because the phrase is a distortion, creating in the public an unjustified sense of alarm.

To set the record straight, there are no coaches among the top two hundred schools who conduct themselves in such a way that it is clear they are out there simply to win-at-any-cost.

The phrase should be retired along with the Tulane jersey of John Williams, who was categorically presumed guilty by the nation's media, by the NCAA, and by the NBA despite the presumption of innocence supposed to be accorded to all Americans by the United States Constitution.

OPEN LETTER TO DIVISION I
UNIVERSITY PRESIDENTS

Dear Presidents:

You are being saluted around the nation for taking a stand in behalf of cleaning up the abuses of major college athletics. I personally do not feel that you have studied the causes and sources of the problems carefully enough to take the best possible actions, but nevertheless I understand your desire to take SOME dramatic action in order to restore public faith in our institutions of higher learning.

Many university presidents, including specifically President Singletary of the University of Kentucky and President Friday of the University of North Carolina, have made it clear that the steps taken during the Special Convention are only a beginning; therefore, I would like to suggest some follow-up steps which should accompany those already taken in order to truly make big-time college sports what you want them to be.

1. Compensate basketball and football players in proportion to their economic value to your universities (and feel free, then, to make them pay their way through school just like all of your other students). It is appalling, in America, that kids responsible for generating millions of dollars often end up leaving your universities after four years without diplomas and with no money to show for their efforts.

2. Cut the number of scholarships in both basketball and football sufficiently, so that each player recruited becomes an important member of the team — whose health and personal development are crucial to the team's success.

3. Let scholarships (to be awarded to high school players) be given directly in proportion to the number of players graduating. No graduates, no scholarships. This will assure you that your coaches will be doing their best to see to it that your athletes graduate; otherwise, the coaches will have no chance for success.

4. Repeal Proposal 4 which takes away a player's eligibility permanently if he is caught accepting inducements beyond those stipulated by NCAA rules. (Once you begin compensating players fairly, you may forget this request, but until then . . .) Realize that many kids truly need money and, in accepting it, they are trusting in some adult who has won their confidence and convinced them of the moral rectitude of their acceptance. You yourself would be hard-pressed to claim that stealing food in behalf of starving loved ones is immoral, and you should know — after a review of past NCAA violations — that cheating in the form of "inducements" nearly always involves a very poor athlete. In other words, although your proposal to punish "cheaters" appears noble enough, it was made with seemingly very little understanding of the

242

actual circumstances of the young athletes tempted to accept money and other benefits.

5. Withdraw your university from the NCAA and establish an RPMCAA so that your athletic program can solve its unique problems along with other like programs, unencumbered by the will of hundreds of tiny, non-revenue producing schools whose problems are simply not the same as yours.

6. Grant your coaches tenure so they feel comfortable to be educators and counselors primarily concerned with the total development of the student-athletes with whom they work.

7. Help your basketball and football players create a PLAYERS EDUCATION FUND with the monies earned from both basketball and football national championships, so that each basketball and football player who enters your university will have sufficient counseling and remedial help to be sure that he can compete successfully in your classrooms, and so that each basketball and football player that leaves your university has the comfort of knowing that he can have free education as long as wishes to continue.

Each of these steps is easily accomplished if you and your Division I colleagues merely wish that they be so.

You have already demonstrated your resolve to clean up big-time college sports and to make them what they should be, so there is no reason you should not complete the task you have so famously begun by adding these next steps.

You were right to think that things needed changing, and it will indeed be wonderful when the finishing touches — that help the athletes themselves — are put on your work.

Your speedy action on these steps will make big-time college athletes highly educated as well as highly competitive, and no doubt — with this unbeatable combination — they will be one of America's greatest resources as we move into the 21st Century.

Thank you for your vision and persistence in making this dream a reality.

Gratefully yours,

Dick DeVenzio

OPEN LETTER TO DIVISION I PLAYERS

Dear Division I Football and Basketball Players:

It would be wonderful if college presidents and athletic directors and coaches would all get in your shoes for a year so they could understand you and your concerns. But they have failed you this long, and there is no reason to believe they will quit failing you now or in the near future.

It appears as though you are going to have to have the courage to act in your own behalf if you want to achieve the results and enjoy the compensation you are entitled to.

You must also realize that making something important happen is rarely easy. You are going to have to have guts and persistence, and you are going to have to weather public abuse at times, the same way you have to on a visitors turf or court.

But you know the feelings, you can take it, and you will benefit gloriously if you have the guts and fortitude to make it happen.

Specifically, I think you are going to have to think in terms of a strike. I can help you, and there are others like me — former players — who will also help you. But you have to demonstrate the willingness to act yourselves, before you can expect to get a lot of help.

Your best bet would be to convince the members of one of the teams winning the PAC-10 or Big-10 football championships to strike the Rose Bowl. Being the biggest of the bowls with the largest payout, something like twelve million dollars for one day's work, you can see that this would be an effort worth pinning demands on.

Of course, if you could pull off a New Year's Day strike, holding up all four games unless your demands would be met, this would be ideal.

I think it is reasonable for you to do this. Naturally, a lot of people will say it is crazy and greedy, but then a lot of people called Abraham Lincoln crazy and greedy too.

Anytime people want to change the status quo, there will always be those who will scream and holler and try to disparage the change.

You must remember, however, that George Washington was a revolutionary, a radical in his own time; and Thomas Jefferson, Benjamin Franklin, Martin Luther King, and nearly everyone we admire had to, at one time in their lives, make decisions to strike or protest or go against the prevailing, established order of things.

I think that time has come for you. When you consider how you are treated, and how the money you generate is used, it becomes clear that you are fully entitled to a dramatic change in the way things are. You have a right in America, as generators of so much money, to demand — at the very least — simple things like remedial help before college, and continuous, free education after your eligibility runs out. These are tiny requests compared with what YOU deserve.

As for basketball players, you may be best off by supporting and encouraging a football Bowl strike, and then by selectively striking various games here and there — without any set pattern.

You could accomplish this easily by simply refusing to play some games — just before game time — by claiming that all of you suddenly felt sick and could not play.

Sick players, of course, can not be expected to play, and neither could they be prosecuted in any way, even by the school. Your school would be powerless to do anything to you if you got sick, as a group, now and then, and refused to play.

If each team just gets sick once during the season, enough havoc would be created to convince the NCAA that something needs to be done — especially because they would have to fear that you might strike the NCAA Tournament, for which CBS has paid 32 million dollars per year.

You need to realize that nothing in your scholarship says that you can not get sick. Nothing even says that you can not get a bad back or a sore neck or a feeling of nausea. You also need to realize that your coaches will be more sympathetic with your cause than they will be able to let on. They know better than others what you go through and what your needs are, and nearly all of them would like to see you get a fair share. They are simply too much under the gun themselves these days to give you much public support.

Let's look at a few other considerations. If you are worried about the entire program being shut down, I suppose that COULD happen, but the public certainly wouldn't like it. And besides, you could get aid, like other students, and work your way through.

I know this is not what you have in mind. You love playing sports. But still, you are people, and you have a lot of critics who gloat over what dumb jocks you are. So maybe this is truly the time to show what you are.

Certainly you could expect that the effort will not be permitted to die after you are finished with school. We could continue working until players ARE fairly compensated, and you would have reason to hope that the players in control of a large PLAYERS' FUND in the future would be eager to pay off the debts you acquired if things didn't work out as we hope they will.

Remember, that is a worst-case scenario. But you would also have an excellent chance of succeeding. Money talks, you know that. When a major football program quits making money, the entire student body will feel the effects. The intramural program will likely be suspended, the minor sports will likely be suspended, and a lot of associated people would be faced with having their jobs suspended. You are valuable. That is what you have to realize, and that is why you are entitled to receive more compensation than you are now getting.

Although the pressure on you will be great, especially at a time when you have decided not to play a game, you can surmount it. Let your most intelligent player speak for the whole team. Let him repeat over and over that all of you love your sport, love being Americans, and love the opportunity you have to get an education. Let him add that all of you regret the sickness and that all of you are looking forward to the coming games.

In other words, be positive. Say you are looking forward to the day when basketball and football players are looked up to on campuses across the nation and looking forward to the day when high percentages of basketball and football players are doctors, lawyers, and professors.

Your cause is just. Don't get mired in answering questions about greed and failure to appreciate the good things you have. Those are red herrings. Say continually how much you appreciate what you have, and thank profusely all of those who have helped to give you what you have.

Show no cynicism or disdain. Be calm and positive.

Those who disparage your efforts will act like what you are doing is against motherhood and apple pie, yet they will terminate your whole football and basketball program immediately — without a second thought — by rule — with a sense of duty — if they merely discover that one member of one of your teams has twice received a hundred dollars to help out his poor family.

Remember this when they are moralizing against you. They do not have YOUR interests at heart as much as they sometimes will appear to. They will give you the sense that they are your allies until they smell just the slightest odor of "wrong-doing," and then they will sniff you out like bloodhounds and treat you as if you have the plague.

Can you recall how many allies stepped forward during the Tulane "scandal" to say that the point-shaving was ALLEGED, not a proven fact? Do you recall how many people stepped forward in behalf of the Tulane players pleading innocent? How many were quick to point out the presumption of innocence, "innocent until proven guilty," that is supposed to be part of the American justice system?

Take time to think carefully about what you are seeking. You are not trying to take away anyone's job. You are not seeking to hurt anyone. All you want to do is benefit from your efforts and your unique position as big-time college football and basketball players. In spite of all the things that your critics will try to muster against you, you are not asking for so much, nor are you asking for the impossible.

Take time to weigh the use of funds now generated against the use you are seeking, and there can be no doubt as to the rightness of what you are trying to accomplish.

Get the facts clear in your mind and then go for it. Do it now, before programs get suspended BY THEM, and before innocent victims permanently lose their eligibility.

The best way to show off just what a student-athlete can be is to take this stand, present your intelligent points, and be calm in the face of their criticism. It won't be easy. But it will be worthwhile — just like any championship in basketball and football.

Best of luck. Let me know if you need some assistance.

Sincerely,

Dick DeVenzio

OPEN LETTER TO BOOSTERS

Dear Boosters:

Will you help?

The charade goes on and on. The NCAA and the media have made student-athletes and boosters into bad words. They have systematically prevented the natural relationship between boosters and athletes from flourishing and being enjoyed; and they, not us, have tarnished the image of big-time sports.

If you agree with me, and if you think it is time for sweeping changes, please get in touch with me. Your financial and moral support could be very helpful.

Obviously, it will take some financial resources to bring cases to court in behalf of student-athletes, as well as to continue organizing them so they can stand up for their rights.

Any help which you can offer will be much appreciated. Please feel free to write to me (the address is in the back of the book) or to call me anytime — 704-537-7375.

I am serious about my commitment, and I will be grateful for any efforts you feel moved to make in behalf of this cause. I am looking forward to hearing from you.

Sincerely,

Dick DeVenzio

APPENDIX

Books and Materials

Index

BOOKS AND MATERIALS

THE LAW OF SPORTS, John C. Weistart and Cym H. Lowell, Bobbs-Merrill Co., NY 1979.

THE LAW OF SPORTS, SUPPLIMENT, 1985.

FINANCING COLLEGE EDUCATION, Kenneth A. Kohl and Irene C. Kohl, Harper & Row, NY 1983.

CHAVEZ, Ronald B. Taylor, Beacon Press, 1975.

NCAA MANUAL, NCAA Publishing, 1985.

NCAA ANNUAL REPORTS, NCAA Publishing, 1985.

REPORT OF THE SELECT COMMITTEE ON ATHLETIC PROBLEMS AND CONCERNS IN HIGH EDUCATION, NCAA Publishing, 1983.

REVENUES AND EXPENSES OF INTERCOLLEGIATE ATHLETIC PROGRAMS, Mitchell H. Raiborn, NCAA Publishing, 1982.

JOURNAL OF COLLEGE AND UNIVERSITY LAW, Association of College and University Attorneys, Volume 10, Number 2, Fall 1983-84.

Also consulted frequently: New York Times, USA Today, Washington Post, The NCAA News, The Sporting News, Eastern Basketball, and other sports publications and newspapers.

INDEX

251

D⁴

SPECIAL PEOPLE, SPECIAL THANKS

There are some special people who have been particularly helpful in making this book possible.

First, my brother Huck. A student-athlete at Cornell University in the late Sixties, he has spent years as an advertising executive. This year he interrupted a world tour to help edit this manuscript. If he says something is wrong, it's wrong. When he said one section was unclear to him, I removed it entirely. Huck is one of those rare people who knows what he is talking about but never tries to pretend he knows something he doesn't. His instincts are infallible.

Second, three athletic friends — Richard Ford, a former Duke basketball player now studying law at the University of Georgia; Jim Ryan, an excellent basketball coach in Nutley, New Jersey; and my brother Dave. All of these guys are intelligent, competitive, and great sports fans who helped with some research and some lively discussions on student-athlete issues.

Third, the Delmar Printing Company, with a team of book production experts who make authorship and publishing easy and enjoyable. Dick Edwards and his son Phil — former athletes themselves — know the ins and outs of composition, and they are great to work with. Nona Latane added her expertise in paste-up; and Christine Townsend is an attractive account executive who made it fun to be making all the trips between home and press while turning a manuscript into a book.

Fourth, there are some current student-athletes — Charles Davis (football star, Tennessee), Spencer Tillman (football star, Oklahoma), and Billy Thompson (basketball star, Louisville) — who demonstrated a high degree of maturity and sensitivity by taking time during the early stages of this movement to express their support and encouragement.

Fifth, a few newspaper sports editors — Virgil Parker (Lincoln, Nebraska), Rick Starr (Tarentum, Pennsylvania), and Al Browning (Knoxville, Tennessee) — perceived immediately the sincerity and logic behind this movement and used their columns to present my views fairly to the public.

Last (and certainly least) I want to thank Barbara Frady for marrying Vernon Nelson. No one else would, and he was bothering me by watching my TV all day while I was trying to write. (Now he has to work or stay home.)